FIELD FORTIFICATIONS

THE ARMY INSTITUTE FOR PROFESSIONAL DEVELOPMENT

ARMY CORRESPONDENCE COURSE PROGRAM

ENGINEER
SUBCOURSE 65

FIELD
FORTIFICATIONS

CORRESPONDENCE COURSE PROGRAM

U. S. ARMY ENGINEER SCHOOL

FORT LEONARD WOOD, MO

INTRODUCTION

Field fortifications are natural or manmade protective features used as defensive obstacles, personnel and weapons shelters, and protected firing positions.

This subcourse teaches you how to construct personnel, vehicle, and weapons emplacements, intrenchments, shelters, entanglements, and obstacles under various climatic conditions. Standard plans, types of material, construction procedures, and estimated time and labor requirements are also given.

The subcourse consists of five lessons and an examination as follows:

Lesson 1. Purpose and Requirements of Field Fortifications.

2. Trenches, and Fieldworks.

3. Obstacle Employment.

4. Barbed Wire Entanglements.

5. Camouflage (Protection Against Enemy Surveillance).

Examination.

Fifteen credit hours are allowed for this subcourse.

The format of this subcourse has been developed to facilitate student self-pacing and self-testing. Each lesson in this subcourse is followed by a number of Self-Test questions and exercises designed for a review of that lesson. After completing study of the lesson, you should answer the Self-Test exercises, then turn to the back of the subcourse booklet where the correct answers to the Self-Test have been included. A comparison of your answers with those given in the back of the subcourse will indicate your knowledge and understanding of the material presented. When you have completed all lessons to your satisfaction, complete and forward the Examination Answer Card which you will find in the subcourse packet. The grade you receive on the examination is your grade for the subcourse.

* * * IMPORTANT NOTICE * * *

THE PASSING SCORE FOR ALL ACCP MATERIAL IS NOW 70%.

PLEASE DISREGARD ALL REFERENCES TO THE 75% REQUIREMENT.

LESSON 1

PURPOSE AND REQUIREMENTS OF FIELD FORTIFICATIONS

CREDIT HOURS.. 3

TEXT ASSIGNMENT.. Attached memorandum.

LESSON OBJECTIVES

Upon completion of this lesson you should be able to --

1. **Basic Requirement of Field Fortifications.** Describe the basic requirements for field fortifications to include efficient employment of weapons, protection qualities, and progressive development.

2. **Protective Measures Against Nuclear Weapons.** Describe protective measures against nuclear weapons to include before, during and after explosion actions and procedures.

3. **Individual Emplacements.** Describe construction methods for individual emplacements to include skirmisher's trench, improve emplacement, one-man fox hole etc.

4. **Crew Served Infantry Weapons Emplacements.** Describe construction of infantry weapons emplacements to include machine gun emplacements, emplacements for recoilless weapons, etc.

5. **Vehicle and Artillery Emplacements.** Describe construction of vehicle and artillery emplacements to include vehicle pit, towed artillery weapons emplacements, and self-propelled and tank-mounted weapons emplacements.

6. **Firebase Construction.** Describe construction of a firebase to include layout, artillery requirements, and construction tasks in Phases I, II, and III.

7. **Deliberate Shelters and Bunkers.** Describe construction of deliberate shelters to include general construction requirements, sectional shelters, bunkers, overhead cover, and standoff.

8. **Prefabricated Shelters and Bunkers.** Describe construction of prefabricated shelters and bunkers to include design considerations of the WES concrete arch bunker, and WES concrete arch shelter.

9. **Protective Shelters for Frozen Environment.** Discuss the barriers and shelters which can be constructed of snow or ice and the qualities of snow and ice as protective materials.

ATTACHED MEMORANDUM

Section I. Purpose and Protective Requirements of Field Fortifications

1-1. USE OF FIELD FORTIFICATIONS

a. On the offense. During offensive operations periodic halts may be required to regroup, resupply, or consolidate positions gained. Where the enemy threat is known to include a counterattack capability (or probability), offensive units should seek available cover or should dig hasty emplacements.

b. On the defense. A defensive position is built around a series of organized and occupied tactical positions. Positions are selected for their natural defensive strength and the observation afforded. Fortification measures include clearing fields of fire, digging weapons emplacements and positions for personnel, strengthening natural obstacles, installing artificial obstacles, and providing camouflage.

c. Fortification plans. Plans for fortification not only provide for the desired degree of protection but also for bringing the enemy under the maximum volume of effective fire as early as possible. Fortification plans are usually based on progressive construction, that is, proceeding from open to covered emplacements and shelters, to the ultimate protection permissible under the circumstances. Characteristics of personnel and individual weapons emplacements are shown in table 1-1 (in back of course booklet).

d. Dispersion. The separation of units and individuals is a primary means of protection, particularly from the effects of nuclear weapons. If the area occupied by a unit is doubled, it is less vulnerable to shell fire or the effects of nuclear weapons. Proper dispersion can greatly reduce the requirements for high level protection from field fortifications. The amount that a unit spreads out depends on the mission, terrain, and the enemy situation. Fortifications, properly employed, can be used in lieu of, or to supplement, dispersion, but fortifications are particularly important for units that cannot disperse sufficiently to obtain adequate protection.

e. Alternate and dummy positions. When time and the situation permit, dummy and alternate positions should be constructed to deceive the enemy and to allow flexibility in the defense.

1-2. RESPONSIBILITIES

Field fortifications are constructed by personnel of all arms and services. Hasty shelters and emplacements are normally constructed by the combat units occupying the position. Some engineer equipment and supervisory assistance are frequently required to assist the combat units. Fortifications of a more complex character may require construction by engineer troops. Actually, engineers at all echelons of command assist in the preparation of plans and orders and furnish technical advice and assistance in the construction of field fortifications.

1-3. BASIC REQUIREMENTS FOR FORTIFICATIONS

a. Employment of weapons. Emplacements must permit effective use of the weapons for which they are designed. This requirement may limit the protection which can be provided and may influence the design and depth of adjacent shelters.

b. Protection. As far as possible, protection should be provided against hazards except a direct hit or a close nuclear explosion. To obtain maximum protection, excavations should be as small as possible, thereby limiting the effective target area for high trajectory weapons and airbursts.

c. Simplicity and economy. The emplacement or shelter should be strong and simple, require as little digging as possible and be constructed with materials that are immediately available.

d. Progressive development. Plans for defensive works should allow for progressive development to improve the usefulness of the fortification. Development fortifications can be accomplished in three steps --

(1) Digging in quickly where speed is the principal consideration and no special tools or materials are required.

(2) Improvising with available materials.

(3) Refining, using stock materials.

e. Camouflage and concealment. Fortifications should be built so that the completed work can be camouflaged. It may not be practical to conceal a defensive position completely, but it should be camouflaged enough to prevent the enemy from spotting the position by ground observation. If possible, dummy positions should be constructed the same time as the actual position.

f. Ingenuity. A high degree of imagination and ingenuity is essential to assure the best use of available materials as well as the best choice and use of the fortifications constructed.

1-4. PROTECTION FROM CONVENTIONAL WEAPONS

a. Digging in. Protection against conventional weapons is best provided by constructing a thickness of earth and other materials. This is done by digging into the ground so that personnel and equipment offer the smallest target possible to the line of sight of weapon. This means of protection is effective against direct fire of small arms and horizontally impelled shell fragments. Digging in also provides some protection against artillery,

infantry heavy weapons, bombs, and other serial weapons. Advantage should be taken of all available natural cover. Improvement of the position continues until the unit leaves the area.

b. Overhead cover. Overhead protection is important particularly in the forward areas where the threat includes airburst shelling in addition to the possibility of nuclear attack. Covered firing positions should be built for individual riflemen. Small readily accessible shelters adjacent to weapons emplacements are also necessary. A minimum of 15-20 centimeters (6-8 inches) of logs, 45 centimeters (18 inches) sandbags, rocks, and dirt, in that order, is required for overhead protection. Any available material may be used but cover should be kept low. However, cover of this type will not protect personnel against direct shell hits. Overhead cover should be strengthened and improved as long as the position is occupied. Only part of the firing position should be covered. Sandbags are placed over the logs to prevent dirt from falling on the occupants.

1-5. PROTECTION FROM CHEMICAL AND BIOLOGICAL WEAPONS

Open or partially open emplacements afford no protection from chemical or biological attack. Personnel in open emplacements should use the poncho for protection against liquid contamination and the protective mask to provide protection from chemical vapors and biological aerosols. Overhead cover will delay penetration of chemical vapors and biological aerosols, thereby providing additional masking time and protection against direct liquid contamination. Covered emplacements with relatively small apertures and entrance areas which can be closed, provide protection from napalm and flame-flamethrowers.

Section II. Nuclear Weapons Protective Methods

1-6. EXPLOSIONS

Since the threat of nuclear weapons is present in modern warfare, it is necessary to

understand the effects of these weapons on personnel and equipment. Well trained and well disciplined soldiers can protect themselves and their equipment against this threat and continue their mission, even though a nuclear weapon has more destructive power than any other device.

1-7. WEAPONS EFFECTS

a. Radiation. The presence of radiation and the high intensity of the blast or earth shock following nuclear explosions distinguishes them from the effects of conventional bombs or other explosives.

(1) Thermal radiation. A nuclear explosion causes extreme **heat** and **light** that are comparable in intensity to the surface of the sun. Heat from nuclear explosions causes varying degrees of burns from the equivalent of a mid sunburn to more severe injuries. The intense heat may also set fire to buildings, forests, and equipment. Light from a nuclear explosion may daze personnel for a short time during daylight, and at nighttime the effects are even more severe, lasting about 10 minutes. Night vision may be impaired for an extended period of time, and permanent injury will result if the eyes are focused in the direction of the burst.

(2) Nuclear radiation. Initial and residual radiation effects are associated with nuclear explosions. **Initial radiation** which is emitted within a minute of the burst travels in straight lines at about the speed of light and has a high penetrating effect. **Residual** or lingering radiation comes from the radioactive materials originally in a nuclear weapon or from normally nonradioactive materials (such as soil or equipment) which have been made radioactive by the nuclear reaction. Substances, including soil or equipment that have become contaminated and remain radioactive emit **induced radiation**, one form of residual radiation. Another form of residual radiation, commonly referred to as **fallout**, is induced when a nuclear explosion occurs under, at, or near the surface of the earth and large quantities of dirt and debris are thrown up, mixing with the fireball. These radioactive particles in the atmosphere gradually fall to earth. Injuries from nuclear radiation are caused by the penetrating rays of the initial and residual radiation. The degree of

injury depends on: (a) amount of body exposure; (b) length of time exposed; (c) previous radiation damage to the body tissue; (d) other injuries received which may contribute to disability; (e) general physical condition.

b. Blast and earth shock. Blast and associated earth shock effects are caused by violent changes in pressure that move out in all directions from the center of the explosion, like a very strong wind. Most direct injuries from the blast effects result when personnel are thrown to the ground by the blast. Indirect blast injuries are sustained from flying debris and the collapse of emplacements, shelters, trenches, or buildings.

1-8. PROTECTIVE MEASURES

Individual protective measures against nuclear weapons should be taken before, during, and after the explosion. All personnel should follow the unit standing operating procedure (SOP) which covers such items as the use of protective equipment, warning signals, first aid, firefighting, reorganization, marking of contaminated areas, and decontamination. The following general procedures are also applicable:

a. Before the explosion. If there is warning of a nuclear explosion, and available time and the tactical situation permit --

(1) Positions should be improved -- dug deeper and covered. Even a shelter half, covering the top of a foxhole, provides some protection. A poncho should not be used because it may get too hot, melt, and cause burns. The position should be revetted if possible.

(2) If there is not enough time to prepare a good position, a shallow trench should be dug deep enough so the body is below the surface of the ground and covered with a shelter half.

(3) Helmet should be worn, and personnel should keep their faces down.

b. During the explosion.

(1) Personnel should crouch low in

their foxholes with their heads down, or lie flat in their trench with shelter halves over them.

(2) If they are in the open, soldiers should try to get into a nearby ditch or behind a wall, but they should not try to get to a shelter if it is more than a few yards away.

(3) If no shelter is available nearby, personnel should turn their backs to the explosion while dropping to a prone position.

(4) The brilliant flash will cause temporary blindness and may cause permanent eye damage if looked at directly.

(5) Personnel should stay where they are until the blast wave passes. By this time, the greatest danger from heat, initial radiation, blast, or shock will be over.

c. After the explosion.

(1) Fallout will usually be present so personnel should --

(a) Keep under cover until fallout has stopped.
(b) Brush the dust from their clothing. Scrape up and throw out any dirt or other material which has fallen into the foxholes. Dig out dirt and pile it several inches deep for at last 1 meter around the hole.
(c) Clean equipment as well as available material permits.

(d) Help others as much as possible.

(2) Be prepared to continue the mission. The enemy can be expected to follow up a nuclear explosion to take advantage of any resulting damage and confusion. Stay in position to repel an attack.

1-9. OTHER MEASURES

a. Friendly nuclear weapons. Nuclear weapons may be used close to our own areas. If used close enough to be dangerous there will be warning and instructions on precautions to take. The individual protective measures discussed above are important in a situation of this kind.

b. Contaminated areas. If required to occupy a contaminated (radioactive) area, the following actions should be taken:

(1) Dig foxholes quickly.

(2) Scrape dirt from around the edge of the foxholes for at least 1 meter, and scatter dirt around the foxholes for 10 meters.

c. Contaminated equipment. Trained personnel in each unit will use instruments to test equipment and supplies for contamination. If instruments are lacking, the urgency of the situation dictates whether equipment is used without being tested. Generally, equipment not damaged by the explosion is safe to use. Washing or brushing will usually make contaminated equipment safe to operate.

Section III. Principles and Methods of Construction

1-10. MATERIALS

a. Natural. Full use is made of all available natural materials such trees, logs, and brush in constructing and camouflaging emplacements, shelters and overhead cover. Usually, enough natural material can be found to meet the requirements for hasty or expedient fortifications. Snow and ice may be used in the construction of emplacement and shelters in cold regions.

b. Other materials.

(1) Manufactured materials, such as pickets, barbed wire, cement, lumber, sandbags, corrugated metal, and other materials for revetting, camouflage, shelter, and concrete construction are supplied by support organizations.

(2) Captured enemy supplies, locally procured material, and demolished buildings are other sources of fortifications construction materials.

1-11. METHODS OF EXCAVATING

a. **Handtools.** The individual soldier is equipped with an intrenching tool and, if necessary, he can use his bayonet to assist in digging. Pick mattocks, shovels, and other tools are also useful, and frequently available for this purpose (fig 1-1). In addition, captured enemy equipment may be available. The relative value of each tool depends on the soil and terrain. In arctic areas, a larger quantity of picks and pick mattocks are required to aid in the preparation of emplacements in frozen ground.

b. **Equipment.** Relatively narrow cuts with steep or nearly vertical sides required for most emplacements or shelters can be excavated more accurately by hand. However, intrenching machines, backhoes, bulldozers, bucket loaders, and scrapers may be where the situation will permit the use of heavy equipment. Usually, these machines cannot dig out the exact shape desired or will dig more earth than necessary, requiring completion of the excavation by hand. Additional revetment material is usually required when machines are used. Distinctive scars on the ground resulting from the use of heavy equipment require more effort for effective camouflage than fortification work performed by hand.

c. **Explosives.** Many fortification tasks are made easier and accomplished more quickly by using explosive in any type of soil. Special explosive digging aids available include the M2A3 and M3 shaped demolition charges, and the field expedient det cord wick.

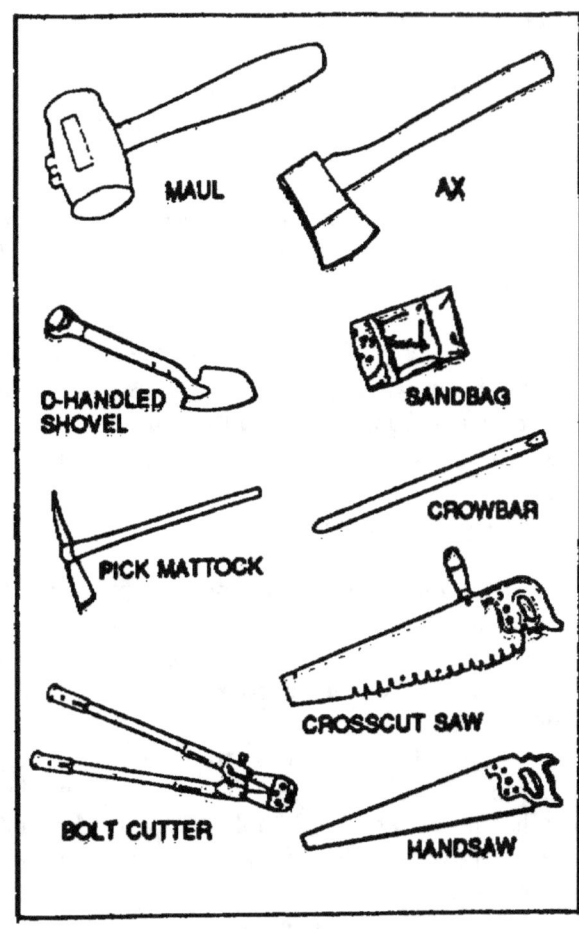

Figure 1-1. Intrenching equipment.

SECTION IV. Construction of Individual Emplacements

1-12. TYPES OF EMPLACEMENTS

a. **Hasty emplacements**. Hasty emplacements are dug by troops in contact with the enemy, when time and materials are limited. Hasty positions should be supplemented with overhead cover and strengthened as conditions permit. If the situation permits, the small unit leader will verify the sectors of observation and fire for the individual members of the squad from their designated positions before they dig individual foxholes. When the situation is stabilized, even temporarily, positions are selected so they can be connected by trenches later. The emplacements described below provide protection against flat trajectory fire. They are used when there is no natural cover. Hasty positions (figure 1-2) are good for a short time because they give some protection from direct fire. If the unit remains in the area, they must be developed into well-prepared positions to provide as much protection as possible.

Figure 1-2. Hasty positions in an open field.

(1) Shell crater. A shell or bomb crater of adequate size, 0.6 to 1 meter (2 to 3 ft), offers immediate cover and concealment and can be quickly made into a hasty position (figure 1-3). By digging the crater to a steep face on the side toward the enemy, the occupant can provide himself with a firing position. A small crater can later be developed into a foxhole. Craters, even if developed, are susceptible to being overrun by tracked vehicles.

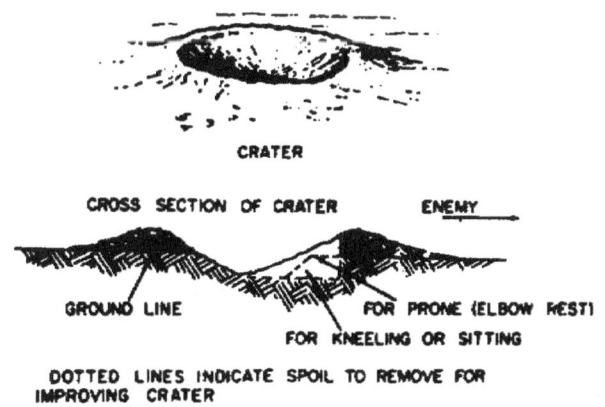

CRATER

CROSS SECTION OF CRATER   ENEMY

GROUND LINE   FOR PRONE (ELBOW REST)
                 FOR KNEELING OR SITTING

DOTTED LINES INDICATE SPOIL TO REMOVE FOR IMPROVING CRATER

Figure 1-3. Improved crater.

(2) Skirmisher's trench. This shallow pit type emplacement (fig 1-4) provides a temporary open prone firing position for the individual soldier. When immediate shelter from heavy enemy fire is required and existing defiladed firing positions are not available, each soldier lies prone or on his side, scrapes the soil with his intrenching tool, and piles it in a low parapet between himself and the enemy. In this manner, a shallow body-length pit can be formed quickly in all but the hardest ground. The trench should be oriented so that it is least vulnerable to enfilade fire. A soldier presents a low silhouette in this type of emplacement and is protected to a limited extent from small arms fire. It can be further developed into foxhole or a prone emplacement.

Figure 1-4. Skirmisher's trench.

(3) Prone emplacement. This emplacement (fig 1-5) is a further refinement of the skirmisher's trench. The berm dimension of this emplacement, as shown in the parapet detail, is varied to conform to the position and arm length of the occupant. It serves as a good firing position for a rifleman and provides better protection against small arms or direct fire weapons than the improved crater or skirmisher's trench.

(4) Rocks, snow, and ice. Limited protection can be provided by piling up rocks, chunks of ice, or packed snow. Icecrete, formed by mixing dirt and water, is very effective as an arctic building material. A minimum of 30 centimeters (12 inches) of this material will resist penetration of small arms fire.

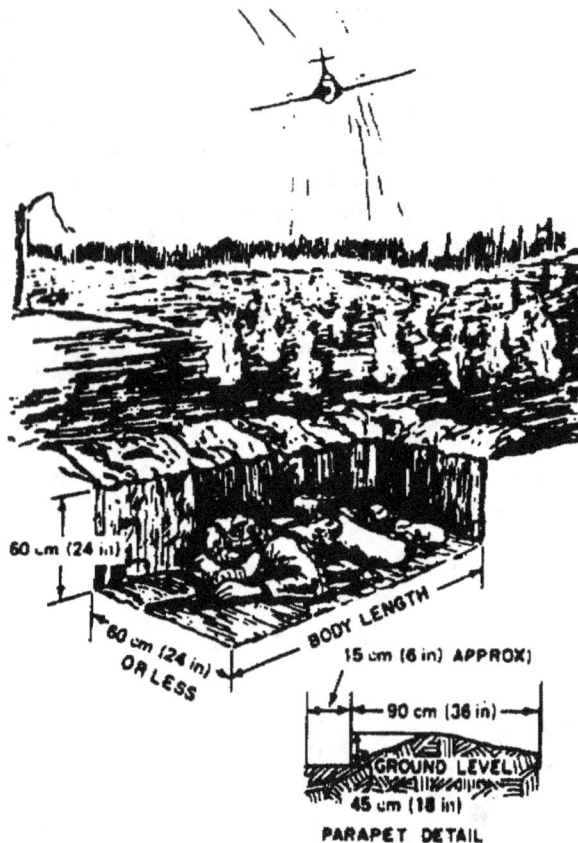

Figure 1-5. Prone emplacement.

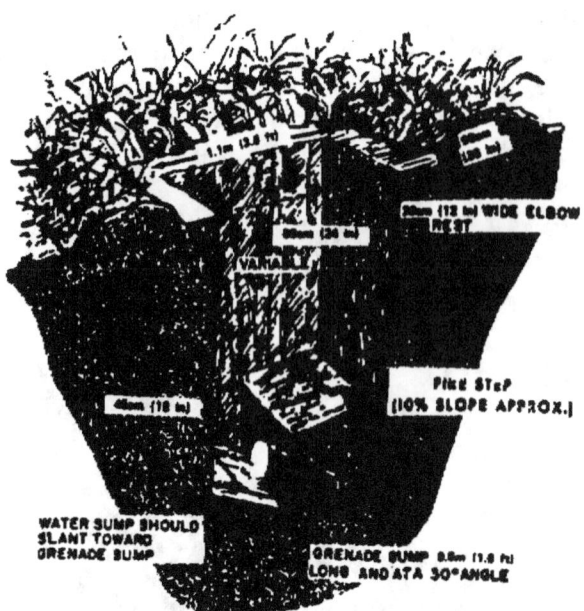

Figure 1-6. One-man foxhole.

b. Foxholes. Foxholes are the individual rifeman's basic defensive position. They afford good protection against enemy small arms fire and can be developed from well chosen craters, skirmisher's trenches, or prone emplacements. Foxholes should be improved, as time and materials permit, by revetting the sides, adding expedient cover, providing drainage, and excavating a grenade sump to dispose of handgrenades tossed into the hole by the enemy.

(1) One-man foxhole. The overall dimensions and layout of the one-man foxhole are shown in figure 1-6.

(2) Construction details.

(a) Fire step. The depth of the fire step will vary depending on the height of a comfortable firing position for the occupant, usually 1 meter to 1.5 meters (3 1/2 to 5 ft). The occupant, crouched in a sitting position on the fire step, must have at least 60 cm (2 ft) of overhead clearance if a tank overruns the foxhole. This will normally provide protection against the crushing action of tanks; however, in loose unstable soils it will be necessary to revet the walls of the foxhole in order to provide this protection.

(b) Water sump. A water sump, 45 cm (18 in.) by 60 cm (2 ft.) and 45 cm (18 inches) deep below the fire step, is dug at one end of the foxhole to collect water and to accommodate the feet of a seated occupant. One or two layers of large stones are then placed at the bottom of the hole with smaller stones on top up to the level of the ground (fig 1-6). The sump may simply provide a collecting basin from which water can be bailed.

(c) Grenade sump. A circular grenade sump large enough to accept the largest known enemy grenade and sloped downward at an angle of 30° is excavated under the fire step beginning at the lower part of the fire step riser. Handgrenades thrown into the foxhole are exploded in this sump, and their fragmentation is restricted to the unoccupied end of the foxhole. For good drainage and to assist in disposing of grenades, the fire step is sloped toward the water sump, and the bottom of the water sump is funneled downward to the grenade sump.

(d) **Parapet.** If excavated spoil is used as a parapet (fig 1-6), it should be placed as a layer about 1 meter (3 feet) wide and 30 cm (6 inches) high all around the foxhole leaving an elbow rest (berm) of original earth about 60 cm (1 foot) wide next to the foxhole. If sod or topsoil is used to camouflage the parapet, the sod or topsoil should be removed from the foxhole and parapet area, set aside until the parapet is complete, and then placed on top in a natural manner.

(e) **Camouflage.** Whether or not a parapet is constructed in wooded or brushy type terrain, a foxhole can be camouflaged effectively with natural materials, as shown in figure 1-7. In open or cultivated areas, it may be preferable to omit the parapet, remove the excavated soil to an inconspicuous place, and improvise a camouflage cover for the foxhole. This can be a light, open frame of branches garnished with grass or other natural foliage to match the surroundings. As an alternate method, the foxhole can be covered with a shelterhalf, poncho, or other expedient material, and further covered with snow or some other material, according to local terrain conditions (fig 1-7). The occupant raises one side of the cover for observation or firing.

(f) **Overhead cover.** A half-cover (fig 1-8) over a one-man foxhole provides good protection for the occupant and permits full use of the weapon. Logs, 10 to 15 cm (4 to 6 in.) in diameter of 14 cm (6 in.) timbers approximately 1.2 meters (4 ft.) in length, support the earth cover. They should be long enough to extend at least 30 cm (1 ft.) on each side of the foxhole to provide a good bearing surface. Dirt should be removed on each side of the foxhole so that the supporting logs or timbers are even with the ground surface. If the ground is soft and tends to break away, a bearing surface of planks or timbers should be provided for cover supports. Logs or timbers of this size will support an earth cover 30 to 45 cm (1 ft to 1 1/2 ft) thick. The walls of the foxhole should be stabilized with revetment material (fig 1-9) at least under the

① FOXHOLE WITH CAMOUFLAGE COVER IN PLACE

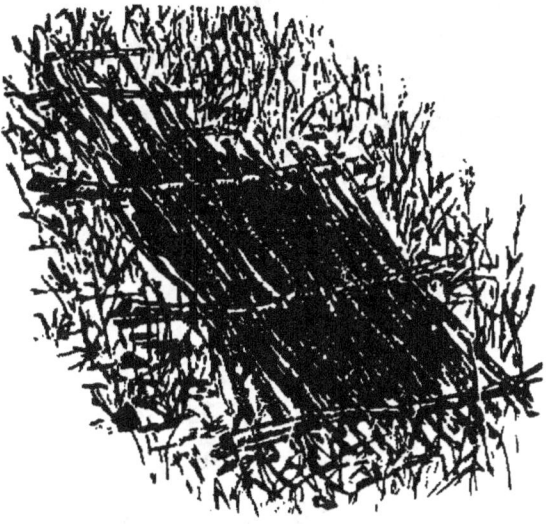

② METHOD OF CONSTRUCTING COVER

Figure 1-7. Camouflaged one-man hole.

overhead cover to prevent a cave-in from the added weight of the cover.

(g) **Revetment material.** Use of different types of revetting material are shown in figure 1-9. Expedient material, such as brushwood, saplings, sheet metal, or dimensioned lumber should be thin and tough so that it will support the sides of the emplacement when properly staked and tied. Revetment stakes, either metal or wood 1.8 meters (6 feet) in length, should be spaced not more than 60 centimeters (2 feet) apart and driven into the ground 30 to 45 centimeters (12 to 18 inches). The revetment stakes are held firmly in place by anchor wires of barbed wire or 14 gage wire attached to anchor

Figure 1-8. One-man foxhole with half cover.

Figure 1-9. Types of revetting material.

stakes (fig 1-10). Five or six strands of wire should be stretched between the revetment and anchor stakes at ground level and tightened by twisting. The distance between the revetment and anchor stakes should be approximately twice the depth of the excavation. The wire between the stakes should not pass over the parapet in any case.

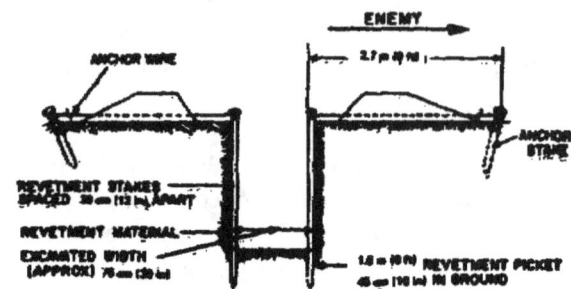

Figure 1-10. Supporting and anchoring revetment.

   (3) **Open two-man foxhole.** In a defensive position, the two-man foxhole (fig. 1-11) is generally preferred to the one-man emplacement.

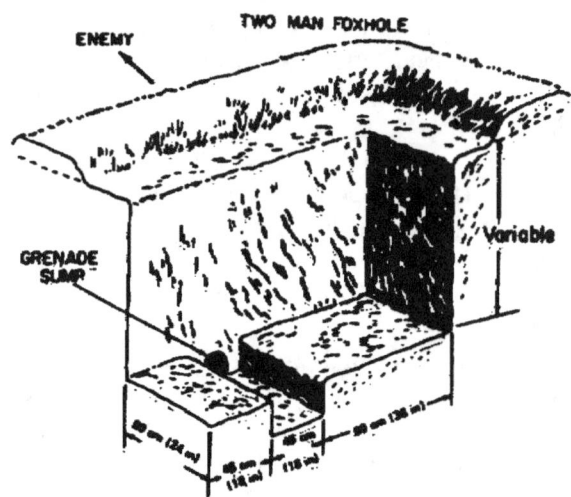

Figure 1-11. Open two-man foxhole.

   (a) **Advantages.** One man can provide protection while the other is digging. It affords relief and rest, for the occupants as one man rests while the other observes. In this manner, firing positions can be effectively manned for longer periods of time. If one

1-10

soldier becomes a casualty, the position is still occupied. The psychological effect of two men together permits positions to be occupied for longer intervals.

(b) **Disadvantages.** If a direct hit occurs, two men will become casualties instead of one. Also, the area that can be occupied may be reduced significantly.

(c) **Construction.** The two-man foxhole is constructed the same as the one-man foxhole except for the location of the grenade sump which is dug into the face of the foxhole towards the enemy.

(d) **Overhead cover.** A substantial overhead cover for a two-man foxhole may be provided by constructing an offset shown and described in figure 1-12. An alternate method is shown in figure 1-13.

c. **Full frontal berm overhead rifle positions.**

(1) Large positions are weak positions. Each rifle position should begin with a rectangular hole as long as the shoulder-to-shoulder length of the men who will fight in it, as wide as a man plus equipment. Spoil should be placed forward and to the sides to form a sloped, progressively packed berm.

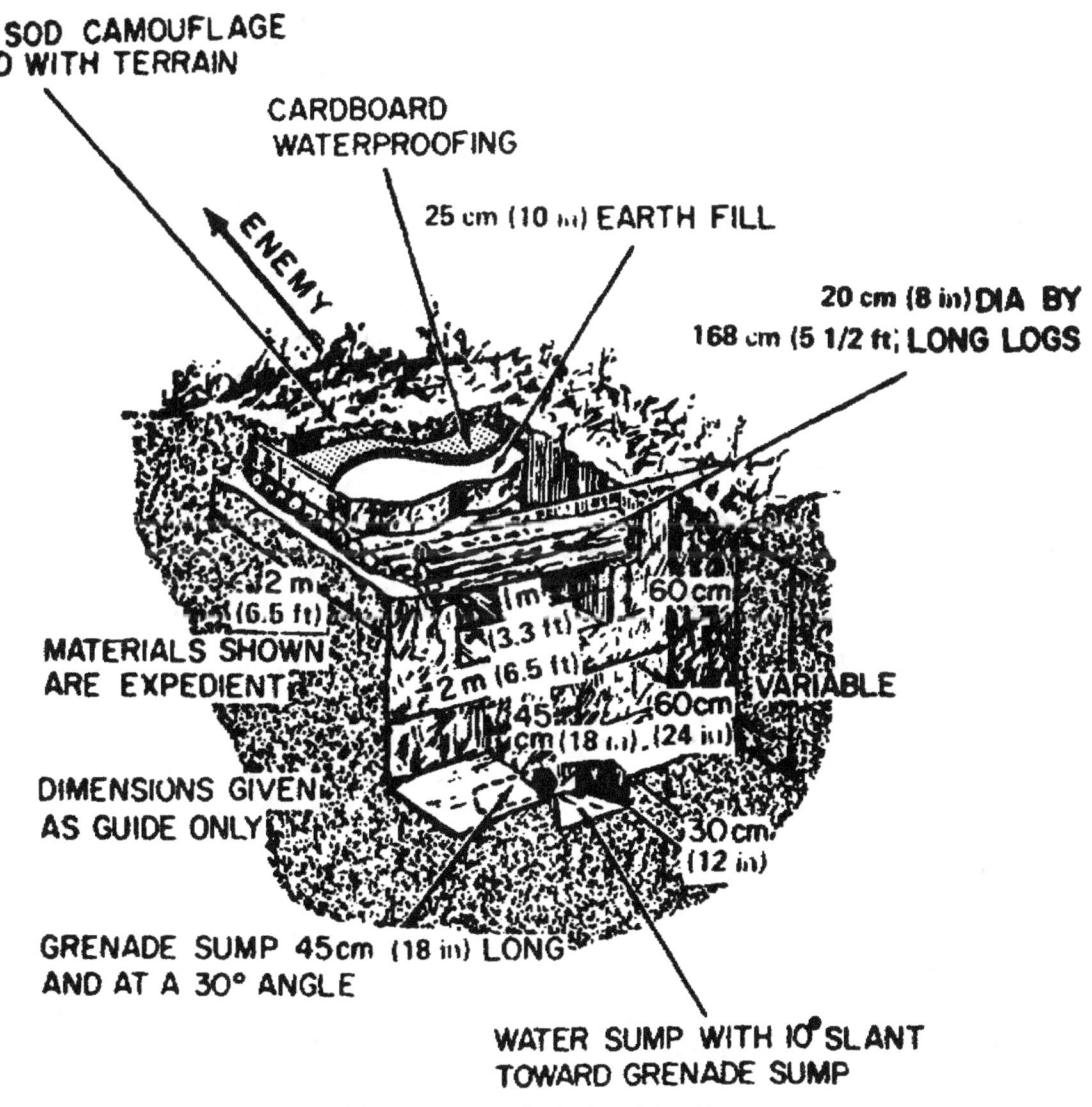

5 cm (2 in) SOD CAMOUFLAGE TO BLEND WITH TERRAIN

CARDBOARD WATERPROOFING

25 cm (10 in) EARTH FILL

20 cm (8 in) DIA BY 168 cm (5 1/2 ft) LONG LOGS

ENEMY

2 m (6.5 ft)

1m (3.3 ft)

60 cm

2 m (6.5 ft)

VARIABLE

MATERIALS SHOWN ARE EXPEDIENT

45 cm (18 in)

60 cm (24 in)

DIMENSIONS GIVEN AS GUIDE ONLY

30 cm (12 in)

GRENADE SUMP 45 cm (18 in) LONG AND AT A 30° ANGLE

WATER SUMP WITH 10° SLANT TOWARD GRENADE SUMP

Figure 1-12. Two-man foxhole with offset.

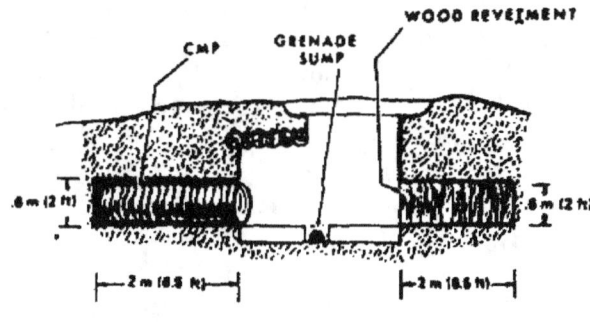

Figure 1-13. Two-man foxhole with offset constructed of timber and culvert.

(2) The next step at the hole is to cut firing apertures at 45 degrees to the direction of the enemy and deepen the hole, tailoring the depth to each man, and carving elbow rests in the parapet for each rifleman to insure solid elbow-under-the piece firing positions. Apertures should be provided with grenade sumps and dug narrow and tapered, just sufficient to command the assigned sector of fire (fig 1-14). Automatic rifles on

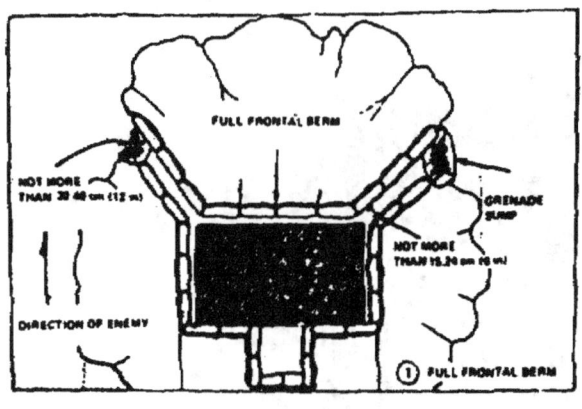

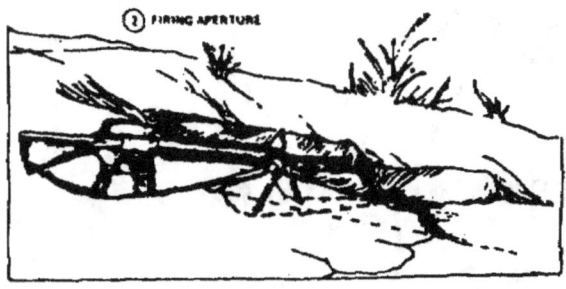

Figure 1-14. Rifle position.

bipods should have bipod rest slot cut forward to the parapet to allow the bipod to be withdrawn easily and to rest the gun muzzle low. The fitting for firing should be undertaken carefully to counter the natural tendency to shoot high at night. This is accomplished by digging each man down so that standing in his hole in firing position his piece is level at height for graze, firmly seated and supported, and as close to the ground as his mission permits.

(3) Overhead cover is now added. Cover can be fabricated from large logs plus sandbags or dirt, or sapling/bamboo mats in three crosslaid laminations plus sandbags or dirt, but should be sturdy enough to take the full weight jumping of a large combat-loaded soldier. Full overhead cover is constructed over all positions; full cover cuts vulnerability to airbursts and grenades, and lessens prospects of flooding in the event of rain. Care must be exercised to hold the silhouette of the position as low as possible, and the apertures as small as sector of fire permits. The height of the cover is determined by placing the firers in the hole, and the cover adjusted a full inch above their helmets while they take up night firing positions -head high over the sights. Berms and apertures should be extended and sloped forward to cut vertical surfacing, and to hide muzzle flash from the front. Construction of revetted, walls and overhead cover should follow principles outlined in **b** above.

(4) Camouflage is now added. Preferably this should be rooted plants and grass sod, calculated to grow naturally in place on the position, and to blend fully with the surrounding vegetation. While digging the fighting position, maximum care should be taken to prevent the destruction of natural camouflage growing near the hole, scaling off the sod to a depth that will maintain the roots, and setting it aside to be used for camouflage upon completion of the overhead cover.

(5) A rear entrance is now dug. This rear entry should be an auxiliary, fully open, individual firing position that can be used for throwing grenades and M79 fires. It should

Figure 1-14. Rifle position (Continued)

be, at minimum designed to allow entry into the hole from the rear, covered with a poncho or similar screen to cut down backlighting the firing apertures. Full consideration should be given to protecting defenders from friendly direct fire weapons located to the rear of the position (including artillery beehive ammunition), and to emergency resupply. The sleeping position should be directly behind the fighting position. A completed rifle position (except for camouflage) is shown in (3), figure 1-14.

(6) A machinegun position is constructed generally following the same procedure as for the rifle position, except that the hole must be designed around the gun. The first step is to emplace the gun on its final protective line and walk the latter to check the site. The hole is then traced to place a sturdy firing table with working room for the loader on the left.

d. **Overhead cover for foxhole (fabric).** When available Overhead Cover for Foxholes (OCF) is an effective protection for 1-and 2-man foxholes (fig 1-15).

(1) **Description.** The foxhole cover is a woven dacron fabric laminated to polyester film. It is 1.5 meters (5 feet 4 inches) long by 1.8 meters (6 feet) wide and weighs slightly less than 2 pounds. Connected to each side of the width are tubular sections, 15 centimeters (6 inches) in diameter and 1.5 meters (5 feet 4 inches) long. It will support 45 centimeters (18 inches) of soil over any emplacement, while simultaneously withstanding the blast effects of a nuclear weapon. The unit will cover 1- and 2-man foxholes and is capable of combining in multiple to cover shelter portions of crew-served weapons emplacements. It will function over emplacements 25 percent larger than standard.

(2) **Installation.**

(a) After completing excavation of the foxhole (trench), unfold the cover (OCF) and place it over the foxhole, locating the pouch at each side of the cover in a position parallel to the edge of the foxhole. Center the cover so that the pouches are approximately the same distance from the edge of the foxhole.

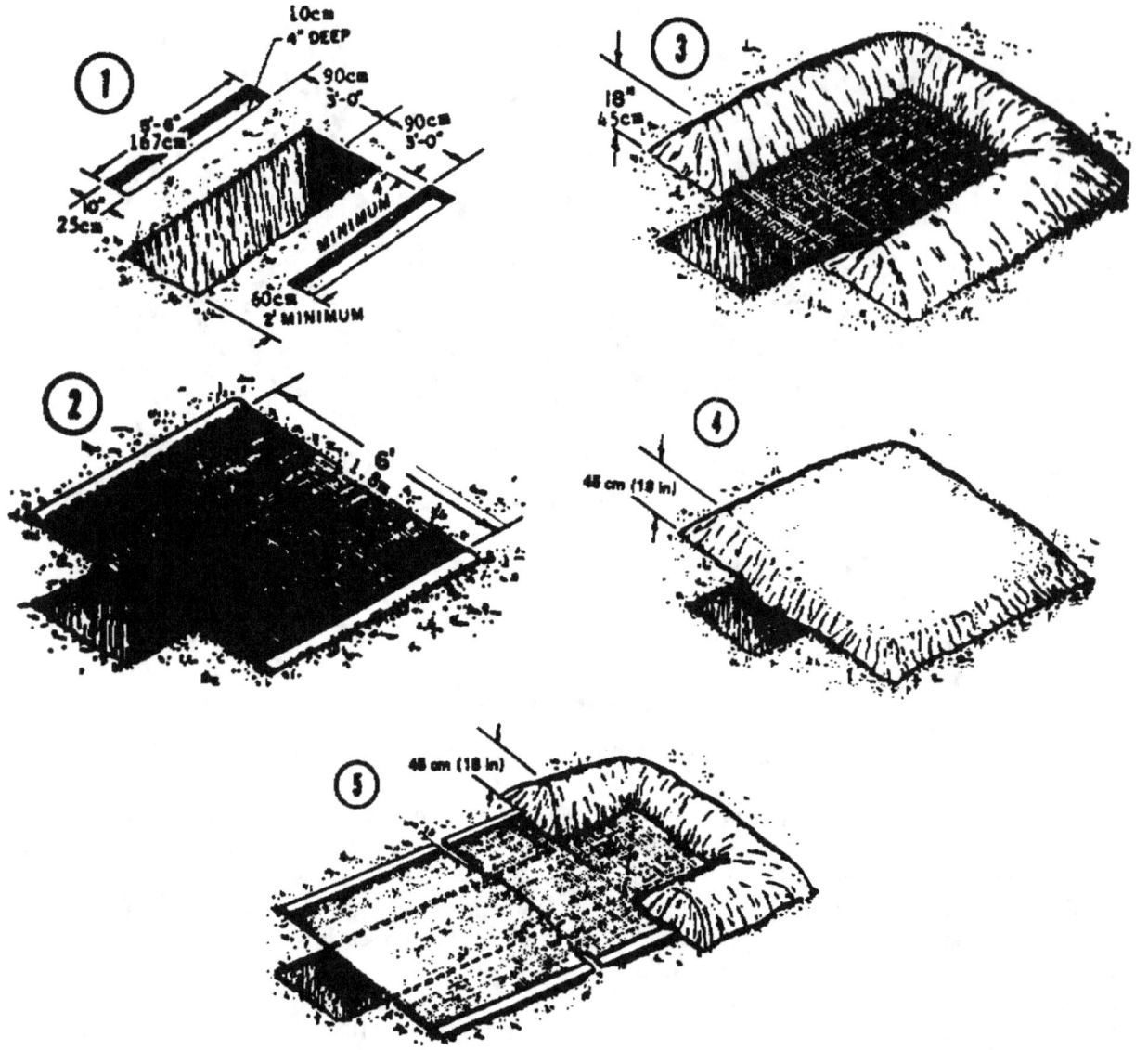

Figure 1-15. Overhead cover for foxhole (fabric).

(b) Allow a minimum of 60 centimeters (2 feet) of open space at one end to permit entrance into the foxhole. Be sure that the cover extends at least 10 centimeters (4 inches) beyond the closed end of the foxhole ((1), fig. 1-16). This will insure that oil does not slide down the end wall of the foxhole.

(c) Mark the inside (nearest foxhole) edge of the pouches in the soil on both sides of the trench. Using the marked lines as the inside edge, dig two (one on each side) shallow trenches approximately 10 centimeters (4 inches) deep, 25 centimeters (10 inches) wide, and 1.67 meters (5 feet

6 inches) long parallel to the length of the foxhole ((1), fig. 1-15).

(d) Using entrenching tool, fill one pouch with soil using both ends as filling points. Fill other pouch in the same manner. Stretch the cover taut between the two pouches because a taut cover does not sag as much as a loose cover ((2), fig. 1-15).

(e) Place soil backfill around the edges of the foxhole to a depth of 45 centimeters (18 inches) minimum. The sloping outside soil edge should cover the soil filled pouch ((3), fig. 1-15).

(f) Complete covering with soil to a uniform depth of 45 centimeters (18 inches) but continue placing soil from the edges toward the center ((4), fig 1-15).

(g) Snap fasteners on each end of the cover provide means of covering a trench by connecting two or more covers ((5), fig 1-15), When connecting two or more units to form a covered trench type structure, it is essential that only steps 1 through 3 should be completed before connecting successive units. Any two units to be connected should be connected with the five middle snaps before the pouches of the second one are filled with soil. After the pouches are filled, the eight remaining snaps should be connected. Step 4 may be completed before all covers are erected over the trench but only on units positioned two or more units back from the last one connected.

1-13. FIELDS OF FIRE

a. Principles. There is little opportunity to clear fields of fire when a unit is in contact with the enemy. Individual riflemen and weapons crews must select the best natural positions available. Usually, there is only time to clear areas in the immediate vicinity of the position. However, in preparing defensive positions for expected contact with the enemy, suitable fields of fire are cleared in front of each position. The following principles are pertinent:

(1) Excessive or careless clearing will disclose firing positions (fig. 1-16)

(2) In areas organized for close defense, clearing should start near the position and work forward at least 100 meters (328 ft) or to the maximum effective range of the weapon if time permits.

(3) A thin natural screen of vegetation should be left to hide defensive positions.

b. Procedure.

(1) Remove the lower branches of large scattered trees in sparsely wooded areas.

(2) In heavy woods, fields of fire may

ORIGINAL TERRAIN

WRONG—AFTER IMPROPER CLEARING

RIGHT—AFTER PROPER CLEARING

Figure 1-16. Clearing fields of fire.

neither be possible nor desirable within the time available. Restrict work to thinning the undergrowth and removing the lower branches of large trees. Clear narrow lanes of fire (fig. 1-17), for automatic weapons.

(3) Thin or remove dense brush since it is never a suitable obstacle and obstructs the field of fire.

(4) Cut weeds when they obstruct the view from firing positions.

(5) Remove brush, weeds, and limbs that have been cut to areas where they cannot be used to conceal enemy movements or disclose the position.

(6) Do only a limited amount of clearing at one time. Overestimating the capabilities of the unit in this respect may result in a field of fire improperly cleared which would afford the enemy better concealment and cover than the natural state.

(7) Cut or burn grain, hay, and tall weeds.

(8) Whenever possible, check position from the enemy side to be sure that the positions are effectively camouflaged and they are not revealed by clearing fields of fire.

WRONG—TOO MUCH CLEARING. DEBRIS NOT REMOVED. ENEMY WILL AVOID

RIGHT—ONLY UNDERBRUSH AND TREES DIRECTLY IN LINE OF FIRE REMOVED. ENEMY SURPRISED

Figure 1-17. Clearing fire lanes.

Section V. Construction of Crew Served Infantry Weapons Emplacements

1-14. PRINCIPAL CONSIDERATIONS

a. **Firing positions.** While it is desirable to give maximum protection to personnel and equipment, the principal consideration must be the effective use of the weapon. In offensive combat, infantry weapons are sited wherever natural or existing positions are available or where weapons can be emplaced with a minimum of digging. The positions described in this section are designed for use in all types of terrain that will permit excavation.

b. **Protection.** Protection of crew-served weapons is provided by emplacements which give some protection to the weapon and crew while in firing positions. As the positions are developed, the emplacements are deepened and provided with half overhead cover, if possible. Then, if the positions are occupied for an extended period of time, shelters adjoining the emplacement or close to it should be built. Characteristics of crew served infantry weapons emplacements are shown in table 1-2. (located in back of book).

c. **Crew shelters.** Shelters immediately adjoining and opening into emplacements improve the operational capability of the crew, since the men are not exposed when moving between the shelter and the weapon.

1-15. MACHINEGUN EMPLACEMENTS

a. **Pit type.** The gun is emplaced initially in a hasty position (fig. 1-18).

b. **Horseshoe type.** The dimensions and layout of the completed emplacement are shown in figure 1-19. The horseshoe shaped trench, about 60 centimeters (2 feet) wide, is dug along the rear and sides, leaving a chest-high shelf in the center to serve as the gun platform. The spoil from this trench is used

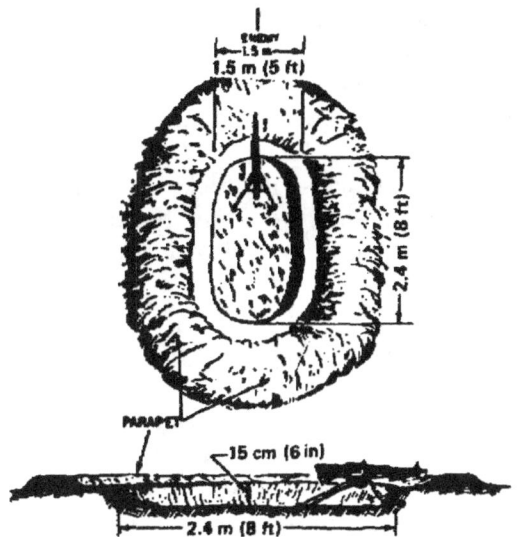

Figure 1-18. Planview and cross section of machinegun emplacement.

to form the parapet, making it at least 1 meter (40 inches) wide and low enough to permit all-round fire. This type emplacement permits easy traverse of the gun through an arc of 180°, but the crew cannot fire to the rear effectively. The firing table must be reverted to prevent the vibrations of the automatic weapons from breaking down the walls of the table.

c. **Two one-man foxhole type.** This emplacement consists of 2 one-man foxholes close to the gun position as illustrated in figure 1-20. The parapet is low enough for all-round fire and good protection for the crew, A foxhole is dug for the gunner at the rear of the gun and another foxhole is dug for the assistant gunner on the left of the gun and 45 cm (18 in.) in front of the gunner's foxhole. The spoil is piled all around the position to form a parapet, care being taken to pile it so as to permit all-round fire of the weapon. Although 360° fire is possible from

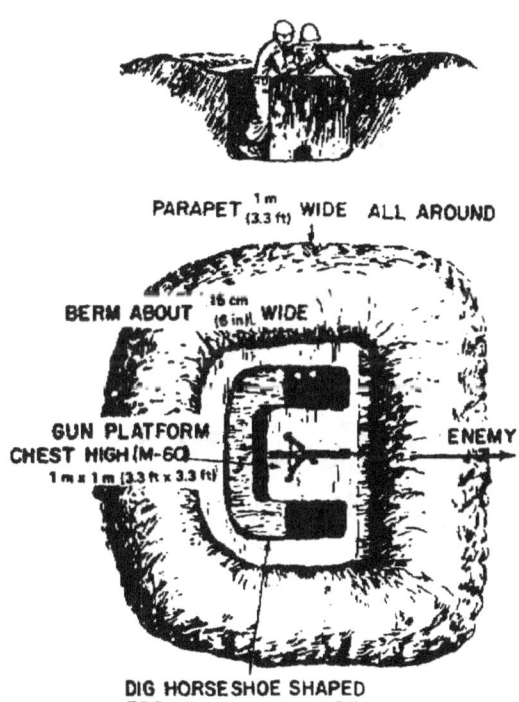

Figure 1-19. Horseshoe type machinegun emplacement.

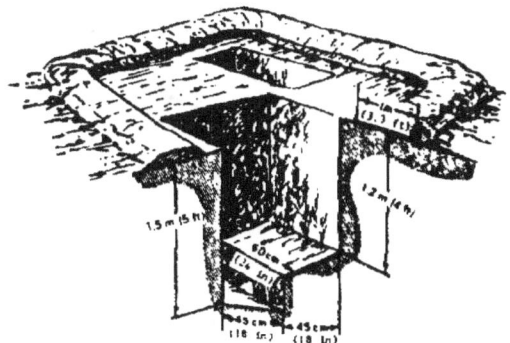

Figure 1-20. Two one-man foxhole type machinegun emplacement.

this position, fire to the front or rear is most effective since the M60 machinegun is fed from the left side.

1-16. EMPLACEMENTS FOR RECOILLESS WEAPONS

a. Types. Two types of open emplacements for recoilless weapons are the pit type and the two two-man foxhole type.

(1) Pit type. This emplacement is a circular pit about 1.2 meters (4 feet) in diameter and about 1 meter (40 inches) deep depending on the height of the occupants. A parapet should not be constructed for this emplacement because of the backblast. It is large enough for two men and permits the assistant to turn with the traversing weapon, to avoid being behind it when it is fired. This emplacement is shallow enough to permit the rear end of the weapon to clear the top at maximum elevation, thus insuring that the hot backblast of the rockets is not deflected to the occupants. Since this emplacement offers protection for the crew against direct fire weapons only, supplementary personnel emplacements should be provided ((1), fig. 1-21).

(2) Two two-man foxhole type. The emplacement shown in (2) figure 1-21 provides

limited protection for the crew against nuclear effects and armor except when actually firing.

b. Blast effects. Due to the backblast effects of the recoilless weapon, it should not be fired from a confined space such as a fully covered emplacement. Because the backblast will reveal the firing position, alternate firing positions with the connecting trenches should be constructed if there is sufficient time.

1-17. MORTAR EMPLACEMENTS

a. General. The emplacement illustrated in (1), figure 1-22 is circular in shape. The emplacement is excavated to the dimensions shown with the sides of the emplacement sloping inward toward the bottom. The floor slopes to the drainage sump located under the open gap in the parapet. An ammunition ready rack or niche, located so that it is convenient for the gunner, is built into the side of the emplacement. The bottom of the ammunition rack is elevated from the floor of the emplacement. Another ready rack may be constructed in one side of the trench leading to the position. The initial emplacement is revetted using sandbags and the improved emplacement is revetted using

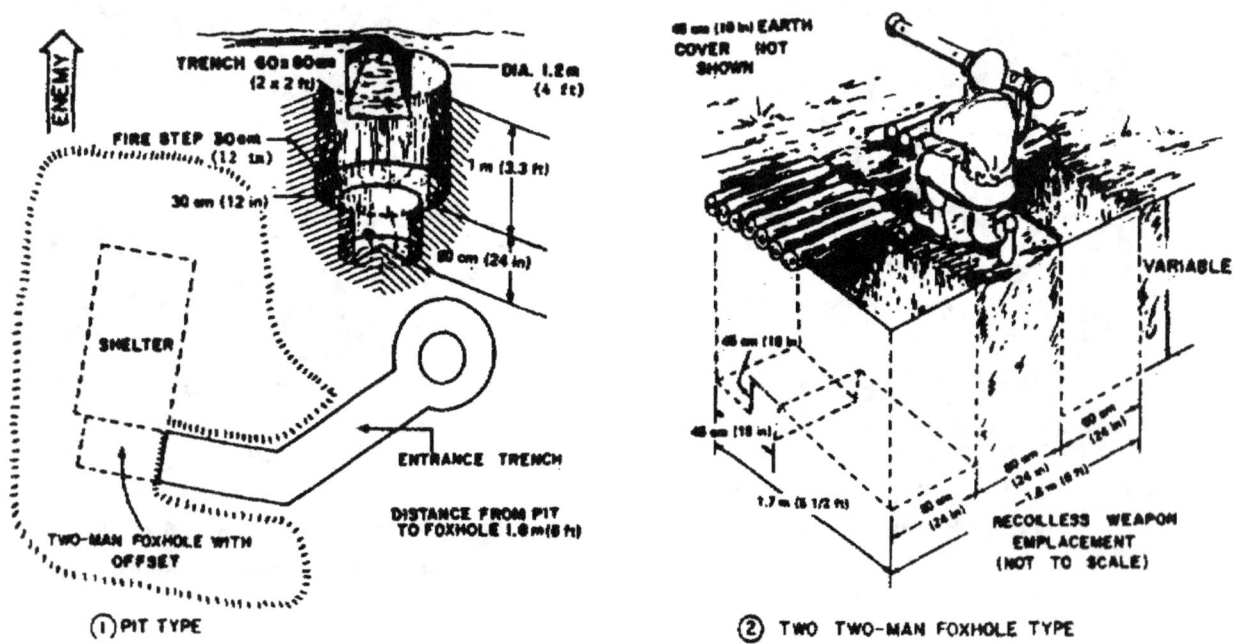

Figure 1-21. Emplacement for recoilless weapons.

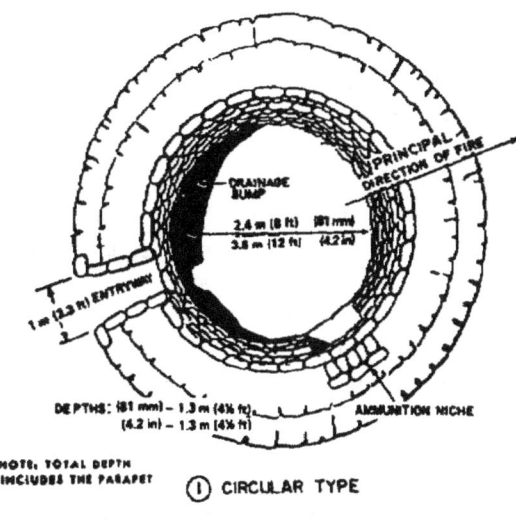

① CIRCULAR TYPE

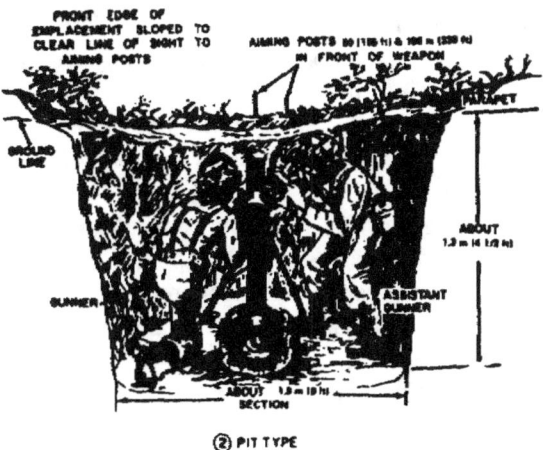

② PIT TYPE

Figure 1-22. Mortar emplacements.

corrugated metal. Before constructing the parapet, the mortar is laid for direction of fire by the use of an aiming circle or alternate means. The parapet should be not more than 50 cm (20 inches) high and a minimum of 1 meter (3 feet) wide. An exit trench may be constructed leading to personnel shelters and to other mortar positions. Construction of the parapet should be coordinated with the infantry commander.

b. The 81-mm mortar. A pit type emplacement for the 81-mm mortar is shown in (2), figure 1-22.

c. Emplacement for 4.2-inch mortar. The 4.2-inch mortar emplacement is identical to the one described above for the 81-mm mortar except for dimension changes shown in (1), figure 1-22.

1-18. EMPLACEMENT FOR 106-mm RECOILLESS RIFLE OR TOW MISSILE (JEEP MOUNTED)

These weapons are often fired from their 1/4-ton truck mounts since the weapons should be mobile and moved to new positions after firing a few rounds. In a defensive operation, several open pits should be constructed with concealed routes from these firing positions to a concealed shelter position with overhead cover. The weapons remain in the shelter until needed, then after firing, they are moved to other firing positions or back to their shelters. The firing pit for these weapons should protect the sides and front of the body of the vehicles. The rifle or TOW should be above the parapet level. The rear of the emplacement should be ramped so the vehicle can move out quickly. Emplacements of this type require approximately 30 manhours to construct since alternate positions are required, so the necessity for using heavy equipment is obvious. Figure 1-23 illustrates an emplacement for the 106-mm recoilless rifle which will permit the weapon muzzle to extend over the parapet to preclude damage to the vehicle from the muzzle blast.

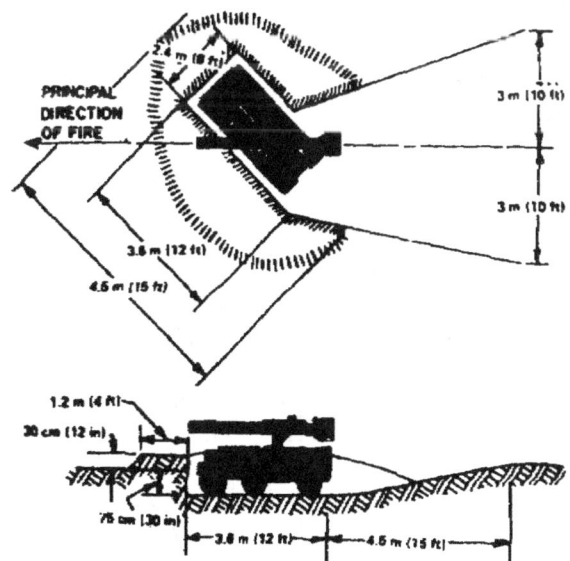

Figure 1-23. Emplacement for 106-mm rifle TOW missile.

Section VI. Construction of Vehicle and Artillery Emplacements

1-19. TYPICAL VEHICLE PIT

Digging in should be restricted to essential vehicles. Vehicle pits should be as narrow and as short as the vehicle size permits. They should be oriented randomly. All canvas should be removed and the top of the trucks should be at least 1 foot below the top of the surrounding parapet. The excavations should be as shown in table 1-3 and figure 1-24. Use of soil in construction of the

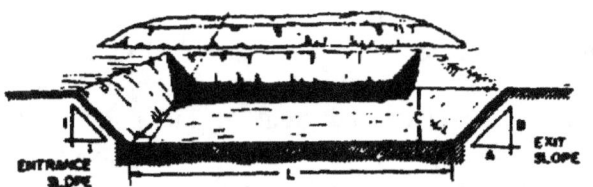

Figure 1-24. Typical vehicle pit.

parapet reduces the depth of cut necessary to properly protect a vehicle. The parapet should be streamlined and as well compacted as possible. The majority of vehicles should be concealed or camouflaged, with advantage taken of natural features such as woods, defilade, hegerows, and buildings.

1-20. TOWED ARTILLERY WEAPONS

a. Purpose. Emplacements for artillery weapons must provide maximum flexibility in the delivery of fire and protect the weapon and its crew against the effects of conventional and nuclear weapons.

b. Emplacement for 105- and 155-mm howitzer. Artillery weapons emplacements are constructed so as to allow for continuous improvement in order to provide additional protection and comfort in the event of prolonged occupation. These emplacements are developed in stages as described in (**1**) through (**4**) below.

(**1**) **Stage 1.** This stage provides open foxholes for the protection of the crew and open emplacements for infantry weapons used to defend the position. Provision is made for only minimum essential shifting of the gun trail and ammunition is stored in the open. Stage-one emplacement for a 105-mm howitzer is illustrated in figure 1-25.

(**2**) **Stage 2.** This stage provides trail logs for all around traverse of the weapon, a low parapet to protect the weapon, and covered emplacements for the crew, defensive weapons, and ammunition. Stage-two emplacement for a 105-mm howitzer is illustrated in (2), figure 1-25.

(**3**) **Stage 3.** In this stage a parapet revetted on the inside which permits all around direction fire is provided. Work is

Table 1-3. Dimensions of Typical Vehicle Pits

	¼-ton truck and trailer, canvas down	¾-ton truck and trailer, with radio shelter	2½-ton truck and trailer, canvas down	5-ton truck and trailer, canvas down
Depth of cut (C)	0.9m (35 in)	1.8m (6 ft)	1.5m (5 ft)	1.5m (5 ft)
Width of pit	2.4m (8 ft)	3.0m (10 ft)	3.5m (11.5 ft)	3.6m (11.8 ft)
Level length of pit (L)	6.0m (20 ft)	8.1m (27 ft)	10.5m (34 ft)	10.8m (35.5 ft)
Thickness of parapet (H)	60cm (2 ft)	75cm (30 in)	75cm (30 in)	75cm (30 in)
Width of parapet (P)	1.2m (47 in)	2.4m (7.9 ft)	2.7m (8.9 ft)	2.7m (8.9 ft)
Exit slope (A:B)*	1:1	2:1	2:1	2:1
Total excavation	19 cu meters (25 cu yd)	61 cu meters (80 cu yd)	71 cu meters (93 cu yd)	76 cu meters (100 cu yd)
Equipment hours**	0.4	0.8	0.9	0.9

*Entrance slope 1:1.
**For cut and rough parapet construction only, at appropriate rates for D7 or D8 type bulldozers.

Figure 1-25. Development of 105-mm Howitzer emplacement.

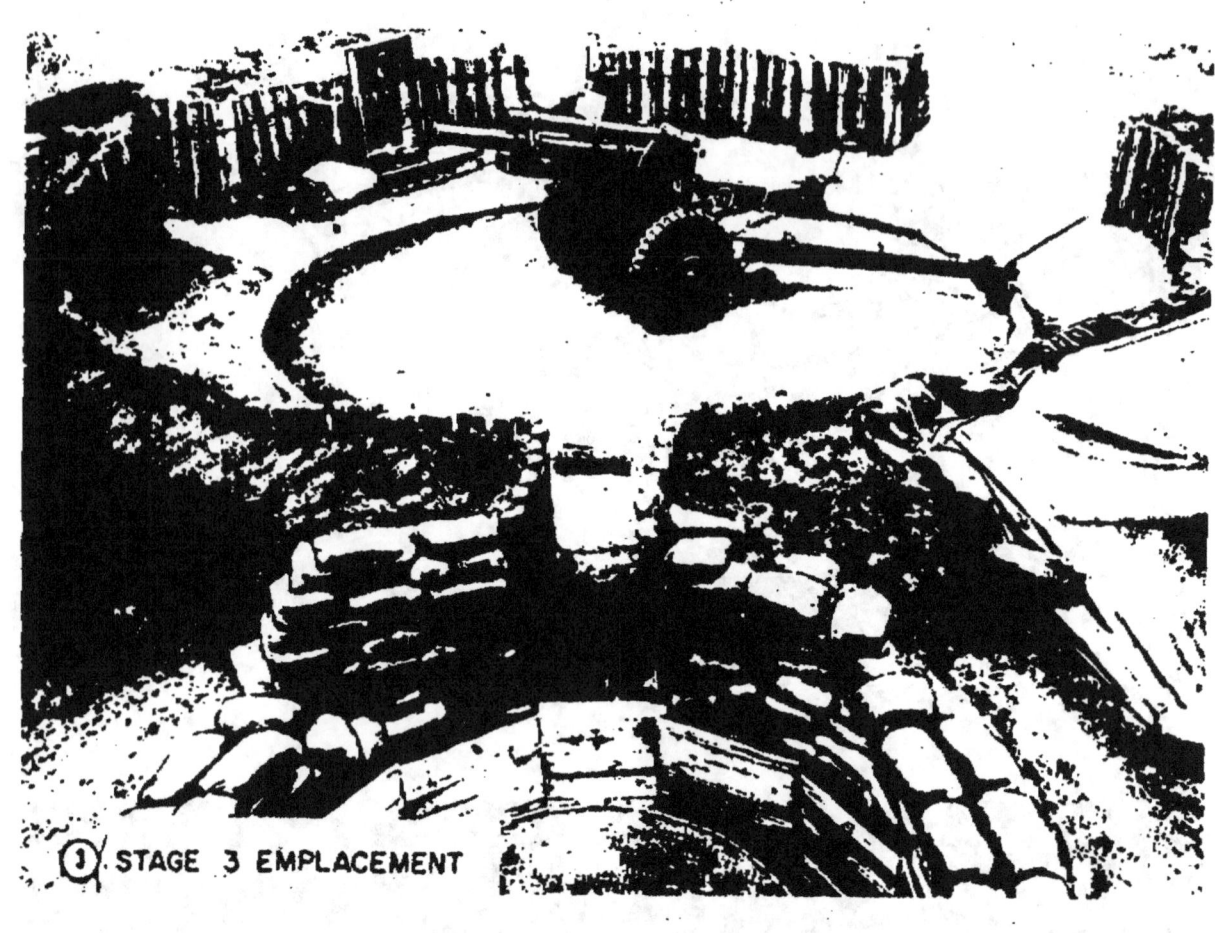

③ STAGE 3 EMPLACEMENT

④ COMPLETED EMPLACEMENT

Figure 1-25. Development of 105-mm Howitzer emplacement. (Continued)

1-22

begun on covered shelters for personnel and ammunition. Stage-three emplacement for a 10-mm howitzer Is illustrated in (3), figure 1-25.

(4) **Stage 4.** In this stage revetment is provided for the round fighting positions and for the outside and top of the parapet. Overhead cover is also provided for the personnel ready position and the ammunition shelter. Stage-four emplacement for a 106-mm howitzer is illustrated in) (4), figure 1-25 and (2), figure 1-26. Dimensions and layout are also shown in figure 1-26. Figure 1-27 shows semipermanent position for 155-mm howitzer.

(5) **Use of overhead cover.** It is usually difficult to provide overhead cover for artillery weapons. The widths and heights involved make such construction impractical under most conditions. Overhead cover would unduly restrict the firing capability of the weapon. In addition, under most conditions, it is not desirable to excavate an emplacement for the weapon much below ground level or to construct a high all-round parapet for the following reasons:

(a) A high all-round parapet restricts the direct fire capability of the weapon.

(b) An emplacement excavated below ground creates difficulty in rapid removal of the weapon from the emplacement.

c. **Accessory structures.**

(1) **Ammunition shelters.** Sectional shelters as described previously may be used with overhead cover as ammunition shelters with the types of weapons emplacements discussed above.

(2) **Accessory shelters.** Ready shelters for personnel and shelters for fire direction centers and switchboards are constructed using standard shelter designs.

1-21. **SELF-PROPELLED ARTILLERY AND TANK-MOUNTED WEAPONS EMPLACEMENT**

a. **Self-propelled artillery.** Large caliber self-propelled weapons have a limited

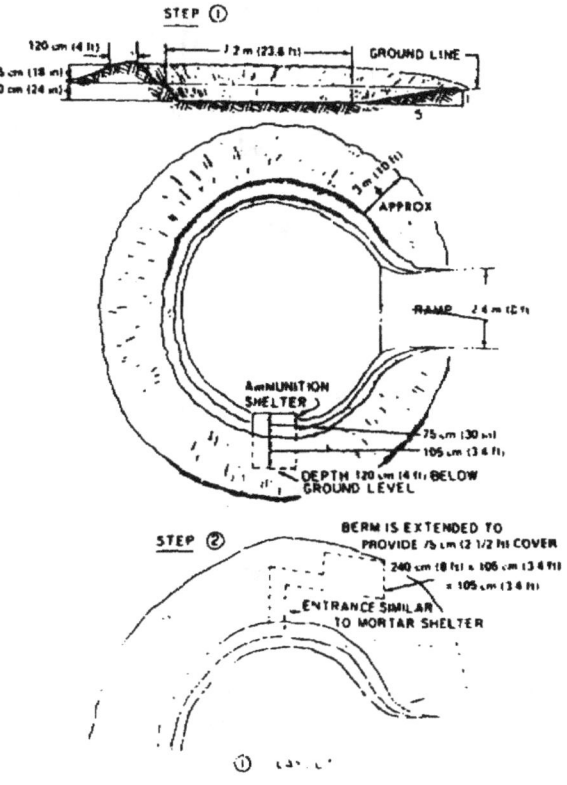

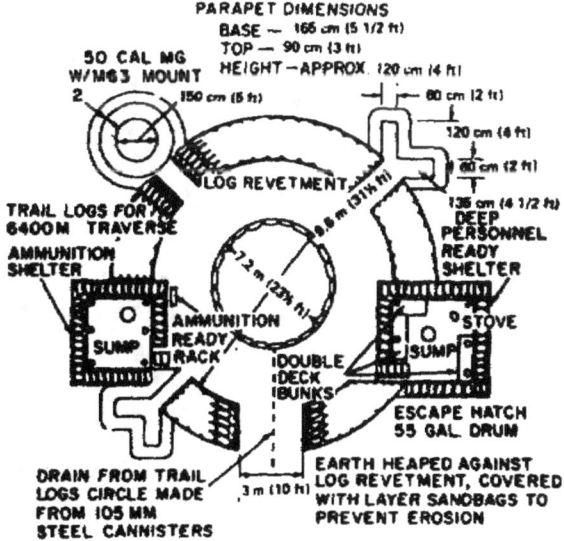

Figure 1-26. Final stage development, howitzer emplacement.

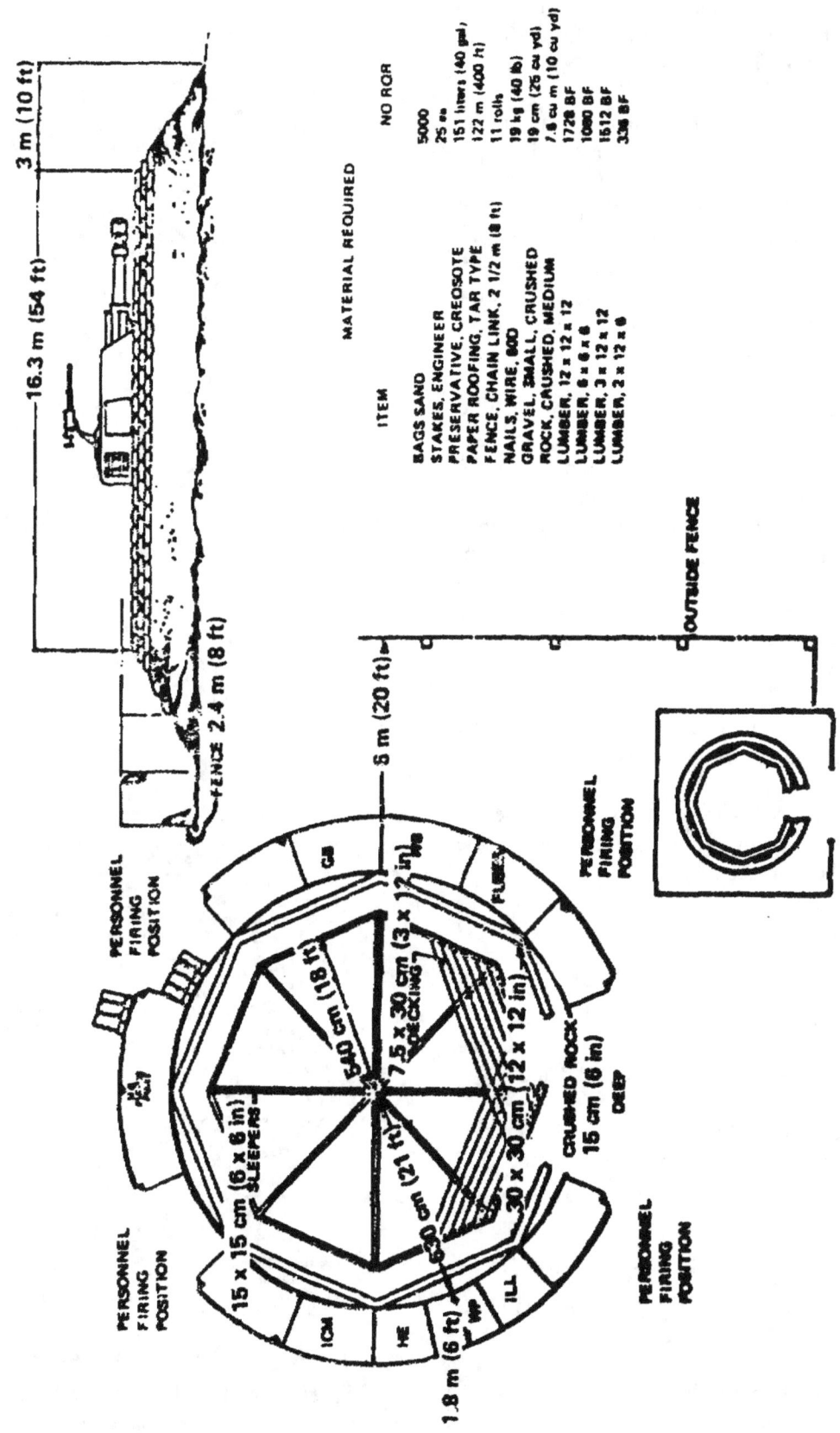

Figure 1-27. Position for 155-mm howitzer, SP (semipermanent installation).

1-24

traverse without turning the vehicle. For this reason it is seldom practical to construct emplacements for this type of weapon. When positions for self-propelled weapons are prepared, a sloped ramp is built to facilitate the vehicle's entry into and withdrawal from the gunpit. In extremely cold weather, gravel, saplings, or similar covering may be necessary for the floor of the pit so that the tracks of the vehicles will not freeze to the ground. The rear of the pit and the sloped ramp should be widened sufficiently to permit driving the vehicle in at an angle in order to compensate for the limited traverse of the weapon.

b. **Tanks.** A tank is emplaced or protected in the same manner as any other vehicle. Natural defilades such as road cuts or ditches are used where available. In open areas, parapets are provided to protect the sides and front of the hull of the vehicle, and the rear is left open. The simplest form of a dug-in position of this type is shown in figure 1-28. Whenever possible, such positions are constructed and occupied during darkness, with all camouflage being completed before dawn. The emplacement

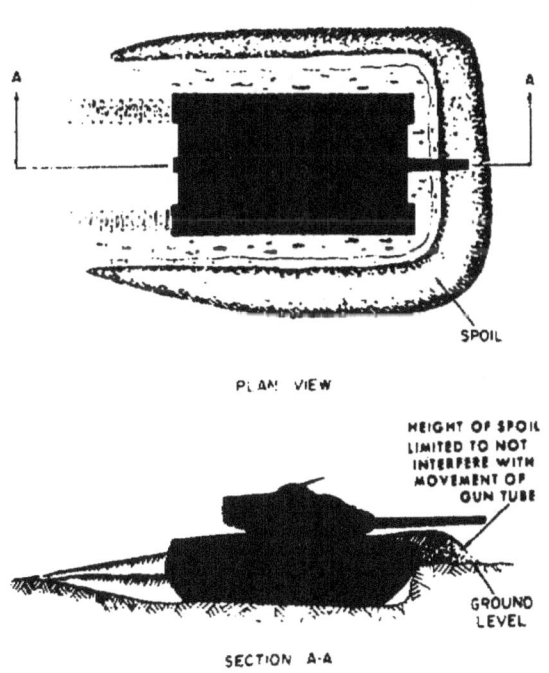

SPOIL

PLAN VIEW

HEIGHT OF SPOIL LIMITED TO NOT INTERFERE WITH MOVEMENT OF GUN TUBE

GROUND LEVEL

SECTION A-A

CAMOUFLAGE NOT SHOWN

Figure 1-28. Dug-in emplacement for self-propelled weapons.

normally includes foxhole protection for relief personnel, preferably connected with the emplacement by a short trench. A dug-in emplacement of this type should have the following:

(1) An excavation deep enough to afford protection for the tracks and part of the hull of the vehicle with maximum thickness of the parapet at the front of the emplacement and the rear left open for entry and exit of vehicle.

(2) Inside dimensions just large enough to permit entry and exit of vehicle.

(3) An inside depth permitting the weapon to depress to its minimum elevation. Tank emplacements must have sufficient space for the storage of ammunition.

(4) Barrel stops, if necessary, to prevent fire into adjacent units.

(5) Provisions for drainage (if possible) and frostproof flooring to prevent tracks from freezing to the ground.

(6) If it is necessary to deliver fire at elevations higher than permitted by the carriage design, the floor must be sloped up in the direction of fire.

1-22. ARTILLERY EMPLACEMENT IN SOFT GROUND

a. The siting of artillery positions in areas where the ground is soft requires the construction of pads to preclude differential settlement and thus the relaying of the weapon after each round is fired. Wooden pads can be built using laminated construction of radial sleepers (fig. 1-29) and other construction techniques. The wooden pad distributes the load over a large area with no significant settlement and is flexible and strong enough to withstand the turning and movement of self-propelled weapons. The trail logs are anchored just outside the pad for towed weapons. For self-propelled weapons, the recoil spades can be set in compacted material or in a layer of crushed rock just off the pad. Figure 1-30 shows position with pad for the 8-inch or 175-mm gun and figure 1-31 shows another pad for these guns which has non-radial sleepers and laminated flooring.

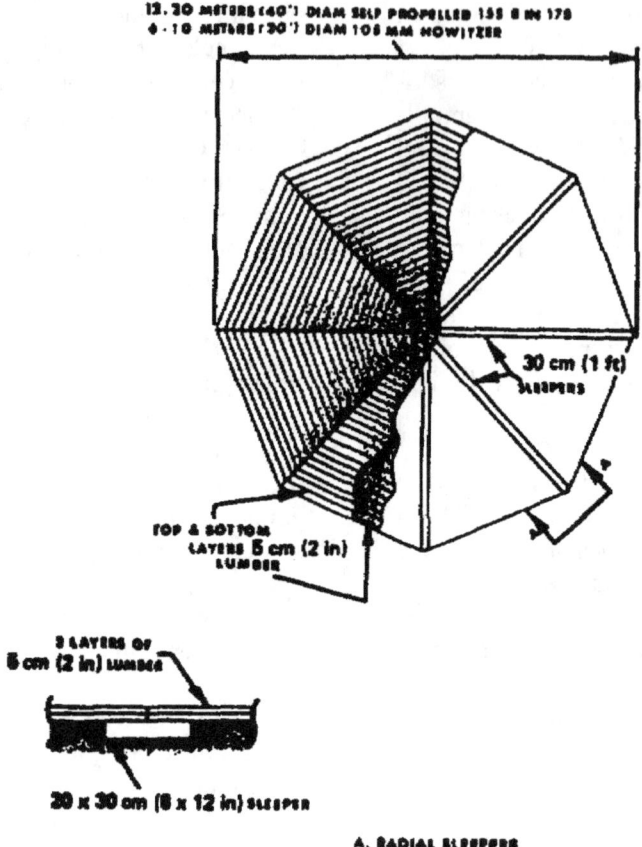

12. 30 METERS (40') DIAM SELF PROPELLED 155 8 IN 175
6 - 10 METERS (30') DIAM 105 MM HOWITZER

30 cm (1 ft)
SLEEPERS

TOP & BOTTOM
LAYERS 5 cm (2 in)
LUMBER

3 LAYERS OF
5 cm (2 in) LUMBER

30 x 30 cm (8 x 12 in) SLEEPER

A. RADIAL SLEEPERS

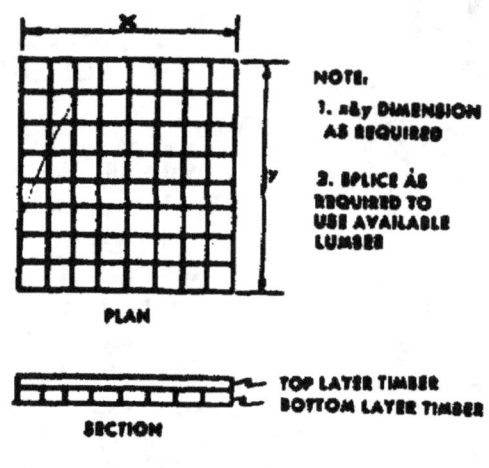

X

Y

NOTE:

1. x&y DIMENSION AS REQUIRED

2. SPLICE AS REQUIRED TO USE AVAILABLE LUMBER

PLAN

TOP LAYER TIMBER
BOTTOM LAYER TIMBER

SECTION

B. LAMINATED CONSTRUCTION

Figure 1-29. Radial and laminated gun pads.

Figure 1-32 shows a concrete gun pad for these weapons. Figure 1-33 shows light and medium artillery battery layouts. Revetments and shelters can be constructed as described in paragraph 1-21.

b. Various synthetic materials, such as fiberglass mats (also used as helicopter landing pads), may be used as gun pads depending on the characteristics of the weapons.

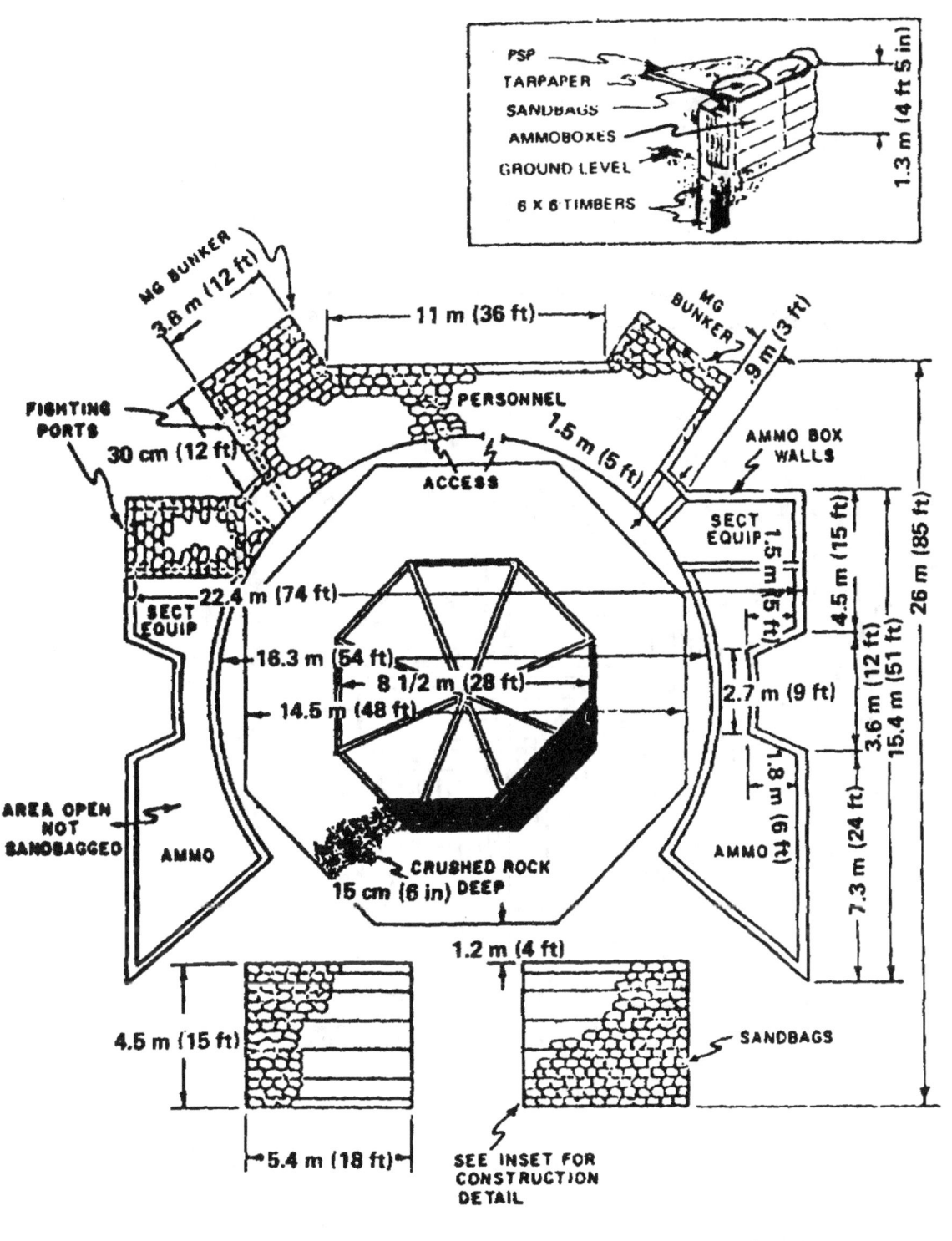

INSET DETAIL:
PSP
TARPAPER
SANDBAGS
AMMOBOXES
GROUND LEVEL
6 X 6 TIMBERS
1.3 m (4 ft 5 in)

MG BUNKER (12 ft)
3.6 m (12 ft)
11 m (36 ft)
MG BUNKER .9 m (3 ft)
FIGHTING PORTS
30 cm (12 ft)
PERSONNEL
ACCESS
1.5 m (5 ft)
AMMO BOX WALLS
SECT EQUIP
1.5 m (5 ft)
4.5 m (15 ft)
26 m (85 ft)
22.4 m (74 ft)
18.3 m (54 ft)
8 1/2 m (28 ft)
14.5 m (48 ft)
2.7 m (9 ft)
3.6 m (12 ft)
15.4 m (51 ft)
SECT EQUIP
1.8 m (6 ft)
7.3 m (24 ft)
AREA OPEN NOT SANDBAGGED
AMMO
AMMO
CRUSHED ROCK 15 cm (6 in) DEEP
4.5 m (15 ft)
5.4 m (18 ft)
1.2 m (4 ft)
SANDBAGS
SEE INSET FOR CONSTRUCTION DETAIL

15,000	SANDBAGS	NAILS, WIRE 60d 15 cm (6 in) 28 kg (60 lbs)
960	105 AMMO BOXES	PRESERVATIVE, CREOSOTE 80 GALS
3,680	ENG STAKES 2.4 m (8 ft) LG	PAPER, ROOFING TAR TYPE .9 m (3 ft) WIDE 121.2 m (400 ft)
150	7.5 cm x 30 cm x 3.8 m (3 in x 12 in x 12 ft)	GRAVEL, SMALL CRUSHED 36 cu m (45 cu yds)
36	15 cm x 15 cm x 3.8 m (6 in x 6 in x 12 ft)	ROCK, CRUSHED, MED. (5- 7.5 cm (2- 3 in DIA)) 73 cu m (95 cu yds)

Figure 1-30. Position with 8-inch or 175-mm gun pad with radial sleepers.

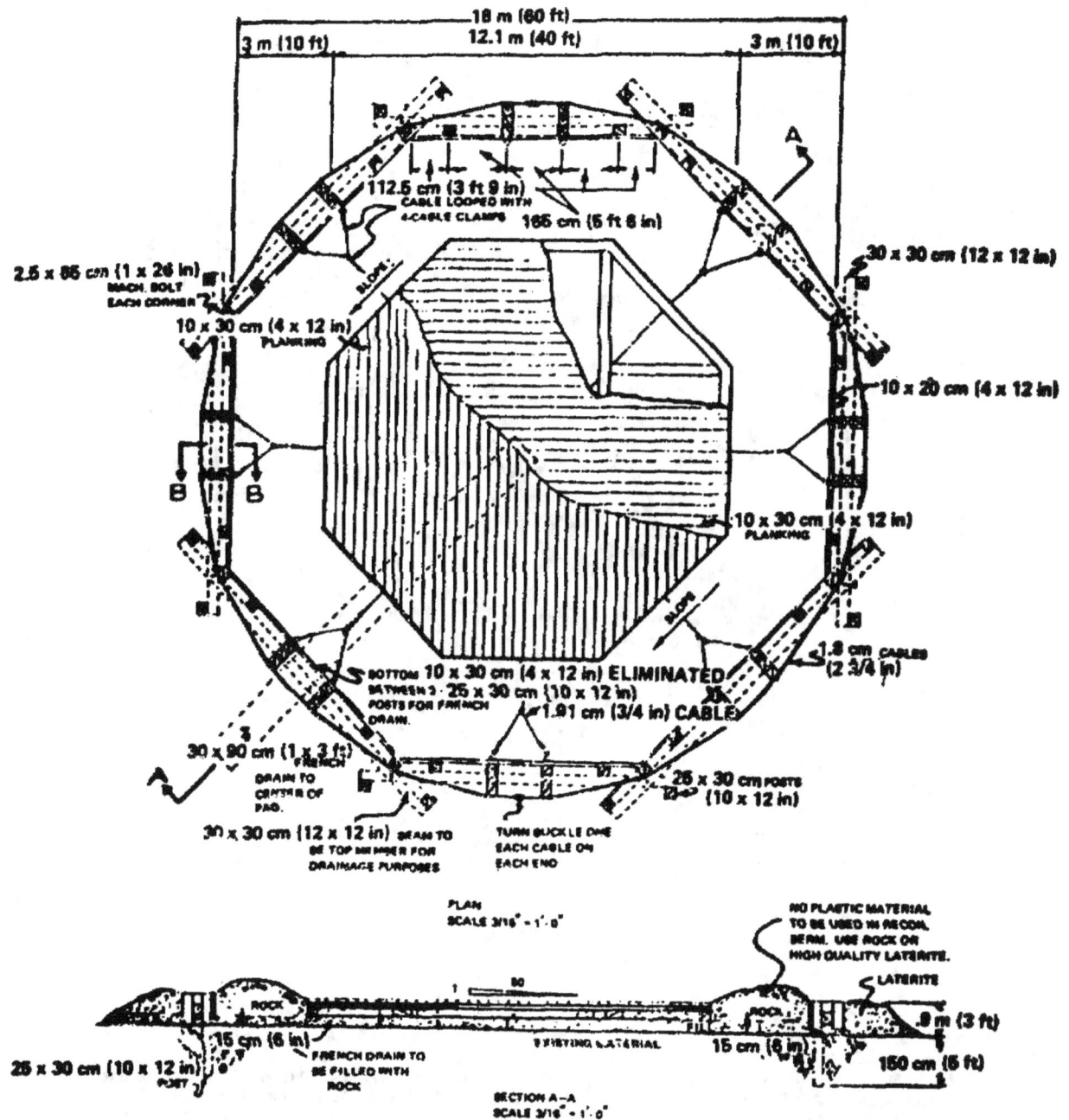

Figure 1-31. Gun pad for 8-inch or 175-mm with non-radial sleepers.

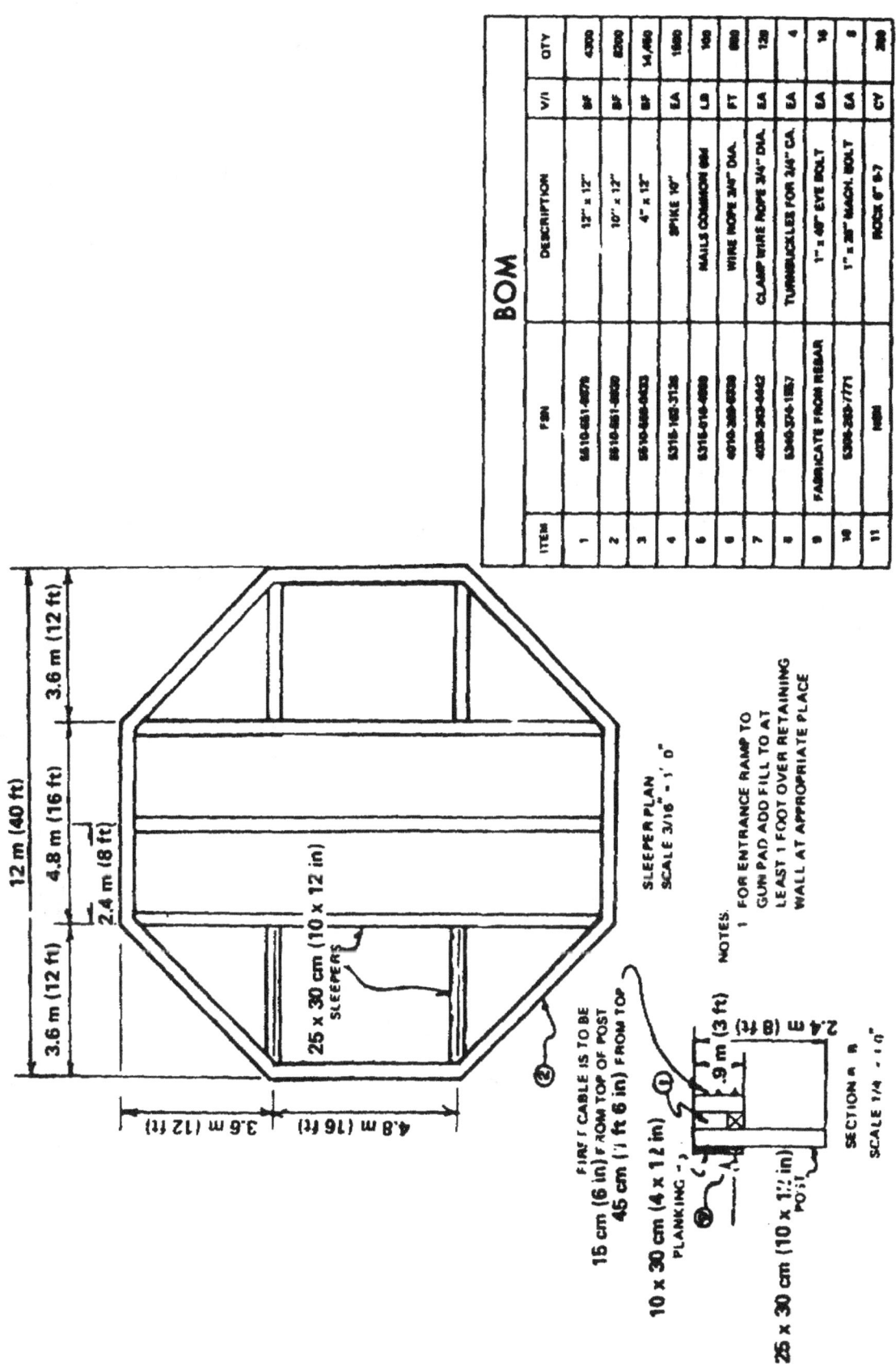

Figure 1-31. Gun pad for 8-inch or 175-mm gun with non-radial sleepers. (Continued)

1-29

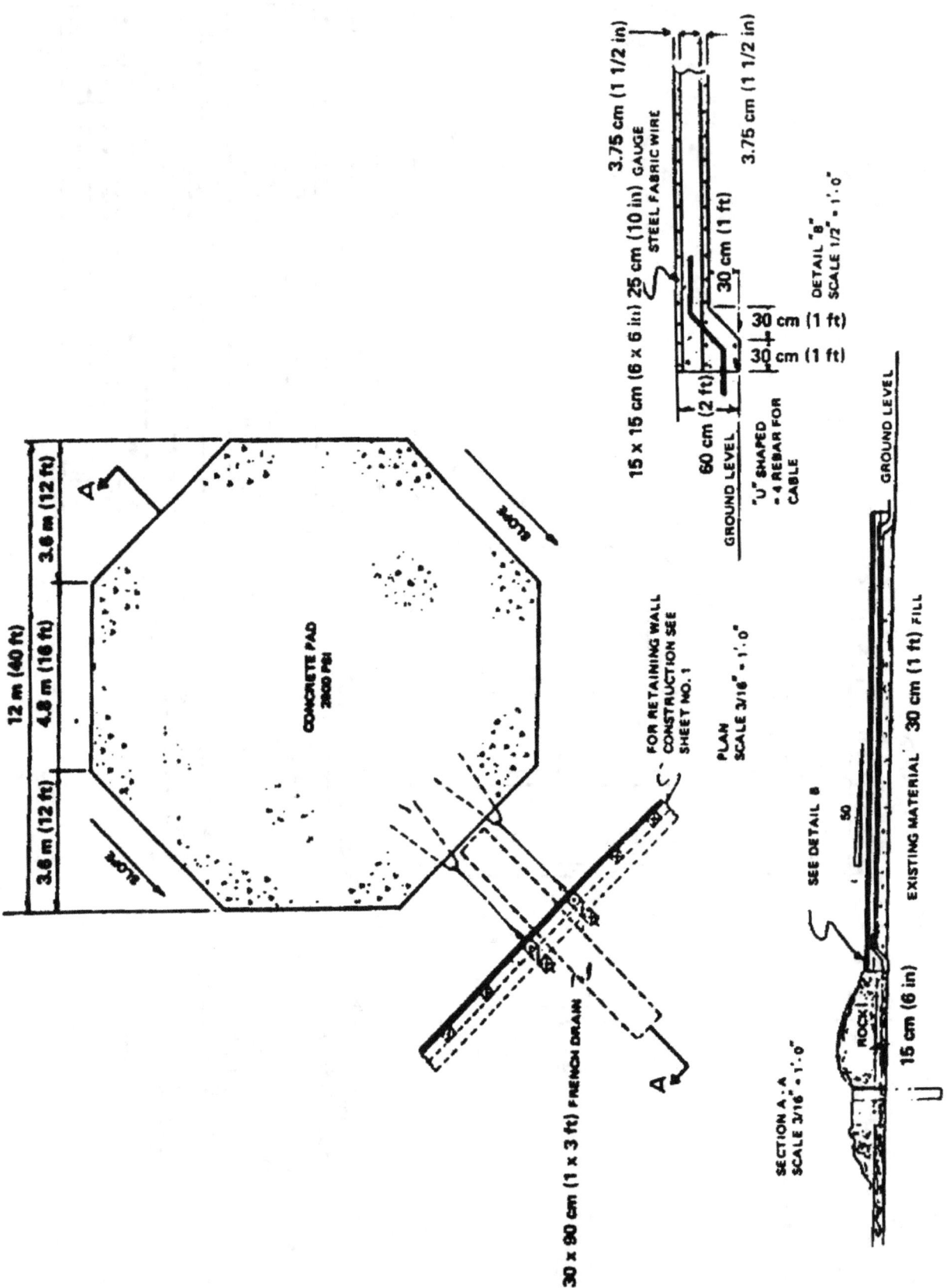

Figure 1-32. Concrete gun pad for 8-inch or 175-mm gun.

1-30

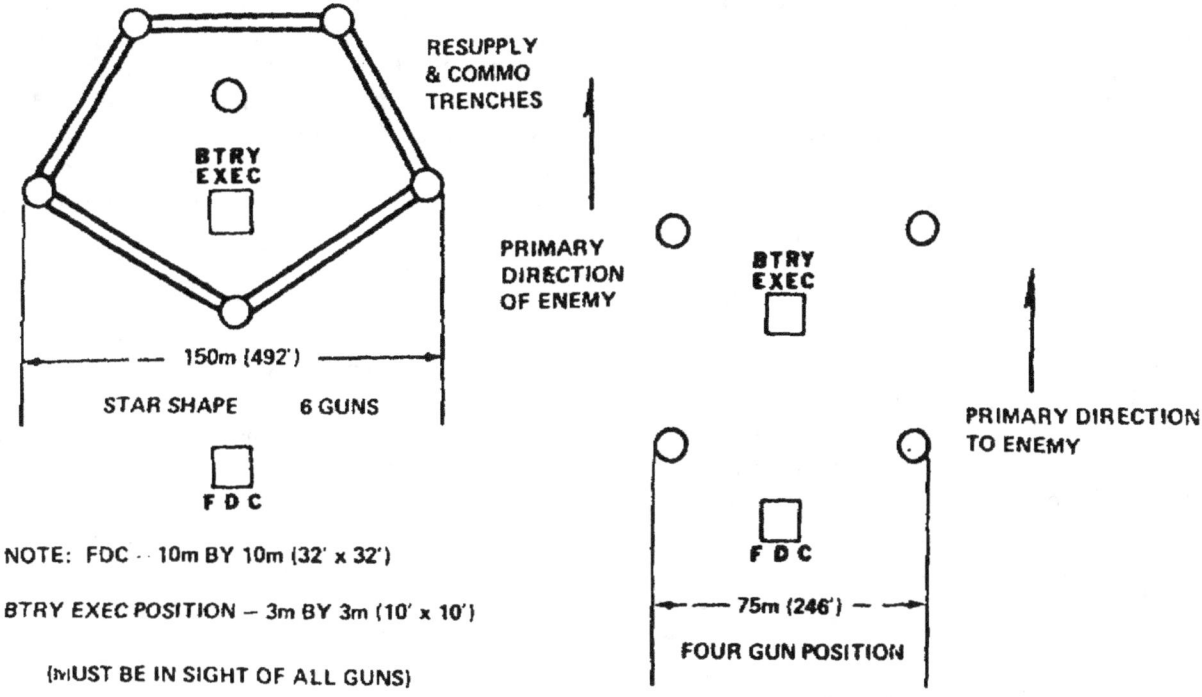

Figure 1-33. Light and medium artillery battery layouts.

Section VII. Firebase Construction

1-23. DESCRIPTION

The airmobile division engineer battalion is equipped to construct artillery firebases in areas where ground transport is prohibitive. Especially in an unsophisticated environment, such as forest and jungle, these firebases play an integral part in airmobile operations, both as command posts and artillery firebases. The most frequently constructed firebase houses an infantry battalion command element, two infantry companies, a 105-mm howitzer battery and three to six 155-mm howitzers. A firebase housing the above units consists of the following facilities: infantry tactical operations center (TOC), artillery fire direction centers (FDC), ammunition storage pits, garbage sump, command and control helicopter pad, logistics storage area and slingout pad artillery firing positions, helicopter marking area and refuel point, and hardened personnel sleeping positions. Firebases usually are surrounded by a protective berm with perimeter fighting bunkers, two or more bands of tactical wire and a cleared buffer zone to provide adequate fields of fire for perimeter defense. If a local water source is available, an airmobile engineer water supply point may be established to provide water for the firebase and units in the local area.

1-24. CONSTRUCTION

Construction of an airmobile firebase may be divided into three phases: combat assault and initial clearing, immediate tactical construction, and final defensive structures.

a. Phase 1. Phase I, combat assault and initial clearing, consists of securing the firebase site and clearing an area large enough to accommodate CH-47 and CH-54 helicopters.

The time required to complete this phase depends on the terrain at the firebase site. If the site is free of trees and undergrowth, or if these obstacles have been removed by artillery and tactical air fire preparation, combat engineers can move immediately to Phase II after the initial combat assault on the site. If the site is covered with foliage and trees, the security force and combat engineers may be required to rappel into the site from hovering helicopters. Depending on the density of the foliage on the site, completion of the initial clearing phase by combat engineers with demolitions and chain saws may take up to three hours to accomplish.

b. Phase II. Phase II, immediate tactical construction, commences as soon as the cleared area can accommodate either medium or heavy lift helicopters. Two light airmobile dozers are lifted to the site and are immediately employed clearing brush and stumps to expand the perimeter and to clear and level howitzer positions. Meanwhile, the combat engineers continue to expand the perimeter with chain saws, demolitions, and bangalore torpedoes. If sufficient area is available, a heavy airmobile dozer usually is committed to clearing a logistic storage area and slingout pad, then to expanding the perimeter and fields of fire. The backhoes are committed to excavating positions for the infantry TOC, artillery FDC and, as soon as the perimeter trace is established, perimeter fighting bunkers. The immediate tactical construction phase is characterized by the coordinated effort of infantry, artillery, and engineer forces to produce a tenable tactical position by nightfall on the first day. It is a time of intense helicopter traffic introducing personnel, ammunition, barrier and bunker materials, rations, fuel, water, and artillery pieces onto the site. Aircraft traffic and logistics input must be rigidly controlled to preclude nonessential supplies and aircraft from hampering engineer effort. Therefore, a coordinated site plan and list of priorities for transportation and construction must be prepared and constantly updated. Priorities and the site plan are established by the tactical commander in coordination with the project engineer. As soon as a perimeter trace is established and the site is capable

of accepting the logistics and artillery lifts, maximum effort is directed toward the defenses of the firebase. Combat engineers and the heavy dozer continue to push back the undergrowth to permit adequate fields of fire. The two light airmobile dozers may be committed to construction of a 1.2 meter (4 ft) berm around the perimeter to protect against direct fire. Infantry troops are committed to constructing perimeter fighting bunkers at sites previously excavated by the backhoes and, assisted by combat engineers, begin erection of the first band of tactical wire, usually triple standard concertina. Artillery troops not committed immediately to fire missions prepare ammunition storage bunkers and parapet around each howitzer.

c. Phase III. Phase III, final defensive structures, is initiated as construction forces complete the immediate defensive structures. Combat engineers who are not placing the tactical wire or clearing fields of fire commence construction of the infantry TOC and artillery FDC. Infantry and artillery troops are committed to the second band of tactical wire and to erecting personnel sleeping positions with overhead cover. Culvert half sections lend themselves to rapid construction of these positions. Phase III is usually a continuous process, involving constant Improvement and maintenance; however, the majority of protective structures, including sandbag protection of the TOC and personnel bunkers, usually are completed by the end of the fourth day. The controlling parameter in construction of a firebase is time; since the firebase is the first phase of the occupation of a hostile area, the battalion command center and the artillery pieces must be operational as soon as possible and protection against direct and indirect fire requires immediate attention. Several techniques have been developed to increase the efficiency and speed with which construction can progress. Among these are precut TOC structures and the use of culvert as molds for protective bunkers. However, the most effective technique yet adopted is a closely coordinated and controlled plan, outlining the location, priority, and construction force for each phase of the mission.

1-25. FIREBASE LAYOUT

a. The primary purpose of the base is to provide positions for artillery. Thus, physical layout of the fire support base (FSB) will give best possible fields of fire to guns.

b. The base TOC will be located as near FDC as the base terrain allows. The TOC should be fairly centrally located and in a position to control base defense by visual means, if necessary.

c. The helicopter logistical pad should be within the base perimeter but be situated so that incoming and outgoing aircraft do not fly through the primary or most likely sector of fire of the artillery.

d. An admin/VIP helipad large enough for two UH-1 type aircraft should be located in the vicinity of the TOC.

e. If a helicopter rearming/refueling facility is located on the FSB, it should not be so near to either the gun positions or artillery ammunition storage pits that a fire or explosion of one will damage the others.

f. A landing zone for troop lift operations may be located outside the FSB but in the immediate vicinity of the perimeter positions.

g. Typical battery layouts are shown in figure 1-33.

1-26. ARTILLERY POSITION REQUIREMENTS

Engineer construction requirements for an artillery position within a firebase are generally as follows:

a. Platforms which allow the howitzers or guns to fire in all directions and be capable of supporting repeated firing shock in any type of soil condition.

b. Shelters capable of providing adequate protection for the firing crew.

c. Separate shelters large enough to contain an artillery section basic load of projectiles, fuzes, and propelling charges.

d. A wall or parapet around each howitzer or gun to protect the crew from fragments and small arms. The wall should be low enough to allow direct howitzer fire.

e. FDC/TOC shelters large enough to contain the personnel and equipment necessary for the operation of the fire direction center and tactical operations center.

Section VIII. Hasty Shelters

1-27. BASIC CONSIDERATIONS

a. Protection. Shelters are constructed primarily to protect soldiers, equipment, and supplies from enemy action and the weather. Shelters differ from emplacements because there are usually no provisions for firing weapons from them. However, they are usually constructed near or supplement the fighting positions. When natural shelters such as caves, mines, woods, or tunnels are available, they are used instead of constructing artificial shelters. Caves and tunnels must be carefully inspected by competent persons to determine their suitability and safety. The best shelter is usually the one that will provide the most protection with the least amount of effort. Actually, combat troops that have prepared defensive positions have some shelter in their foxholes or weapon emplacements. Shelters are frequently prepared by troops in support of front unit. Troops making a temporary halt in inclement weather when moving into positions prepare shelters as do units in bivouacs, assembly areas, rest areas, and static positions.

b. Surface shelter. The best observation is from this type of shelter and it is easier to enter or leave than an underground shelter. It also requires the least amount of labor to construct, but it is hard to conceal and requires a large amount of cover and revetting material. It provides the least amount of protection from nuclear weapons of the types of shelters discussed in this manual. Surface shelters are seldom used for personnel in forward combat positions unless they can be concealed in woods, on reverse slopes, or among buildings. It may be necessary to use surface shelters when the water level is close to the surface of the ground or when the surface is so hard that digging an underground shelter is impractical.

c. **Underground shelters.** Shelters of this type generally provide good protection against radiation because the surrounding earth and overhead cover are effective shields against nuclear radiation.

d. **Cut-and cover shelters.** These shelters are dug into the ground and backfilled on top with as thick a layer as possible of rocks, logs, sod, and excavated soil. These and cave shelters provide excellent protection from weather and enemy action.

e. **Siting.** Whenever possible, shelters should be sited on reverse slopes, in woods, or in some form of natural defilade as ravines, valleys, and other hollows or depressions in the terrain. They should not be in the path of natural drainage lines. All shelters must be camouflaged or concealed.

1-28. CONSTRUCTION

a. **Principles.** Hasty shelters are constructed with a minimum expenditure of time and labor using available materials. They are ordinarily built above ground or dug in deep snow. Shelters that are completely above ground offer protection against the weather and supplement or replace shelter tents which do not provide room for movement. Hasty shelters are useful in the winter when the ground is frozen, in mountainous country where the ground is too hard for deep digging, in deep snow, and in swampy or marshy ground.

b. **Sites for winter shelters.** Shelter sites that are near wooded areas are the most desirable in winter because these areas are warmer than open

fields. They conceal the glow of fires and provide fuel for cooking and heating. In heavy snow tree branches extending to the ground offer some shelter to small units.

c. **Materials.**

(1) **Construction.** Work on winter shelters should start immediately after the halt so that the men will keep warm. The relaxation and warmth offered by the shelter is usually worth the effort expended in constructing them. Beds of foliage, moss, straw, boards, skis, parkas, or shelter halves may be used as protection against dampness and cold from the ground. Snow should be removed from clothing and equipment before entering the shelter. The entrance of the shelter is located on the side that is least exposed to the wind, is close to the ground and has an upward incline. Plastering the walls with earth and snow reduces the effect of wind. The shelter itself should be as low as possible. The fire is placed low in fire holes and cooking pits.

(2) **Insulating.** Snow is windproof, so to keep the occupant's body heat from melting the snow, it is necessary only to place a layer of some insulating material such as a shelter half, blanket, or other material between the body and the snow.

1-29. TYPES

a. **Lean-to shelters.** This shelter (fig. 1-34) is made of the same material as the wigwam (natural saplings woven together and brush). The saplings are placed against a rock wall, a steep hillside, a deadfall, or some other existing vertical surface, on the leeward side. The ends may be closed with shelter halves or evergreen branches.

b. **Two-man mountain shelter.** This shelter (fig. 1-35) is useful, particularly in winter or in inclement weather when there is frequent rain or snow. It is basically a hole 2.1 meters (7 feet) long, 1 meter (40 inches) wide and 1 meter (40 inches) deep. This hole is covered with 6 to 8 inch diameter logs; then evergreen branches, a shelter half, and local material such as topsoil, leaves, snow, and twigs are added. The floor may be

PERSPECTIVE VIEW

SNOW

GROUND
LEVEL

SHELTER HALF
AT ONE OR BOTH
ENDS

SIDE VIEW

Figure 1-34. Lean-to shelter.

Figure 1-35. Two-man mountain shelter.

covered with evergreen twigs, a shelter half, or other expedient material. Entrances are provided at both ends if desired. A fire pit may be dug at one end for a small fire or stove. A low parapet is built around the emplacement to provide more height for the occupants. This shelter is very similar to an enlarged, roofed, prone shelter (figure 1-5).

Section IX. Deliberate Shelters and Bunkers

1-30. TYPES

The most effective shelters are deliberate, underground, cut-and-cover shelters. Shelters should be provided with as deep overhead cover as possible. They should be dispersed and have a maximum capacity of 20 to 25 men. Supply shelters may be of any size, depending on location, time, and materials available. The larger the shelter the greater the necessity for easy entrance and exit. Large shelters should have at least two well camouflaged entrances spaced widely apart. The farther away from the frontlines the larger, deeper, and more substantial shelter may be constructed because of more freedom of movement, easier access to materials and equipment, and more time to spend constructing it.

1-31. CONSTRUCTION REQUIREMENTS

a. Drainage. Drainage is an important problem particularly in cut-and-cover and cave shelters. After the shelter is dug, drainage work usually includes keeping the surface and rain water away from the entrance, preventing the water from seeping into the interior by ditching, and removal of water that has collected inside the shelter. The floors of shelters must have a slope of at least 1 percent toward a sump (fig. 1-36) near the entrance, while the entrance should be sloped more steeply toward a ditch or sump outside the shelter (fig. 1-37).

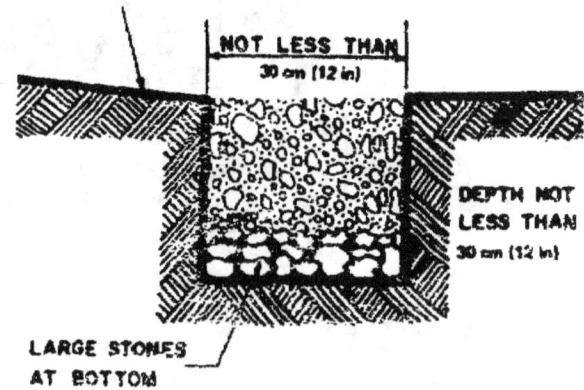

Figure 1-36. Sump for shelter drainage.

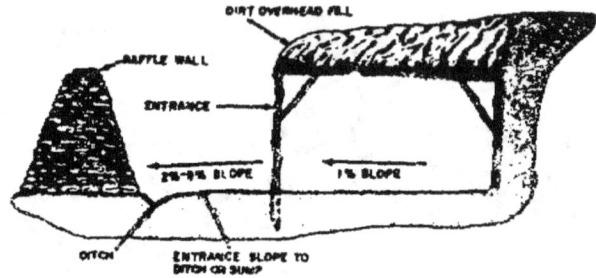

Figure 1-37. Floor and entrance drainage.

b. Ventilation. It is particularly important to ventilate cave shelters, especially if it is necessary to close the entrances during an attack. In surface and cut-and-cover shelters, enough fresh air usually is obtained by keeping entrances open. Vertical shafts bored within cave shelters are desirable if not absolutely essential. A stovepipe through a shaft assists the circulation of air. Shelters that are not provided with good ventilation should be used only by personnel who are to remain inactive while they are inside. Since an inactive man requires about .03 cubic meters (1 cu ft) of air per minute, unventilated shelters are limited in capacity. Initial airspace requirements for shelters for not over 12 men are 10 cubic meters (350 cu ft) per man.

c. **Entrance covering.** If gasproof curtains are not available, improvised curtains made of blankets hung on light, sloping frames may be used. They should be nailed securely to the sides and top entrance timbers. Curtains for cave shelters should be placed in horizontal entrances or horizontal approaches to inclines. Windows should be covered with single curtains. All crevices should be caulked with clay, old cloths or sandbags. Flooring or steps in front of gas curtains should be kept clear of mud and refuse. Small, baffled entrances and/or right angle turns will reduce the effects of nuclear blasts and will keep debris from being blown in. Baffle walls may be constructed of sods or sandbags. Materials which may be injurious to the occupants should be avoided.

d. **Sanitary conveniences.** Sanitary conveniences should be provided in all but air-raid emergency shelters and surface-type shelters, where latrines are available. Disposal is by burial or chemical treatment. When waterborne sewage facilities are available, disposal can be into septic tanks or sanitary sewers.

e. **Light security.** Blackout curtains should be installed in the entrance to all shelters to prevent light leakage. To be most effective, blackout curtains are hung in pairs so that one shields the other. Blankets, shelter-halves, or similar material may be used for this purpose.

f. **Emergency exits.** Emergency exits in larger shelters are desirable in case the main exit is blocked. If possible, the emergency exit should be

more blast-resistant than the main entrance. This can be done by making it just large enough to crawl through. Corrugated pipe sections or 55-gallon drums with the ends removed are useful in making this type of exit. A simple emergency exit which is blast resistant can be constructed by sloping a section of corrugated pipe from the shelter up to the surface, bracing a cover against the inside, and filling the section of pipe with gravel. When the inside cover is removed, the gravel will fall into the shelter, and the occupants can crawl through the exit without digging.

g. **Interior marking of shelter.** The entrances or interior walls of shelters whose personnel capacity makes it desirable may be marked by reflective tape or paint to facilitate the entry of troops under darkened conditions. There should be no sacrifice of camouflage discipline.

1-32. LOG SURFACE SHELTER

A log shelter (fig. 1-38) can be constructed in form of a box braced in every direction. The framework must be strong enough to support a minimum of 45 cm (18 in.) of earth cover and to withstand the concussion of a near-miss of a shell or bomb or the shock of a distant nuclear explosion. The size of the logs used is limited by the size of available

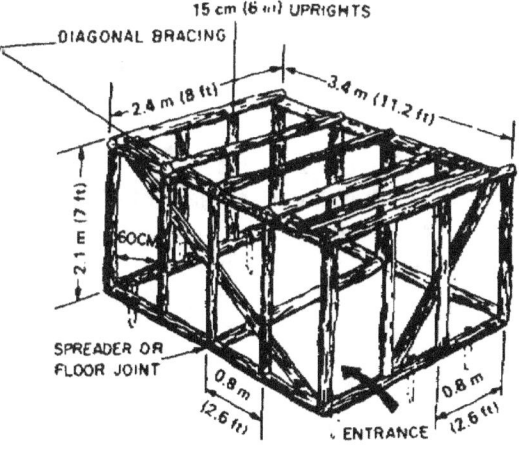

Figure 1-38. Log framed shelter.

logs for the roof supports and by the difficulty of transporting large timbers.

a. Size. Shelters 2 to 3 meters (6.5 to 10 ft) wide by 4.2 meters (14 ft) long are suitable for normal use.

b. Timbers. All timbers should be the same size, if possible, approximately 15 to 20 cm (6 to 8 in.) in diameter depending on the width of the shelter (table 1-4). The uprights should be approximately 60 cm (2 ft) apart except at the entrance where they may have to be spaced farther apart. The roof supports should be spaced the same as the uprights. Holes should be drilled for driftpins at all joints.

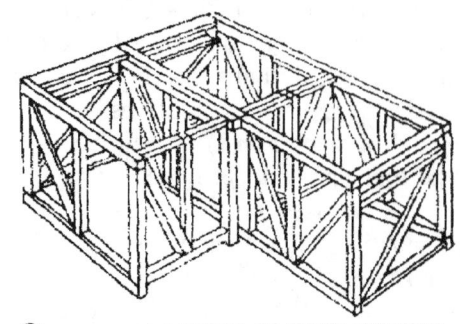

① TYPICAL CONNECTION OF THREE SECTIONS

Table 1-4. Size of Roof Supports

Size of timber (diameter)	Maximum span when used to support 45 cm of earth
10 cm (4 in.)	1.2 meters (4 feet)
12.5 cm (5 in.)	1.5 meters (5 feet)
15 cm (6 in.)	2.1 meters (7 feet)
17.5 cm (7 in.)	2.7 meters (9 feet)
20.0 cm (8 in.)	3.3 meters (11 feet)
22.5 cm (9 in.)	3.9 meters (13 feet)

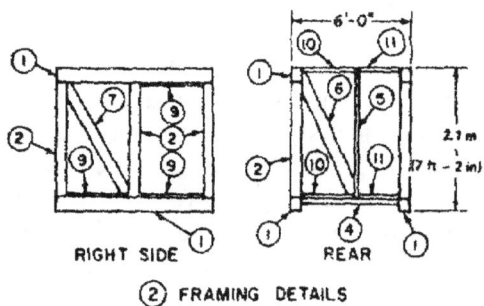

② FRAMING DETAILS

c. Bracing. Boards 2.5 by 10 cm (1 in. by 4 in.) in size for the diagonal bracing are nailed to caps, sill, and uprights.

d. Walls. The log shelters should be covered with board or saplings and backfilled with approximately 60 cm (2 ft) of earth, or hollow wall may be constructed around the buildings and filled with dirt.

e. Cover. A roof of planks, sheet metal, or other material is then laid over the roof supports and perpendicular to them to hold a minimum of 46 cm (18 in.) of earth cover which is effective against fragmentation (shrapnel) effects of mortars, artillery, and rockets.

③ FRAMING DETAILS

Figure 1-39. Sectional shelters.

1-33. SECTIONAL SHELTERS (SURFACE OR SUBSURFACE)

Shelters of the type in figure 1-39 are designed so that the 1.8 by 2.4 meters (6 by 8 ft) sections may be assembled for use individually or in combinations of two or more

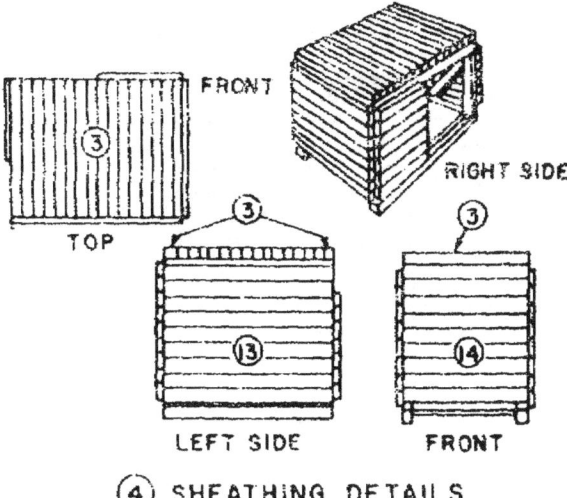

(4) SHEATHING DETAILS

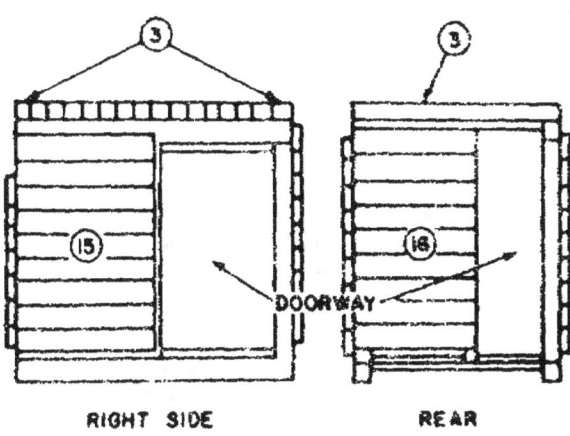

(5) SHEATHING DETAILS

Figure 1-39. Sectional shelters. (Continued)

sections to provide the required shelter area. They may be surface or subsurface. The advantages of sectional shelters for the purpose of command post or aid stations are the flexibility of the shelter area that can be provided, the depth of cover the shelter will support, the facet that the design lends itself to prefabrication, and their airtransportability by Huey helicopter, except for the cover. The principal disadvantage is the degree of skill required in constructing the sections from dimensional lumber or logs of comparable strength, necessitating engineers assistance and supervision.

a. **Siting.** The shelter should be sited on a reverse slope for cut-and-cover construction.

b. **Excavation.** Assuming that each bent or side unit (fig. 1-39 and table 1-5) is sheathed before installation, the excavated area should be 2.1 meters (7 ft) wide and 3 meters (10 ft) long for one section. The additional length of the excavated area will provide working space to install sheathing on the rear unit. The area for the shelter should be excavated to a depth of 3.6 meters (12 ft) to allow for a heavy overhead cover laminated roof and 3.2 meters (10 ft 6 in.) for heavy overhead cover stringer roof.

c. **Assembly.** The two bents or side units may be assembled and sheathed before they are placed in the excavated area. In this manner driftpins are installed in the sill, caps and posts before units are placed in the excavated area. Bracing on the side units as well as the bracing and spreaders on the front and rear units are toenailed.

d. **Organization of work crews.** An engineer squad, or a squad other than engineer under engineer supervision, can be used economically at the worksite to excavate the shelter area, assemble the roofing and cover materials, and construct the overhead cover. Under favorable conditions a trained engineer squad can excavate the area required for the shelter and install the shelter and overhead cover in 18 to 20 hours. However, if a backhoe or bucket loader is available for the excavation, the time can be reduced to approximately 6 hours.

1-34. USE OF STANDOFF

a. **Definition.** A standoff is a steel or wood curtain or chain link fence erected approximate 3 meters (10 feet) in front of a protective structure to detonate shells and thereby reduce their subsequent penetrating effect. Its use is optional but desirable as additional protection of those protective structures most likely to sustain enemy fire.

Table 1-5. Bill of Materials for One 6' x 8' Sectional Shelter With Post, Cap, and Stringer Construction- Dimensional Timber

No.	Nomenclature	Rough size	Roof	Front	Right	Left	Rear
1	Cap or sill	6"x8"x8'0" (15cm x 20.5cm x 246cm)			2	2	
2	Post	6"x6"x5'10" (15cm x 15cm x 180cm)			3	3	
3	Stringer**	6"x6"x6'0" (15cm x 15cm x 184cm)	16				
4	Spreader	3"x6"x5'0" (7.5cm x 15cm x 150cm)		2			1
5	Post, door	3"x6"x6'6" (7.5cm x 15cm x 195cm)					1
6	Brace	*3"x6"x7'0" (7.5cm x 15cm x 215cm)					1
7	Brace	*3"x6"x6'10" (7.5cm x 15cm x 210cm)			1	2	
8	Brace	*3"x6"x8'0" (7.5cm x 15cm x 246cm)		2			
9	Spreader	2"x6"x3'3" (5cm x 15cm x 97.5cm)			3		
10	Spreader	2"x6"x2'9" (5cm x 15cm x 82.5cm)					2
11	Spreader	2"x6"x2'0" (5cm x 15cm x 60cm)					2
12	Scab	3"x6"x2'0" (7.5cm x 15cm x 60cm)					
13	Siding	3"xRWx8'0" (7.5cm x RW x 246cm)				41 1/3SF	
14	Siding	3"xRWx6'0" (7.5cm x RW x 184cm)		36SF			
15	Siding	3"xRWx4'0" (7.5cm x RW x 120cm)			24SF		
16	Siding	3"xRWx3'6" (7.5cm x RW x 107cm)					21SF
17	Roll roofing	100 sq ft roll (9.3 sq meters)	6				
18	Driftpin	1/2"x14" (1.25cm x 35cm)	32		6	6	
19	Nails	60d		8 lb	8 lb	8 lb	8 lb

*Allowance for double cut ends of braces is included in overall length as shown under rough size.
**Laminated wood roof (fig 3-21) may be substituted if desired.

Size of rectangular timber	Size of round timber required to equal (in inches)
6x6	7
6x8	8
8x8	10
8x10	11
10x10	12
10x12	13
12x12	14

Construction Notes

1. Any combination of the four types of side panels shown may be used in regard to location and number of doors required.

2. In the construction of two or more basic units, the exterior wall panels should be based on the number and position of doorways required. Panels to be coupled in the interior of the shelter, forming a double wall, must be of the same type wall construction and provide doorways. Siding is not required on interior walls.

b. **Construction "condition".** A construction "condition" (fig. 1-40 and table 3-3) refers to protective structure with or without a standoff. Condition I means the protective structure has no standoff, condition II - the structure has a steel standoff, and condition III - the structure has a wood standoff (fig. 1-41 and 1-42). A chain link fence standoff is shown in figure 1-43. Table 1-6 shows comparison of relative thicknesses of protective materials needed to withstand penetration of various types of ammunition - with and without standoffs.

1-35. SUBSURFACE SHELTERS

a. **Cut-and-cover shelters.** The log shelter shown in figure 1-38 is suited to cut-and-cover construction or surface construction. The best location for cut-and-cover shelters is on the reverse slope of a hill, mountain, ridge, or steep bank as shown in figure 1-44. The shelter shown provides 1.8 to 2.1 meters (6 to 7 feet) headroom. The shelter frame is built in the excavation; the spoil is backfilled around and over the frame to ground level, or somewhat above, and camouflaged. The protection offered depends on the type of construction (size of timbers) and the thickness of the overhead cover. As in the case of a surface shelter of similar construction, approximately 45 centimeters (18 inches) of earth cover can be supported.

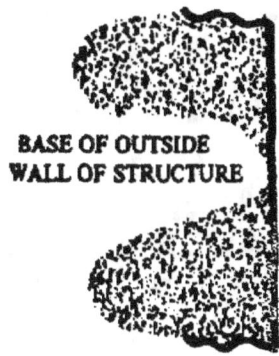

BASE OF OUTSIDE
WALL OF STRUCTURE

NO STANDOFF

1   NO STANDOFF – CONDITION I

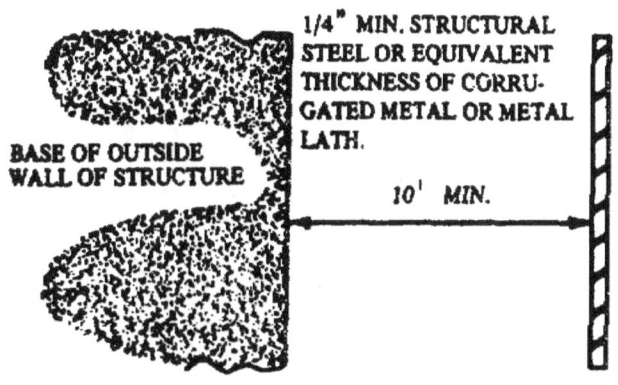

BASE OF OUTSIDE
WALL OF STRUCTURE

1/4" MIN. STRUCTURAL
STEEL OR EQUIVALENT
THICKNESS OF CORRU-
GATED METAL OR METAL
LATH.

10'   MIN.

2   STEEL STANDOFF – CONDITION II

BASE OF OUTSIDE
WALL OF STRUCTURE

1/2" MIN. STRUCTURAL
GRADE DIMENSIONAL
LUMBER OR 1" TO 3"
∅ SAPLINGS.

10'   MIN.

3   WOOD STANDOFF – CONDITION III

Figure 1-40. Standoff condition.

Table 1-6. Minimum Thickness of Protective Material Required to Resist Penetration of Rounds[1]

Condition I—No Standoff
Material in Inches

Types of ammunition	Soil [a]	Sand [a]	Clay [a]	Soil cement bituminous concrete	Concrete	Timber	Aluminum	Steel
.30 cal. ball (AP)............	24	24	30	18	9	60	2.6	1.3
.50 cal. ball (AP)..........	36	30	54	18	9	120	4.4	2.2
57-mm recoilless rifle......	12	12	24	20	10	20	9.0	5.0
82-mm recoilless rifle......	27	27	54	42	23	48	21.0	12.5
90-mm recoilless rifle......	40	42	80	66	33	76	32.0	19.5
107-mm recoilless rifle.....	48	48	96	84	42	88	40.0	22.5
60-mm mortar.............	48	30	64	20	10	20	2.8	1.0
81-mm mortar.............	60	42	90	26	18	27	3.7	1.3
120-mm mortar............	70	48	120	32	16	36	4.7	1.7

Condition I—No Standoff
Material in Metric Measurement
(cm)

Types of ammunition	Soil [a]	Sand [a]	Clay [a]	Soil cement bituminous concrete	Concrete	Timber	Aluminum	Steel
.30 cal. ball (AP).........	60	60	75	45	22.5	150	6.6	3.2
.50 cal. ball (AP).........	90	75	135	45	22.5	300	11	5.5
57-mm recoilless rifle......	30	30	60	50	25	50	22.5	12.5
82-mm recoilless rifle.....	67.5	67.5	135	105	55	120	52.5	31.2
90-mm recoilless rifle......	100	105	200	165	82.5	190	80	48.7
107-mm recoilless rifle....	120	120	240	212	105	200	100	56.2
60-mm mortar...........	120	75	160	50	25	50	7	2.5
81-mm mortar...........	150	105	225	65	45	67.5	9.2	3.2
120-mm mortar.........	175	120	300	80	40	90	11.7	4.2

Conditions II and III — .6cm (¼-inch) Steel or 1.3 cm (½-inch) Timber Standoff[3]
With a .6cm (¼-inch) steel or 1.3cm (½-inch) timber standoff, reduce by 50% the value shown under Condition I.

[1] Refers to depth a delay fused round will penetrate into the various materials. The amount of material required to defeat fragments from the fragmentation ammunition given would be considerably less than shown.

[2] Add 50% if wet.

[3] Timber standoffs are ineffective against .30 and .50 cal. ball (AP) ammunition. Increase the thickness of the material to the values found in the table for condition I opposite .30 and .50 cal. ball (AP) ammunition.

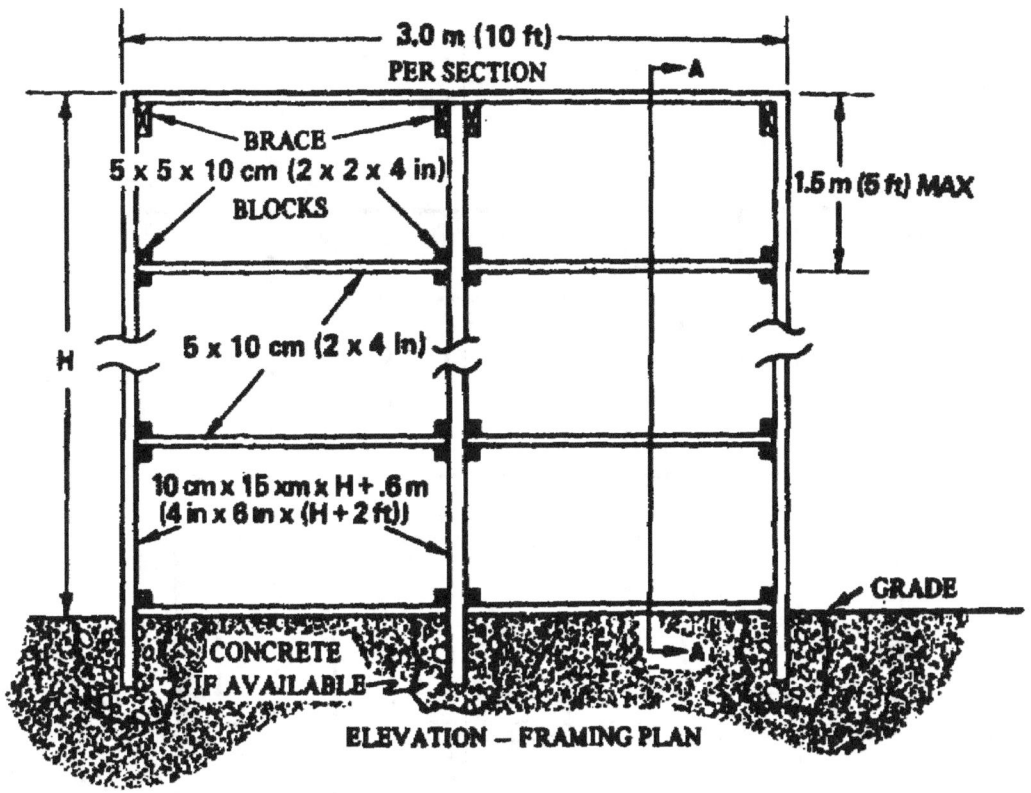

3.0 m (10 ft)
PER SECTION

A

BRACE
5 x 5 x 10 cm (2 x 2 x 4 in)
BLOCKS

1.5 m (5 ft) MAX

H

5 x 10 cm (2 x 4 in)

10 cm x 15 xm x H + .6 m
(4 in x 6 in x (H + 2 ft))

GRADE

CONCRETE
IF AVAILABLE

A

ELEVATION – FRAMING PLAN

CONDITION III

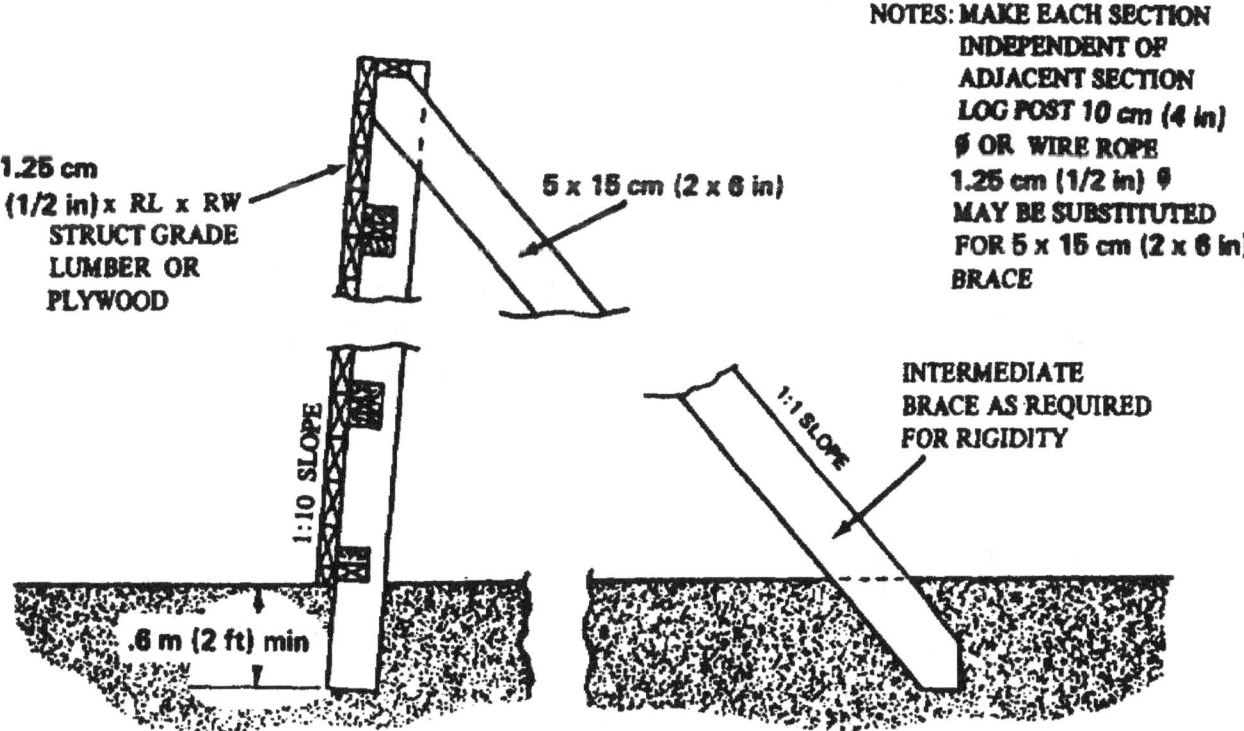

1.25 cm
(1/2 in) x RL x RW
STRUCT GRADE
LUMBER OR
PLYWOOD

5 x 15 cm (2 x 6 in)

NOTES: MAKE EACH SECTION
INDEPENDENT OF
ADJACENT SECTION
LOG POST 10 cm (4 in)
∅ OR WIRE ROPE
1.25 cm (1/2 in) ∅
MAY BE SUBSTITUTED
FOR 5 x 15 cm (2 x 6 in)
BRACE

1:10 SLOPE

.6 m (2 ft) min

1:1 SLOPE

INTERMEDIATE
BRACE AS REQUIRED
FOR RIGIDITY

Figure 1-41. Wooden standoff.

1-43

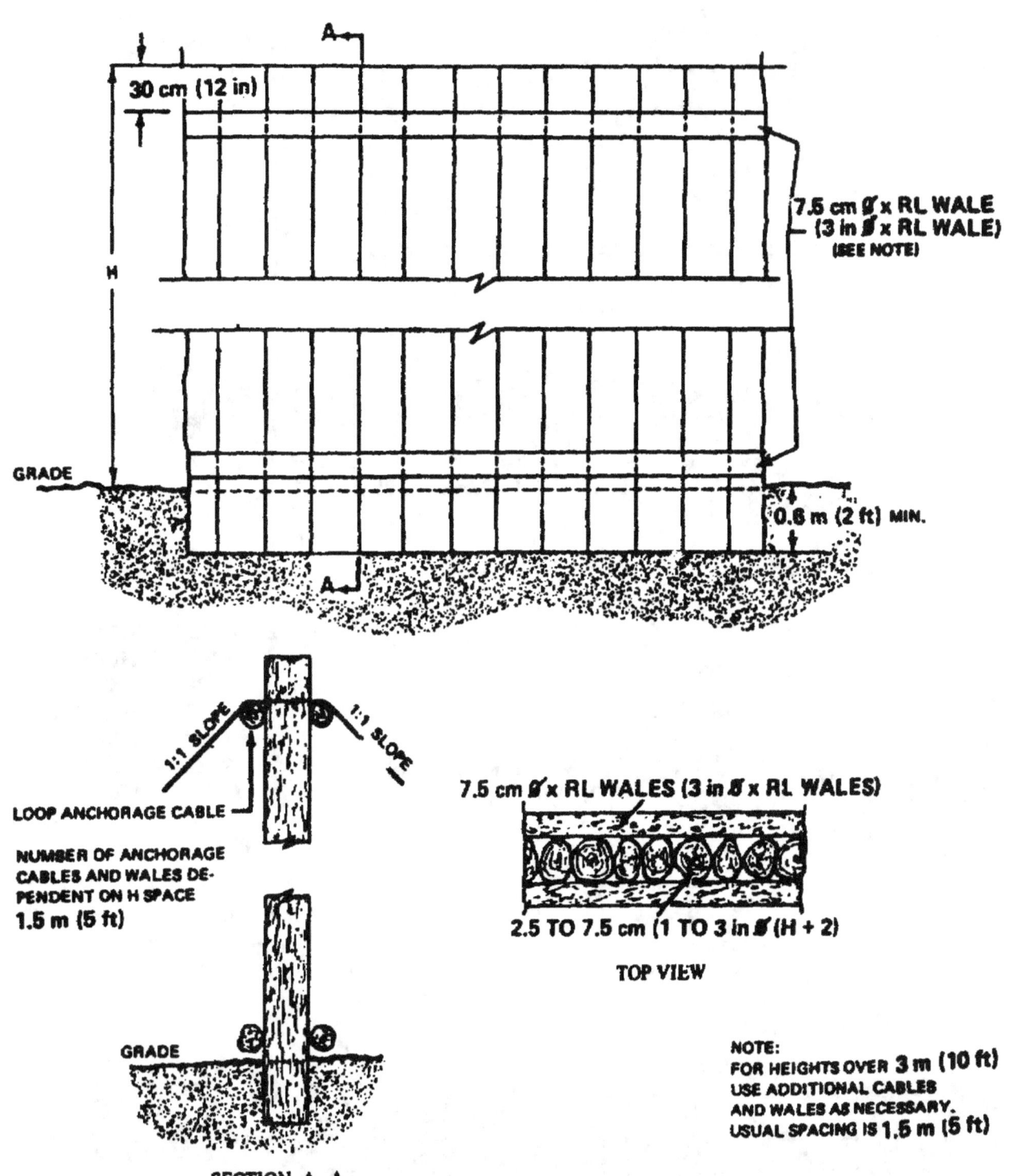

30 cm (12 in)

H

7.5 cm ∅ x RL WALE
(3 in ∅ x RL WALE)
(SEE NOTE)

GRADE

0.6 m (2 ft) MIN.

A

LOOP ANCHORAGE CABLE

NUMBER OF ANCHORAGE
CABLES AND WALES DE-
PENDENT ON H SPACE
1.5 m (5 ft)

1:1 SLOPE

1:1 SLOPE

GRADE

SECTION A-A

7.5 cm ∅ x RL WALES (3 in ∅ x RL WALES)

2.5 TO 7.5 cm (1 TO 3 in ∅ (H + 2)

TOP VIEW

NOTE:
FOR HEIGHTS OVER 3 m (10 ft)
USE ADDITIONAL CABLES
AND WALES AS NECESSARY.
USUAL SPACING IS 1.5 m (5 ft)

Figure 1-42. Log standoff.

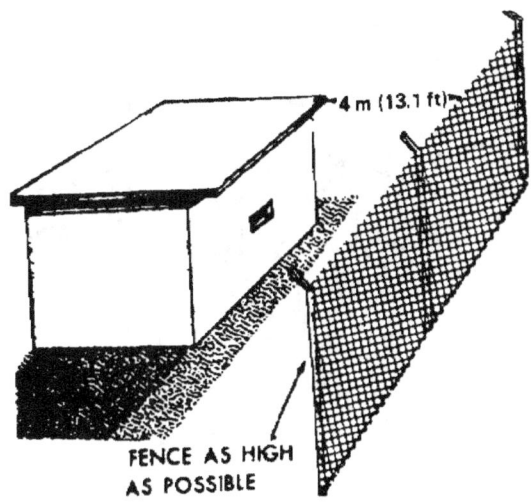

Figure 1-43. Chain link fence standoff.

b. **Cave shelters.** Caves are dug in deliberate defensive positions, usually by tunneling into hillsides, cliffs, cut, or ridges or excavating into flat ground. Because of the undisturbed overhead cover, a cave is the least conspicuous of all types of shelters if the entrance is covered. One of the best locations for a supply cave entrance is shown in figure 1-45. The disadvantages of cave shelters include limited-observation, congested living conditions, small exits, and difficult drainage and ventilation. Their construction is difficult and time consuming. Exits may be blocked or shoring crushed by a direct hit from a conventional weapon or ground shock from a nuclear explosion.

1-36. SPECIAL USE SHELTERS

a. **Observation posts.** These are located on terrain features offering as good a view as possible of enemy-held areas (fig. 1-46). The ideal observation post has at least one covered route of approach and cover as well as concealment, while offering an unobstructed view of enemy-held ground.

b. **Command posts.** Small unit command posts may be located in woods, ravines, in the basements of buildings, or former enemy fortifications. When none of these are available, surface or cut-and-cover shelters previously described may be modified for this purpose.

c. **Medical air stations.** Cut-and-cover shelters are especially adaptable as aid stations since they are easily cleaned and ventilated. Suitable sites may be found in pits, quarries, under banks, or in small buildings or ruins.

d. **Ammunition shelters.** Ammunition shelters should be located and constructed so that they protect ammunition against the

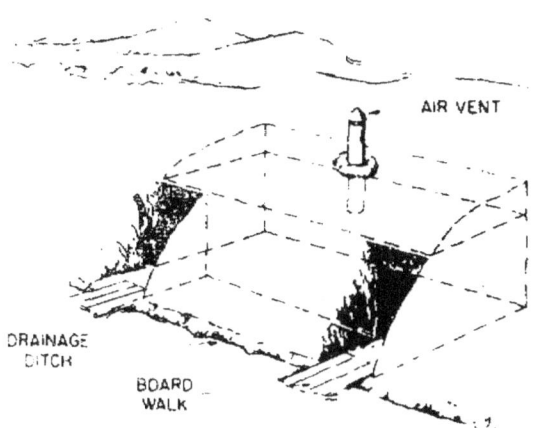

CUT-AND-COVER SHELTER IN A HILLSIDE (BAFFLE WALL OF ENTRANCE CAMOUFLAGE OMITTED) SHADED AREA AND BROKEN LINES SHOW CUT-AND-FILL SECTION

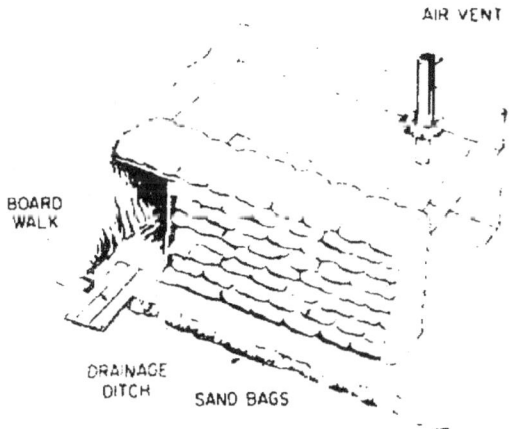

CUT-AND-COVER SHELTER IN A CUT BANK SHOWING SAND-BAGGED OUTER WALL SHADED AREA AND BROKEN LINES SHOW AREA OF CUT-AND-FILL

Figure 1-44. Cut-and-cover shelters.

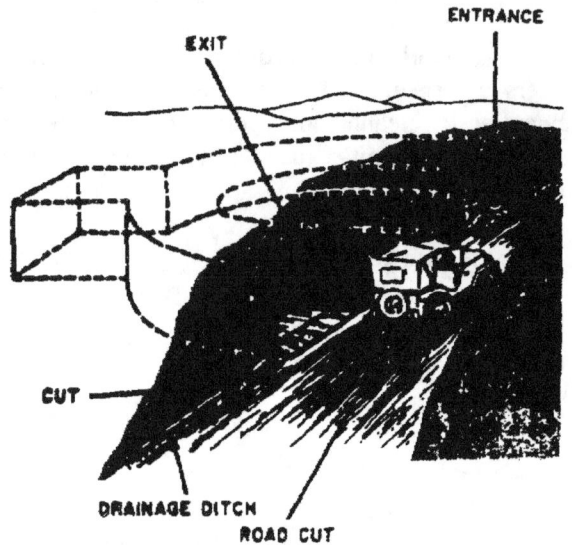

EXIT
ENTRANCE
CUT
DRAINAGE DITCH
ROAD CUT

Figure 1-45. Supply cave in a road cut.

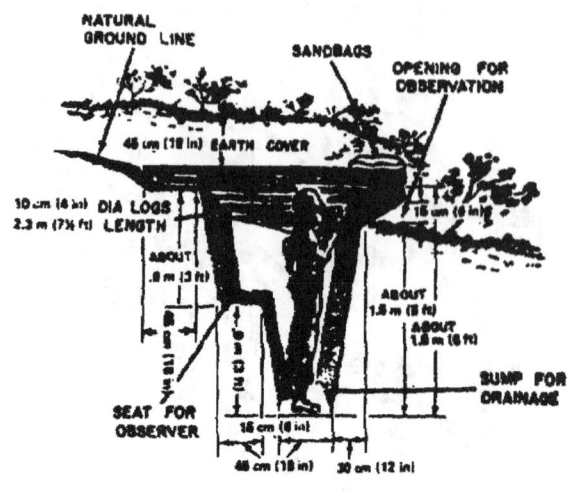

NATURAL GROUND LINE
SANDBAGS
OPENING FOR OBSERVATION
45 cm (18 in) EARTH COVER
10 cm (4 in) DIA LOGS
2.3 m (7½ ft) LENGTH
15 cm (6 in)
ABOUT .9 m (3 ft)
ABOUT 1.5 m (5 ft)
ABOUT 1.8 m (6 ft)
SEAT FOR OBSERVER
SUMP FOR DRAINAGE
15 cm (6 in)
45 cm (18 in)
30 cm (12 in)

CROSS-SECTIONAL VIEW
(ENTRANCE NOT SHOWN)

Figure 1-46. Observation post.

weather and enemy fire. They should be well concealed, and large enough to hold the desired quantity of ammunition close to the firing position. Figure 1-47 shows an ammunition shelter which may be constructed in an emplacement parapet. If it is necessary to construct ammunition shelters above ground, particularly where the water level is close to the surface, a log crib built up with dirt is suitable.

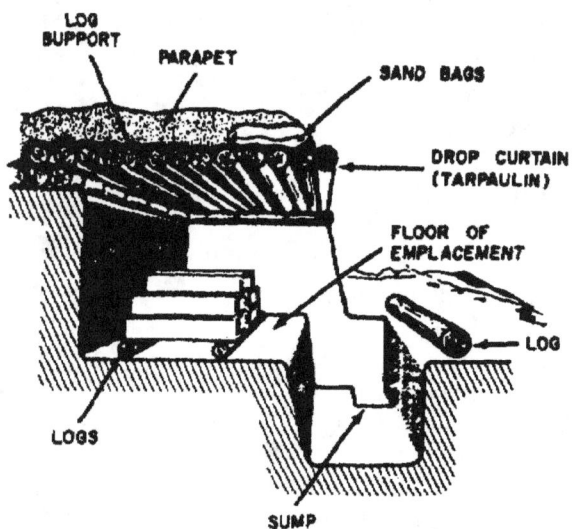

LOG SUPPORT
PARAPET
SAND BAGS
DROP CURTAIN (TARPAULIN)
FLOOR OF EMPLACEMENT
LOG
LOGS
SUMP

PERSPECTIVE VIEW

Figure 1-47. Ammunition shelter.

1-37. HEAVY OVERHEAD COVER

To provide adequate protection against both penetration and detonation of artillery shells and bombs, a structure would require overhead earth cover so thick as to be impracticable. By combining materials and using them in layers in a logical sequence, the required protection is provided with less excavation and construction effort. Two designs of overhead cover in functional layers which protect against the penetration and explosion from a hit by a 155-mm artillery round are shown in figure 1-48 and described, below.

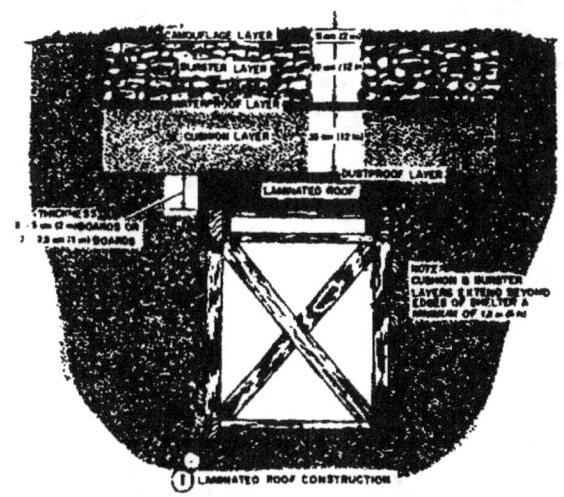

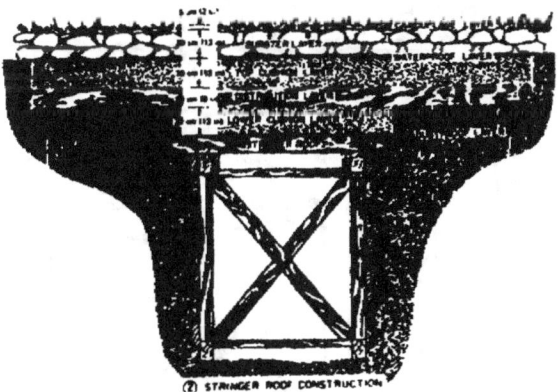

Figure 1-48. Heavy overhead cover.

a. Laminated roof construction. In this design either five 5 centimeters (2 inch) or seven 2.5 centimeters (1 inch) layers of lumber are used for laminated roof as shown in (1), figure 1-48.

(1) Dustproof layer. Tar paper, canvas, or tarpaulins lapped and places above the laminated roof is used to prevent dust and dirt from shaking down on equipment, weapons, and personnel.

(2) Cushion layer. The cushion layer is intended to absorb the shock of detonation or penetration. Untamped earth in the best material for this purpose and should be at least 30 centimeters (12 inches) thick. Materials such as loose gravel transmit excessive shock to the layer below and should not be used in the cushion layer. This layer extends on all sides for a distance equal to the depth of the shelter floor below the ground surface or a minimum of 1.6 meters (5 feet).

(3) Waterproof layer. The waterproof layer is constructed of the same material as the dustproof layer or similar materials. It is intended to keep moisture from the cushion layer in order to retain the cushioning effect of the soft dry earth, and minimize the dead load the structure must carry.

(4) Burster layer. The burster layer is intended to cause detonation of the projectile before it can penetrate into the lower protective layers. This layer is made of 15 to 20 cm (6- to 8-in.) rocks placed in two layers with the joints broken. This layer should be at least 30 cm ((12 in.) thick. Irregular-shaped rocks are more effective for this purpose than flat rocks. If rocks are not available, 20 cm (8-in) logs may be used. They must be wired tightly together in two layers. The burster layer should extend on each side of the shelter a minimum of 1.5 meters (6 ft).

(5) Camouflage layer. The burster layer is covered with about 5 cm (2 in.) of untamped earth or sod, as a camouflage layer. A greater thickness of camouflage

material will tend to increase the explosive effect.

b. Stringer reef construction. Figure (2), 1-48 illustrates stringer roof construction of heavy overhead cover. The construction is similar to laminated roof construction with the addition of --

(1) A lower cushion layer 30 cm (12 in.) thick on top of the dustproof layer. This layer of untamped earth does not extend beyond the sides of the shelter.

(2) A distribution layer consisting of 20 cm (8 in.) timbers. This layer extends beyond each side of the shelter a minimum of 1.5 meters (5 ft) and rests on undisturbed earth to transmit part of the load of the top layers to the undisturbed earth on each side of the shelter.

c. Overhead cover for fight bunker. Figure 1-49 shows the details for the construction of a fighting bunker with heavy overhead cover. The material requirements

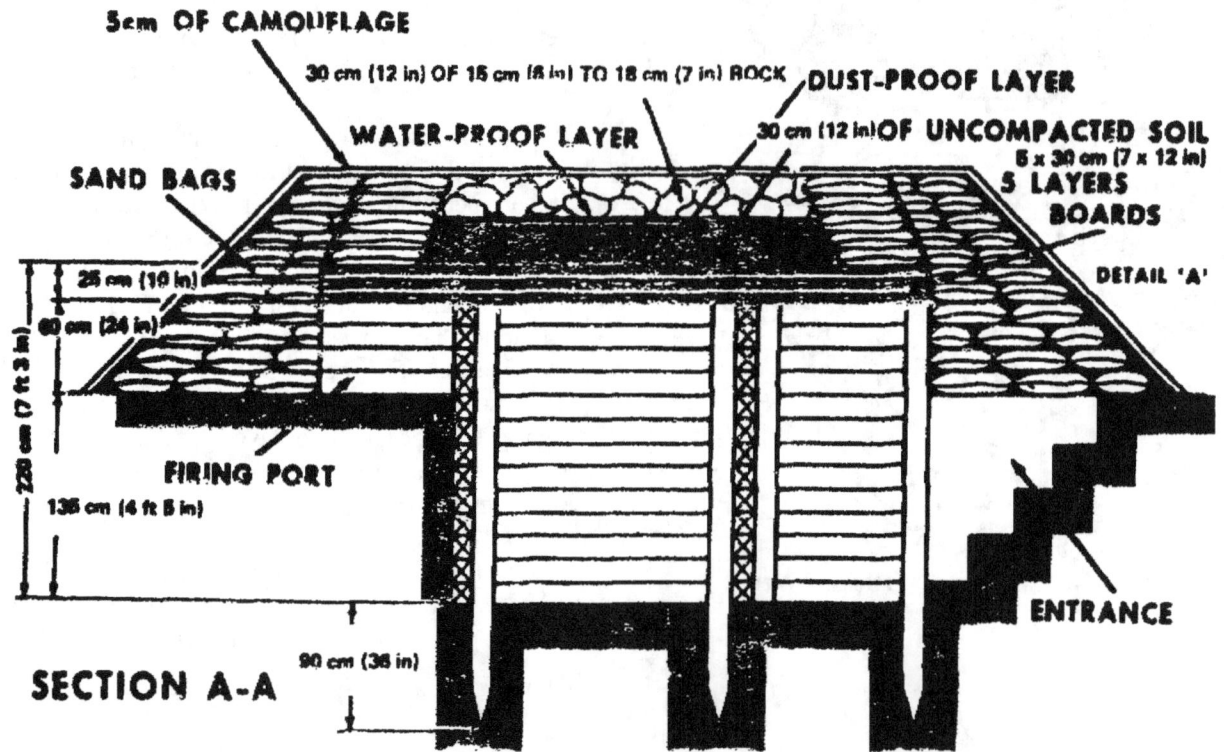

Figure 1-49. Fighting bunker with heavy overhead cover.

for the construction of this bunker are found in table 1-7.

d. Heavy overhead cover protection. Heavy overhead cover protects against the following Soviet weapons:
152-mm gun-howitzer
122-mm howitzer
85-mm gun
120-mm mortar
82-mm mortar
140-mm rocket
122-mm rocket

1-38. ENTRENCHMENT COVER SUPPORT

a. Overhead cover is normally supported on the roof of the structure and the resultant load is transmitted through the cape and posts to the foundation on which the structure rests. It may be necessary, in some instances, to support the roof directly on the earth outside a revetted position. When this must be done, the roof timber should not bear directly on the earth outside the excavation. The added load may use the wall to buckle or cave in. Instead, the roof structure is carried on timber sills or foundation logs bedded uniformly in the surface at

Table 1-7. Bill of Materials, Fighting Bunker, (Laminated Construction)

No.	Nomenclature	Description	Quantities
1	Roof	5cm x 30cm x 2.11m wood (2″ x 12″ x 6′ 11″)	48 pcs
		5cm x 30cm x 4.54m wood (2″ x 12″ x 14′ 11″)	14 pcs
2	Sidewalls	15cm x 15cm x 2.42m wood (6″ x 6″ x 7′ 11″)	26 pcs
3	Entrance wall	15cm x 15cm x 1.21m wood (6″ x 6″ x 4′ 0″)	26 pcs
4	Firing port & entrance door	15cm x 15cm x 30cm wood (6″ x 6″ x 1′ 0″)	26 pcs
5	Front & rear walls	15cm x 15cm x 1.51m wood (6″ x 6″ x 4′ 11″)	13 pcs
6	Firing port & retaining wall	15cm x 15cm x 1.00m wood (6″ x 6″ x 3′ 3″)	8 pcs
7	Side post	15cm x 15cm x 2.85m wood (6″ x 6″ x 9′ 4″)	6 pcs
		15cm x 15cm x 1.95m wood (6″ x 6″ x 6′ 5″)	2 pcs
8	Sandbags		300 each
9	Roofing paper	9.3 sq m (100 sq ft) rolls	8 each
10	Driftpins	1.25cm x 30cm (½″ x 12″)	210 each
11	Nails	16d	30 lb

a safe distance from the cut. This distance should be at least one-fourth the depth of the cut and in no case less than 30 cm (12 in.) to the nearest edge of the sill. Round logs used for this purpose are embedded to at least half their diameter to provide maximum bearing area of log to soil. These principles are illustrated in figure 1-50.

b. Laminated planks or stringers are used to support the roof cover.

(1) Table 1-8 shows the thickness of laminated plank roof required to support various thicknesses of earth cover. The planks should extend from support to support in all layers, and adjoining edged should be staggered from one layer to the next.

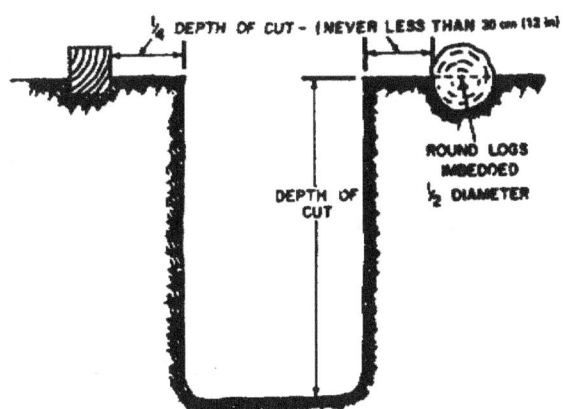

Figure 1-50. Support of overhead cover on earth banks.

Table 1-8. Thickness of Laminated Wood Required to Support Various Thicknesses of Earth Cover Over Various Spans

Thickness in Inches

Thickness of earth cover in feet	Span width in feet					
	2½	3	3½	4	5	6
1½	1	1	2	2	2	2
2	1	2	2	2	2	3
2½	1	2	2	2	2	3
3	2	2	2	2	3	3
3½	2	2	2	2	3	3
4	2	2	2	2	3	4

Thickness in Centimeters

Thickness of earth cover in meters	Span width in meters					
	.75	.9	1.05	1.2	1.5	1.8
.45	2.5	2.5	5.1	5.1	5.1	5.1
.6	2.5	5.1	5.1	5.1	5.1	7.6
.75	2.5	5.1	5.1	5.1	5.1	7.6
.9	5.1	5.1	5.1	5.1	7.6	7.6
1.05	5.1	5.1	5.1	5.1	7.6	7.6
1.2	5.1	5.1	5.1	5.1	7.6	10.2

(2) Table 1-9 shows the spacing of stringers required to support 2.5 cm (1-in.) plank roof under various thicknesses of earth over various spans. Stringers are 5 cm x 10 cm (2 in. x 4 in.) unless otherwise indicated.

(3) The roofs shown with the cover indicated are fragment proofs and will give substantial radiation protection, if properly designed entrances are provided.

c. Sandbags are never used to support overhead cover.

1-39. FIGHTING BUNKER WITH LIGHT OVERHEAD COVER

When establishing positions in wooded areas, it is very important to provide overhead cover to protect personnel from the shrapnel of tree bursts. A fighting bunker with light overhead cover is shown and described in figure 1-51. The overhead cover will stop fragments from trees and airburst artillery, and it is strong enough to withstand the effects of a direct hit by an 81-mm

Table 1-9. Center to Center Spacing in Inches of Wooden Stringers Required to Support a 1-inch Thick Wood Roof with Various Thicknesses of Earth cover over Various Spans

Thickness of earth cover in feet	Span width in feet					
	2½	3	3½	4	5	6
1½	40	30	22	16	10	18*
2	33	22	16	12	8/20*	14*
2½	27	18	12	10	16*	10*
3	22	14	10	8/20*	14*	8*
3½	18	12	8/24*	18*	12*	8*
4	16	10	8/20*	16*	10*	7*

*Stringers are 2" by 4" except those marked by an asterisk (*) which are 2" by 6".

Center to Center Spacing, in Centimeters, of Wooden Stringers Required to Support a 2.54cm Thick Wood Roof with Various Thicknesses of Earth Cover Over Various Spans

Thickness of earth cover in meters	Span width in meters					
	.75	.9	1.05	1.2	1.5	1.8
.45	101.6	76.2	55.9	40.6	25.4	45.7*
.6	83.8	55.9	40.6	30.5	20.3/50.8*	35.6*
.75	68.6	45.7	30.5	25.4	40.6*	25.4*
.9	55.9	35.6	25.4	20.3/50.8*	35.6*	20.3*
1.05	45.7	30.5	20.3/50*	45.7*	30.5*	20.3*
1.2	40.6	25.4	20.3/50.8*	40.6*	25.4*	17.8*

See note above.

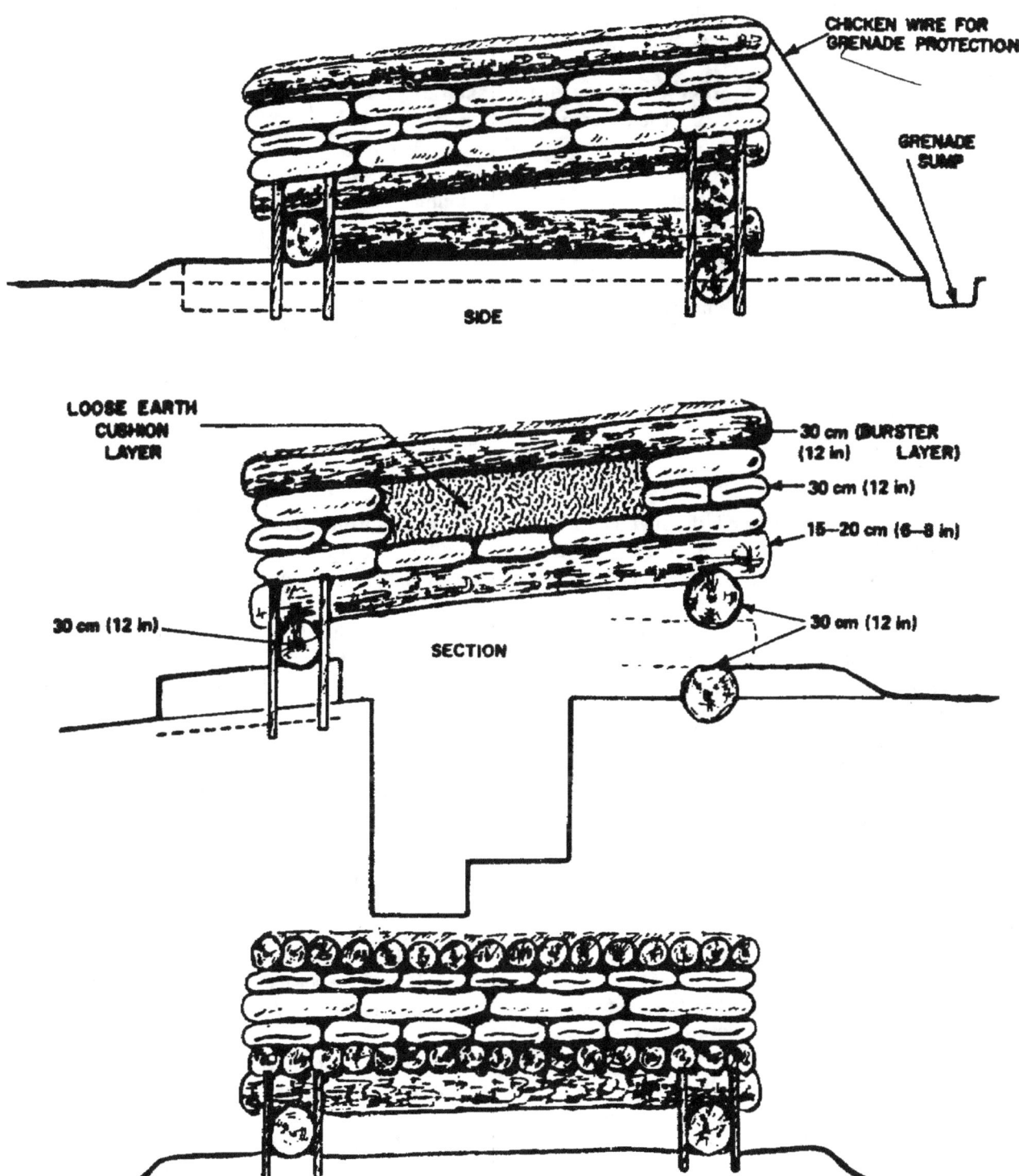

CHICKEN WIRE FOR GRENADE PROTECTION

GRENADE SUMP

SIDE

LOOSE EARTH CUSHION LAYER

30 cm (BURSTER (12 in) LAYER)

30 cm (12 in)

15—20 cm (6—8 in)

30 cm (12 in)

SECTION

30 cm (12 in)

FRONT

Figure 1-51. Fighting bunker with light overhead cover.

mortar. If the side openings are closed with sandbags to prevent the entry of grenades, the fields of fire and observation are limited to the front only. This is a serious disadvantage with this type of position. Chicken wire can be placed over the firing apertures to prevent grenades from entering the bunker. The chicken wire should be sloped with a ditch dug at the base to catch grenades as they roll off the wire.

Section XI. Prefabricated Shelters and Bunkers
(Semipermanent Construction)

1-40. DESIGN CONSIDERATIONS

Designs presented are applicable to all levels of operations and geographic areas. They are especially applicable to operations requiring rapid construction of semipermanent emplacements and shelters that provide protection against mortar and artillery fire in forward areas.

a. Shelters. Design considerations for the shelter design are set forth in the following guideline criteria:

(1) Must be constructed from materials available in the theater of operations or constructed of components readily procured and fabricated.

(2) Must be capable of prefabrication by combat engineer units in rear areas, transportation to forward areas by 25-ton tractor traders, and erection by 20-ton crane and combat engineers.

(3) Should be capable of being transported by CH-47 helicopter and be erectable by normally available materiel handling equipment such as motorized crane or combat engineer vehicle (CEV).

(4) Must provide a large reduction in erection time in-forward areas as compared with previous in-place construction of shelters.

(5) Should be capable of forward area assembly (less site preparations, entrances, cover, and antispall) by six men in 1 hour.

(6) Must permit addition of cover with available combat engineer equipment.

(7) Must be a buried structure composed of modular units of 3.6 meters (12 feet) in width that can provide shelter lengths of least 3.6, 7.2 and 10.8 meters (12, 24 and 36 feet).

(8) Facility, with earth cover and add-on-features, must provide protection from the Soviet 152-mm rounds detonating close by. Reinforced concrete structures must provide protection from 155-mm artillery shell detonated from a distance of 9 meters (30 ft) from the bare concrete without earth backfill.

b. Fighting bunkers. Design considerations for the fighting bunker design are set forth in the following guideline criteria:

(1) Must use only those construction materials that are available in the theater of operations or of components readily procured and fabricated.

(2) Must be capable of being prefabricated by combat engineers, transported to forward areas by means of 25-ton tractor-trailers or equal, and emplacement by combat engineers using 20-ton crane or equal.

(3) Should be capable of being transported by CH-47 helicopter and be erectable by normally available materiel-handling equipment such as motorized crane or CEV.

(4) Must have uniform design and be comprised of multi-use modular units.

(5) Should be capable of being assembled in forward area (less site preparation, entrances, and cover) by six men in 1 hour.

(6) Bunker roof must be capable of supporting 1.2 meters (4 feet) of saturated earth cover.

(7) Must accommodate at least four fighting men with sleeping space for two.

(8) Must provide protection from 152-mm rounds detonating close by the completed bunker.

(9) Must provide protection from 82-mm mortar round detonating on the surface of the earth cover.

1-41. WES CONCRETE ARCH SHELTER (FIG 1-52)

a. Description. A basic unit of Waterways Experiment Station (WES) prefabricated concrete arch-type shelter is 3.6 meters (12-feet) wide and 1.2 meters (4-feet) long. A 3.6 meters (12-feet) long structure consists of three 1.2 meter (4-foot) long arch sections and two end wall sections, together with necessary hardware, waterproofing membrane, and earth cover.

(1) The 15 centimeter (6-inch) -thick arch sections have a 1.8 meter (6-foot) inside radius with a 45 centimeter (18-inch) vertical wall extension and 10 centimeter (4-inch) floor. The floor is framed into the vertical wall section through a 45 centimeter (18- inch) -wide by 30 centimeter (12-inch)-thick footing which is chambered 15 centimeter (6 inches) at the top corners. Monolithically cast, each arch section weighs 10,200 pounds.

(2) The 15 cm (6-in) -thick end wall section consists of a 2.1 meter (7-ft) radius semicircle and a 0.6 meter (2-ft) by 4.2 meter (14-ft) rectangle. A door opening 0.71 meters (2-ft, 4-in), by 1.68 meters (5-ft, 6-in) is provided in each end wall section. Monolithically cast, each end wall weighs 7,000 pounds.

b. Design. This concrete arch shelter is designed to meet the essential and desired characteristics outlined in paragraph 1-45 and is subject to the following additional design factor assumptions:

(1) Dead load consists of the weight of the concrete shell and 2.4 meters (8-ft) of saturated earth cover above the crown of the arch.

(2) Safety factor is 1.5.

(3) Material properties:

(a) Concrete compressive strength of 3,000 psi after 28-day cure.

(b) Reinforcing steel tensile strength of 40,000 psi.

(c) Soil unit weight (wet) of 110 pcf.

c. Transportation. Movement of the prefabricated arch sections and end walls to the emplacement site is accomplished by truck, trailer, or helicopter. Weight and dimensions are shown in table 1-10.

d. Site preparation. Location and position of the shelter can be determined by the function of the shelter, the tactical conditions, the topography and other similar considerations which are determined by the field commander. The depth of excavation is determined by the elevation of the ground water table during the wet season. A bulldozer, scooploader, or crane-shovel with attachments is used to excavate a trench to receive the arch sections. A soft bedding or cushion layer of sand should be provided as a base upon which to set the arch sections to avoid structural stress concentrations, to absorb shock blast, effects, and to minimize unequal settlement between the arch sections, and walls, and entrance structures. Footings for each end wall consists of fourteen timbers 4 inches by 12 inches by 3 feet placed side by side and centered normal to the plane of the end wall. Typical trench excavation is shown in figure 1-53.

e. Emplacement. The shelter sections can be emplaced by six men and one truck-mounted crane in 1 hour after site is prepared. The rough terrain crane which is available in the combat engineer battalion can be used effectively for final excavation, lifting the shelter sections into place and backfilling. The sections are firmly seated, aligned, and secured with five wire rope tie assemblies. The four joints between the arch sections and end walls are covered with any durable, flexible, waterproof material such as salvaged

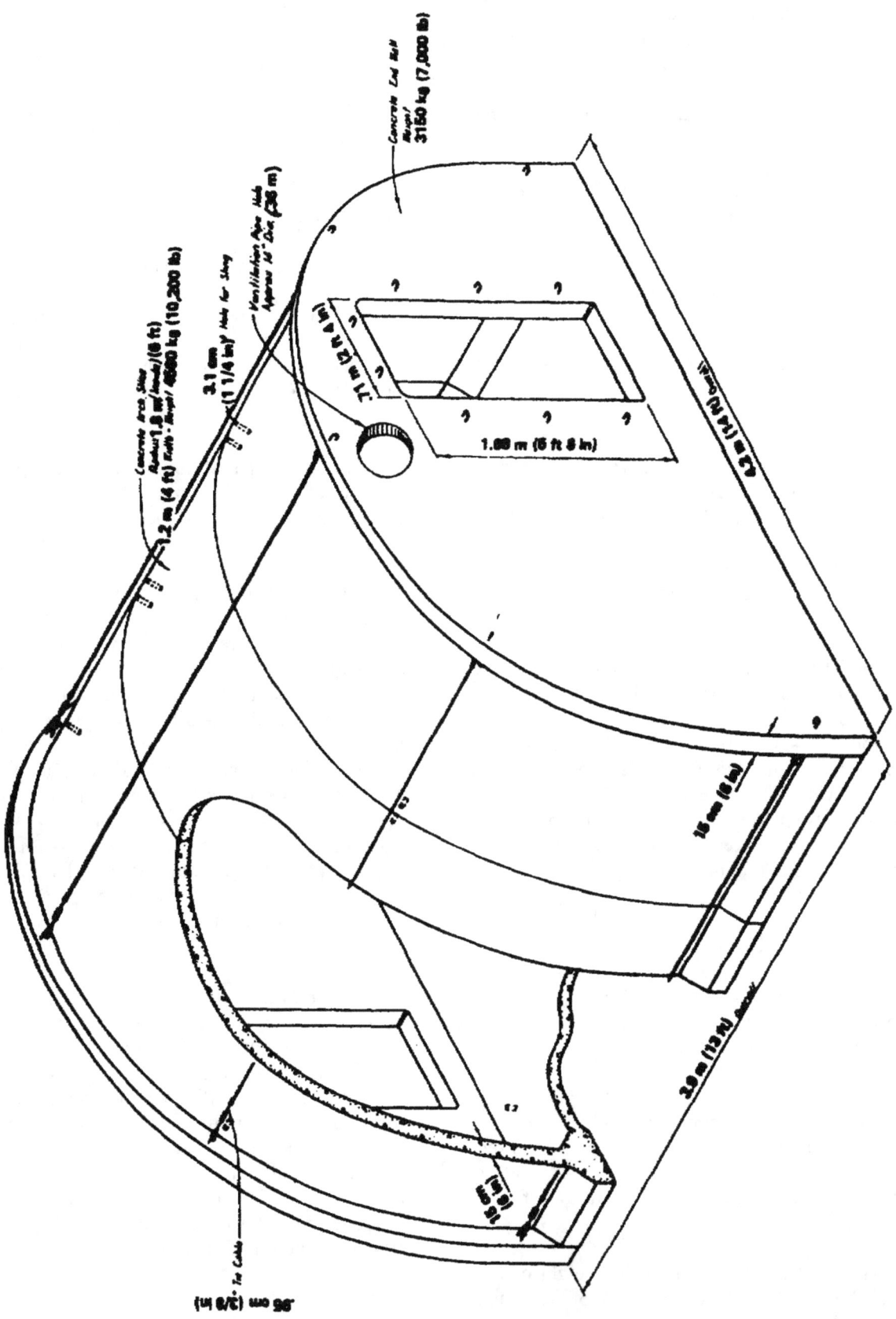

Figure 1-52. WES concrete arch shelter design, isometric.

1-54

Table 1-10. WES Concrete Arch Shelter (Transportation Data)

Items	Number per shelter	Weight each (kilograms/pounds)	Weight total (kilograms/pounds)	Length (meters/feet)	Width (meters/feet)	Height (meters/feet)	Cubage, total (cu meters/cu feet)
Arch section	3	4,636 kg (10,200 lb)	13,909 kg (30,600 lb)	1.2m (4'-0")	.24m (14'-0")	2.55m (8'6")	404 cu m (1,428 cu ft)
End wall section	2	3,181.8 kg (7,000 lb)	6,363 kg (14,000 lb)	4.2m (14'-0")	.35m (1'-2")	2.7m (9'-0")	83 cu m (294 cu ft)
Tie cable and rigging	5	9 kg (20 lb)	45.4 kg (100 lb)	varies	varies	varies	1.12 cu m (4 cu ft)
Waterproof membrane (T-17 mat or equal)	2	136.3 kg (300 lb)	272 kg (600 lb)	varies	varies	varies	8.40 cu m (30 cu ft)
Total			20,590 kg (45,300 lb)				497 cu m (1,756 cu ft)

Note. Total cubage is reducible to 440 cubic meters (1,254 cu ft) by nesting. Entrances, revetting material, buster rock, and add-on items vary; compute separately.

Figure 1-53. Typical trench excavation for shelter.

T-17 membrane. Entrance structures at each end are fabricated from local or manufactured material including timber frame, concrete arch, corrugated metal pipe (CMP), cattle pass, or landing mat. Drainage structures are provided as required. The shelter is then backfilled with sod material. Sandy material, if available, will offer better protection than a clay type sod. The backfill placement should be carried on until a minimum depth of 4 feet and maximum depth of 8 feet insured; the depth of cover includes waterproof membrane, burster course, and camouflage.

1-42. MULTIPLATE PIPE ARCH SHELTER (FIGURE 1-54)

a. Description. The basic multiplate pipe arch shelter is a 3.6 meter by 3.6 meter (12-ft by 12-ft)

prefabricated corrugated steel arch shelter consisting of one 3.6 meter (12-ft) multiplate pipe arch section and two precast reinforced concrete end walls, together with necessary hardware, waterproofing membrane, and earth cover.

(1) The multiplate pipe arch section consists of seven 3.6 meter (12-ft) long corrugated galvanized steel plates of differing curvature which are bolted together along the longitudinal joints. The assembled pipe arch has a span of 3.8 meters (12-ft, 8-in) a rise of 2.4 meters (8-ft, 1-in), and weighs 4 pounds.

(2) The 15 cm (6-in) thick end wall sections are identical to the end wall sections for the WES concrete arch shelter.

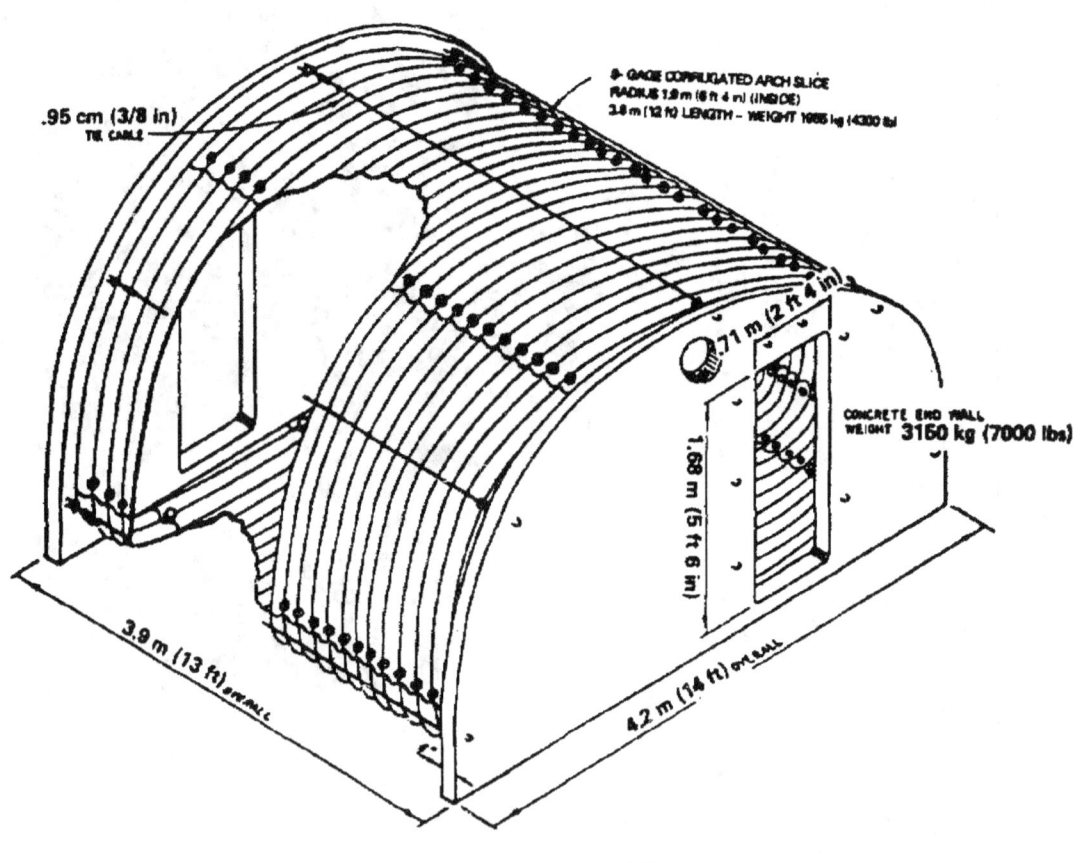

Figure 1-54. Multiplate pipe arch shelter.

b. Design. The multiplate pipe arch shelters use commercial pipe arch which is available in a range of spans, rises, and areas and are tabulated in drainage products handbooks and manufacturer's catalogs. This multiplate arch is designed to meet the criteria outlined in paragraph 1-45 and is subject to the following design factor assumptions:

(1) A minimum of 8-gage-thick steel is required for the arch pipe.

(2) Dead load of 8 feet of saturated earth cover is developed at the crown. Soil unit weight (wet) is 110 pcf.

(3) Properties of the 8-gage corrugated steel plate are --

(a) Pitch of corrugation is 6-inches.

(b) Depth of corrugation is 2-inches.

(c) Uncoated thickness of steel is (0.1644 inches).

(4) Properties of the reinforced concrete are:

(a) Compressive strength is 3,000 psi after 28-day cure.

(b) Reinforcing steel has tensile strength of 40,000 psi.

c. Prefabrication of multiplate pipe arch section. The two slightly curved floor plates, the two curved (1-ft, 6-in. radius) corner plates, the two haunch plates, and the crown plate are lapped and secured with four 3/4-inch-diameter by 1 1/4-inch-long bolts per linear foot of seam. Bolts are staggered in two rows per seam with one bolt in each valley and each crest of the corrugation. Bolts should not be tightened until all bolts have been installed. Manufacture' catalogs, when available, should be consulted for detailed instructions on assembly technique.

d. Transportation. Movement of the prefabricated arch sections and end walls to the emplacement site is accomplished by truck, trifler, or helicopter. Weights and dimensions are shown in table 1-11.

e. Site preparation. Location and position of the shelter can be determined by the

Items	Number per shelter	Weight each (kilograms/pounds)	Weight total (kilograms/pounds)	Length (meters/feet)	Width (meters/feet)	Height (meters/feet)	Cubage, total (cu meters/cu feet)
Arch section	1	1,954 kg (4,300 lb)	1,954 kg (4,300 lb)	3.6m (12'-0")	3.8m (12'-8")	2.4m (8'-1")	362 cu m (1,280 cu ft)
End wall section	2	3,181 kg (7,000 lb)	6,362 kg (14,000 lb)	4.2m (14'-0")	.35m (1'-2")	2.7m (9'-0")	83 cu m (294 cu ft)
Tie cable and rigging	5	9 kg (20 lb)	45 kg (100 lb)	varies	varies	varies	1.1 cu m (4 cu ft)
Waterproof membrane (T-17 mat or equal)	2	136 kg (300 lb)	273 kg (600 lb)	varies	varies	varies	8.5 cu m (30 cu ft)
Total			8,634 kg (19,000 lb)				455 cu m (1,608 cu ft)

Note. Cubage is reducible to 455 cubic meters (1,608 cu ft) by nesting. Excludes revetting material, bracket rods, and add-on items vary; compute separately.

function of the shelter, the tactical conditions, the topography and other similar considerations which are determined by the field commander. The depth of excavation is determined by the elevation to which the ground water table can be expected to rise during the wet seasons. A bulldozer, scoop loader, CEV or crane-shovel with attachments is used to excavate a trench to receive the prefabricated pipe arch section and end walls. A soft bedding or cushion layer of sand should be provided as a base upon which to set the pipe arch section in order to avoid structural stress concentrations, absorb the shock of blast effects, provide drainage, and minimize unequal settlement between the arch section, end walls, and entrance structures. Timber footings under the end wall sections are required where the strength of subgrade is not capable of supporting the 1,000 psf load of end walls.

f. Emplacement. The shelter sections can be emplaced by six men and one truck-mounted crane in 1 hour after site is prepared. The rough terrain crane which is available in the combat engineer battalion can be used effectively for emplacement, to include final excavation, lifting the shelter sections

into place, positioning entrances, and back-filling. Wire rope slings are used to aid the placement of the structure. Entrance structures at each end are fabricated from local or manufactured material such as timber frame, concrete arch, CMP, cattle pass, or landing mat. After excavation has been completed to the proper elevation, a waterproof membrane is installed prior to placing the structure. All bolts should now be checked for tightness and the membrane material wrapped completely around the shelter. Backfill material, dry coarse sand if available, is now placed and compacted. Special attention should be given to the placement and compaction of the soil material under the upturn area of the floor section. Additional backfill material is placed and compacted in 15 cm (6-in.) lifts to an elevation of at least three-fourths of the height of the structure. These procedures are necessary to provide symmetrical loading and to insure proper setting of the structure. To complete the emplacement, the backfill material is placed to a minimum height of 4 feet or up to a maximum height of 8 feet over the crown of the structure including burster layers and camouflage layers. Drainage is provided as required by the topography.

Section XII. Prefabricated Fighting and Command Post Bunkers (Semipermanent Construction)

1-43. CONCRETE LOG BUNKER (fig 1-55)

a. Description. The concrete log bunker is a 4-man fighting bunker, 2-3 meters (7 ft, 6 in) square and 1.8 meters (6 ft) high. The bunker is constructed of 90 precast reinforced concrete logs 15 cm (6 in) wide by 20 cm (8 in) deep of various lengths (.6, .9, 1.2, 1.8, 2.4 and 3.0 meters (2, 3, 4, 6, 8, and 10 ft)) that weigh approximately 164 pounds per meter (50 lb per ft). The bottom of the bunker is set 102 cm (3 ft, 4 in) below the ground surface. The roof is made by placing 3 meter (10 ft)-long concrete logs side by side and pinning them together to make a 20 cm (8 in) -thick roof with 30 cm (1 ft) overhang on all sides. The bunker has a 20 by 45 cm (8- by 18-in.) firing port on each of the four

sides; the bottom of each firing port is 1.2 meters (4 ft) above the floor level. The logs are joined together with steel pins, 1.9 cm (3/4 in.) in diameter, which are dropped through holes, 3.8 cm (1 1/2 in.) in diameter, aligned at 30 cm (1 ft) intervals and cast in the logs. Normal entrance/exit is by means of .9 meter (3 ft) and 1.2 meter (4 ft) diameter corrugated metal pipe (CMP), and an emergency exit is provided by means of two removable logs at the rear face firing port.

b. Design (fig 1-56). This concrete log bunker is designed to meet the characteristics outlined in paragraph 1-45.

Figure 1-55. Concrete log bunker.

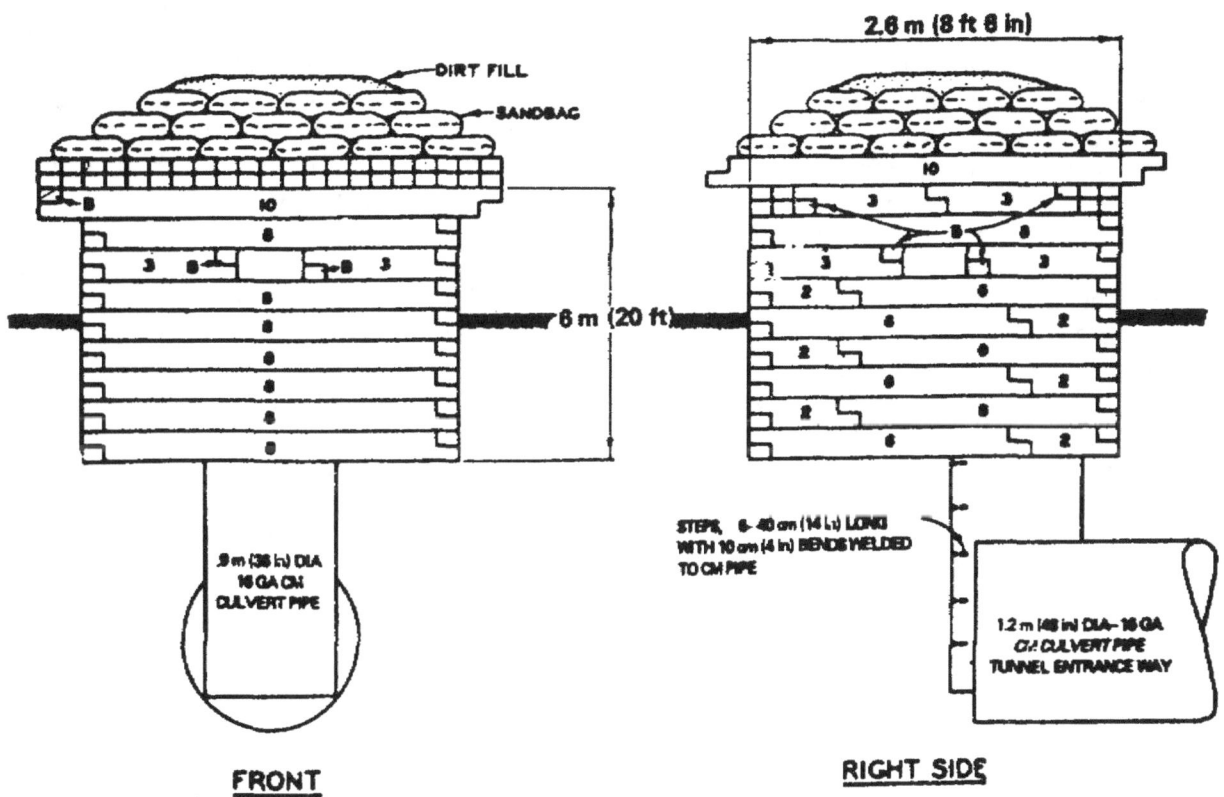

FRONT

RIGHT SIDE

BILL OF MATERIAL

CONCRETE	5 cm (6.5 cu yds)
REINFORCING STEEL, # 4 x 6 m (20 ft)	98 BARS
VERTICAL RODS, # 6 BARS x 6 m (20 ft)	11 BARS
"U" SHAPED ROOF PINS, # 6 BOX x 6 m (20 ft)	11 BARS

NOTE: 1.8 cm (3/4 in) PIPE MAY BE USED FOR VERTICAL RODS.

Figure 1-56. Concrete log bunker design.

c. Forming, steel placement, and casting. The concrete logs are precast in a staging area and transported to the emplacement site. The forms are constructed in the field on a 3.6 by 4.8 meter (12- by 16-ft) casting bed which permits casting of numerous logs of various lengths at one time. The concrete is mixed, poured, vibrated, and cured in accordance with standard procedures. Two to five days' moist cure is required before the precast logs can be moved safely.

d. Transportation. Movement of the precast concrete logs to the emplacement site is accomplished by truck, trailer, or helicopter.

e. Site preparation. Location of the fighting bunker is determined by the tactical commander. The design depth of excavation is 2.54 meters (8 ft, 4 in.), including 102 cm (3 ft, 4 in.); below grade for bunker floor and 1.5 meters (5 ft) below bunker floor for the entrance; however, the elevation to which the ground water table can be expected to rise during the wet season may require a field modification of this design depth. The emergency exit, located above the normal ground level, allows siting of this bunker in locations where the normal entrance may be subject to temporary flooding. Excavation is accomplished by combat support earthmoving equipment or by hand digging.

f. Emplacement. The concrete log fighting bunker can be assembled by six men in 1 hour after the site is prepared and the CMP entrance structure is in place. For poor soils, a footing will be required for this structure to prevent excessive settlement. Cushion, waterproofing, and burster layers, retained with sandbags, are placed on the roof to develop capability to withstand a direct hit from the equivalent of an 82-mm mortar round. Steel mesh grenade gratings are hinged over the firing ports. Standoff screening against AT rockets, fields of fire, communications, camouflage, firing shelves, and bunks should be provided as required. The modular design of the basic concrete logs permits a wide variety of original designs to suit specific requirements. This flexibility of design may be exploited by testing different arrangements using either full scale or model logs.

1-44. CONCRETE ARCH BUNKER (fig 1-57)

a. Description. The concrete arch bunker is a four-man fighting bunker, semi-circular in plan, 3.6 meters (12 ft) wide at the rear by 2.25 meters (7 ft, 6 in.) deep at centerline of the arch width by 1.8 meters (6 ft.) inside height. The bunker consists of three precast reinforced concrete components: a 1.8 meter (6 ft.)-high arch section, a rectangular back wall section, and a semi-circular roof section. Each of the sections is 15 cm (6 in.) thick and reinforced with No. 4 1.25 cm (0.5-in. diameter) steel rebars. The arch section has a 1.8 meter (6-ft) interior radius plus a 45 cm (1 ft, 6 in.) horizontal extension. The roof section overhangs the arch section providing a 45 cm (18-in.)-wide shield. The back wall section and the roof section each have a 20 cm (8-in.)-thick by 45 cm (18-in.)-wide bulkhead beam. The arch section has four 20- by 45-cm (8- by 18-in.) firing ports, and the back wall has one 20- by 45-cm (8- by 18-in.) firing port and a 20- by 75-cm (8- by 30-in.) emergency exit which can be used for a quick exit or grenade throwing.

b. Design. This concrete arch bunker is designed to meet the characteristics outlined in paragraph 1-45. Design is shown in figure 1-58.

c. Forming, steel placement, and casting.

(1) Arch section. Steel forms for the arch section can be fabricated in the field from 16-gage black sheet steel, which is spot welded to 5 cm (2 in.) angles. The form used in the arch shelter can be adapted to casting the arch bunker by omitting the floor portion and adding 0.6 meter (2 ft) of form to the height. The same procedures are used in the steel placement and casting of the 1.8 meter (6 ft) bunker arch as for the 1.2 meter (4 ft) shelter arch, with particular care required in placement, vibrating, and adequate curing before moving to site.

(2) Back wall section and roof section. Forms for casting the back wall and roof are

Figure 1-57. Concrete arch fighting bunker.

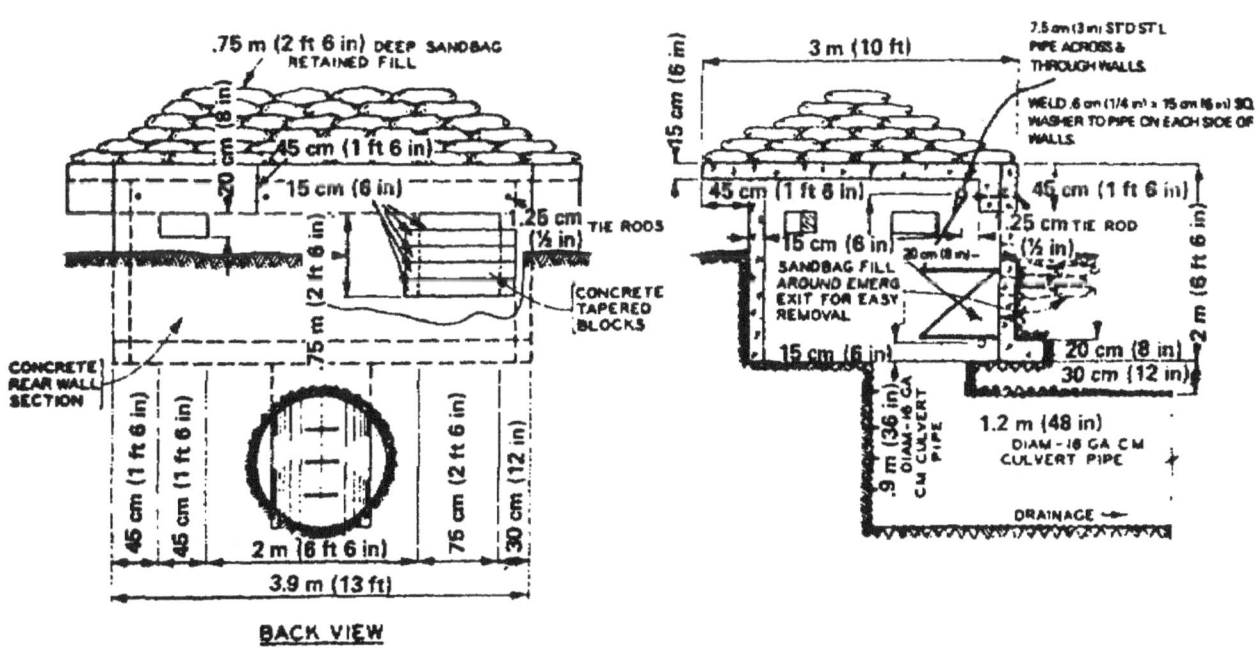

Figure 1-58. Concrete arch fighting bunker design.

built at the prefabrication site using conventional wood forms. Reinforcing steel details are as described for the WES concrete arch. The bulkhead beams for the roof and back wall sections are reinforced with two No. 5 bars placed with 5 cm (2 in.) of concrete cover from the outside edges of the beam.

d. Transportation. Movement of the three precast sections is accomplished by truck, trailer, or helicopter.

e. Site preparation. Location of the concrete arch fighting bunker is determined by the tactical commander. The design depth of excavation 2.5 meters (5 ft 4 in.) including 1 meter (3 ft, 4 in.) below-grade for the bunker floor and 1.5 meters (5 ft) below the bunker floor for the entrance; however, the elevation to which the ground water table can be expected to rise during the wet season may require a field modification of this depth. The emergency exit, located at the firing port level, allows siting of the arch fighting bunker where the deep entrance may be subject to temporary flooding. Excavation is accomplished by combat support earthmoving equipment or by hand labor.

f. Emplacement. The three sections of the arch fighting bunker can be employed by six men and one heavy crane in one hour after site is prepared and the CMP entrance structure is in place. The rough terrain cane which is available in the combat engineer battalion can be used effectively for emplacement especially for positioning of entrance and lifting and positioning bunker sections. The back wall is bolted to the 20- by 45-cm (8- by 18-in.) bulkhead beam at the rear of the roof section to secure the entire structure against displacement when under attack. Except in very good soil conditions, footings will be required under the modified arch section to prevent excessive settlement. Cushion, waterproof, burster layers, retained with sandbags, are placed on the roof to develop capability to withstand direct hit from the equivalent of an 82-mm Soviet mortar round. Steel mesh gratings are hinged over the firing ports. Standoff screening against antitank (AT) rockets, as well as fields of fire, communications, camouflage,

firing shelves, and bunks should be provided as required.

1-45. AIR-TRANSPORTABLE UNDER-GROUND ASSAULT BUNKER (Prefab)

a. Description. This is a prefabricated plywood bunker (fig 1-59) suitable for a command

Figure 1-59. Air-transportable underground assault bunker (prefab).

post or fire-direction center, which can be moved (completely assembled except for the roof) from site to site as the tactical situation demands. Its sloping walls make for easier pulling from the ground by helicopter for relocation. The bunker can be erected and emplaced by means of handtools only.

b. Construction. The bunker walls and floor may be prefabricated (fig 1-60) in rear areas and then be trucked or flown, assembled or disassembled, to the erection site. Fasteners are provided along the edges of each wall and the floor to allow the Individual members to be locked together into a complete unit. The walls of the bunker should extend below the floor section so that the floor can act as a support for the bottom edge of the walls. The longer side walls are abutted against the shorter end walls. Two large straps, completely around the structure, and placed during construction are used to attach bunker to helicopter lifting hook for bunker pullout and transport The underground site can be excavated by means of explosives and handtools (fig 1-61). The floor

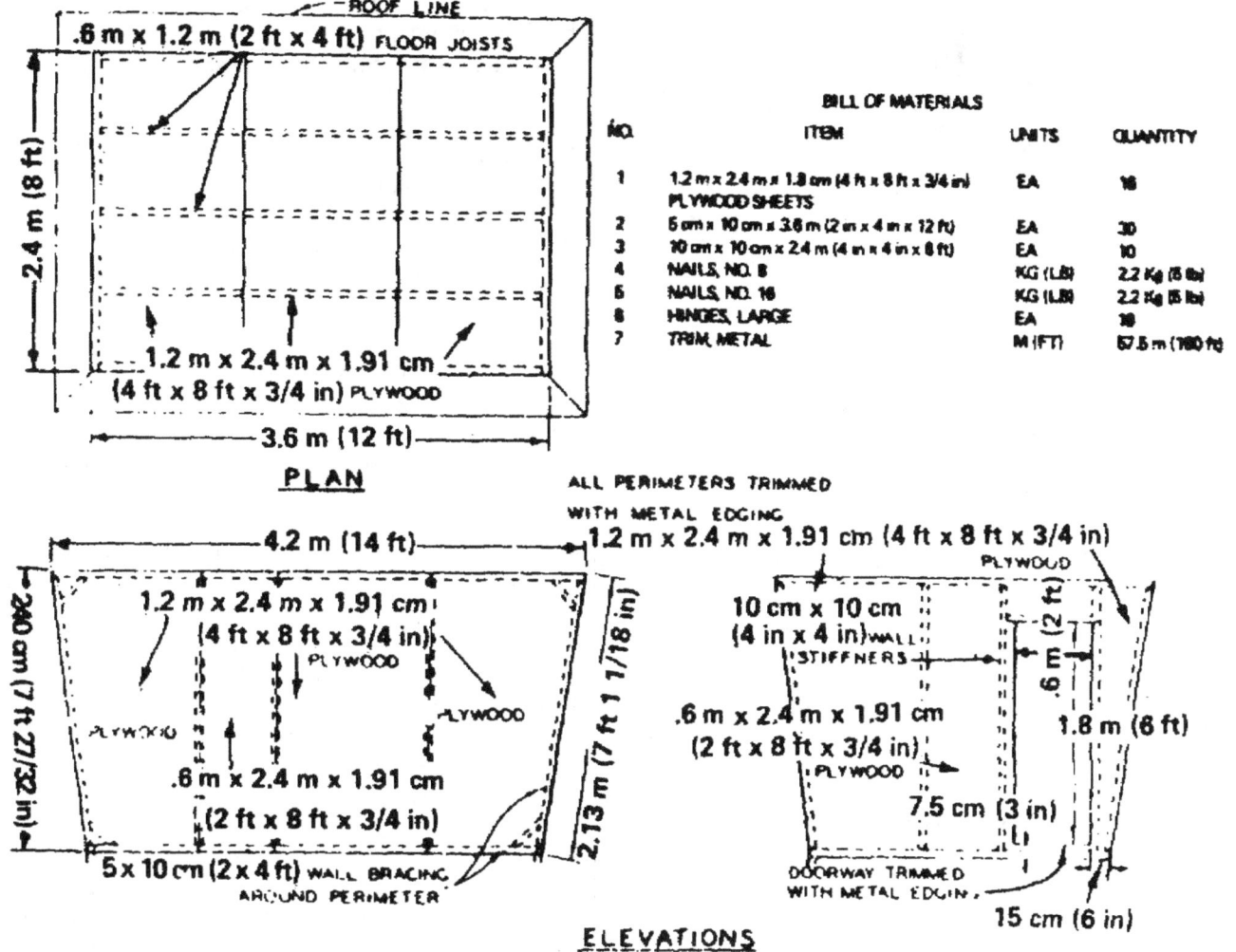

Figure 1-60. Plans of air transportable underground assault bunker (prefab).

area of the excavation should be .6 meter (2 ft.) longer and .6 meter (2 ft.) wider than the area of the bunker floor to allow working space during construction. The roof is concentric to and larger than the floor section and may be fabricated in the rear area or at the erection site. The roof overlaps the walls to be supported on firm (unexcavated) ground - not on the bunker walls. Additional construction recommendations for the bunkers are as follows:

(1) Abut longer side walls against shorter end walls because the longer walls must sustain the greatest load. The shorter walls then act as a support. (Miter corners if possible.)

(2) Provide for wall bracing at the top of the bunker. Brace from the center of each wall to the center of each adjacent wall (diamond pattern).

(3) Attach a sheet of plastic or other thin waterproof covering around the outside before backfilling to minimize friction between earth and the walls and increase moisture resistance.

(4) Make the bunker no larger than necessary. It should be no more than 6 1/2 feet high and the floor area should be less than 100 ft unless special effort is made to provide adequate structural members in addition to those used in the test bunker.

I EXCAVATE WITH EXPLOSIVES

2 SHAPE EXCAVATION WITH SHOVELS TO FIT BUNKER

3 ERECT BUNKER

4. BACKFILL

5. FINISH BY CONSTRUCTING ROOF, DIGGING DOORWAY AND PROVIDING DRAINAGE DITCHES

Figure 1-61. Installation of airtransportable underground assault bunker (prefab).

(5) Backfilling should be accomplished by hand labor, maintaining a uniform load around the perimeter as backfilling progresses.

(6) Although nails are satisfactory as fasteners for wood members, screws or bolts will offer greater holding strength.

(7) If possible, select fasteners for connecting walls and floors that are simple and adjustable.

(8) Make the bottom of the excavation 2 feet longer and 2 feet wider than the length and width of the structure floor to increase working room during erection and provide adequate clearance for the walls.

(9) Use explosives as extensively as practical during excavation to minimize required hand digging.

(10) Prior to lifting the structure from the installed portion, remove some of the backfill with hand tools to reduce effects of wall friction.

(11) Provide for more than one means of employing lifting devices for removal of the structure. Two large straps completely around the structure, placed during construction, seem to be the best method. U-bolts should be used in the floor through 4- by 4-inch members. To help distribute the load, a metal bearing plate should be placed where the U-bolt bears against the underside of the 4- by 4-inch floor joists.

c. **Data.** The bunker weighs approximately 1,600 pounds without the roof. It can be pulled from the ground by a lift of 10,000 pounds (CH-47 helicopter). The bunker should be no more than 1.95 meters (6 1/2 ft) high and the floor space should be under 9.3 square meters (100 sq ft). Excavation, erection, backfilling, and construction of roof and entrance can be completed in less than 10 hours.

1-46. PLYWOOD PERIMETER BUNKER (fig 1-62)

This bunker has plywood revetment (soilbin) walls approximately .6 meter (2 ft) thick. The walls are topped with a plywood cap

Figure 1-62. Plywood perimeter bunker.

to prevent entrance of moisture into the soil fill. The bunker may be provided with a column foundation or be constructed directly on the ground. The bunker soilbin revetment walls withstand small arms fire. The bunker walls, by insertion of landing mat, offer additional cushioning effect against heavy caliber rounds that may penetrate the revetment (soilbin).

1-47. BUILDINGS AS SHELTERS OR FIRING POSITIONS

a. Protection. Some protection from enemy fire may be achieved for occupants in a building used as a shelter by strengthening the building, by shoring up ceilings, and bracing walls. Men inside buildings are reasonably well protected against thermal effects and radiation unless they are near doors or windows. The principal danger is from falling masonry and from fire in the building.

b. Basic considerations.

(1) A ground floor or basement is more likely to make a suitable shelter than any other floor. The risk of being trapped must be guarded against. Heavy bars, pieces of pipe, or timbers, should be available in each room that is occupied, for use by the occupants in the event the building is demolished.

(2) Small arms fire will not penetrate the walls if they are 45 cm (18 in.) thick. The walls will not usually splinter from small arms fire if they are 30 cm (12 in.) thick. Additional protection can be obtained by building sandbag walls. If sandbags are used inside the building they reduce the usable space, but last longer and are not conspicuous. Care should be exercised in using sandbags above the first floor due to the weight involved.

(3) Window glass should be removed since it gives no thermal protection and is dangerous when shattered. If it is retained as protection from the weather, it should be screened or boarded.

(4) Several exits are necessary.

(5) Provisions for fighting fire should be made.

(6) Blackout arrangements should be made, if not already provided by thermal screening of doors and windows.

c. Use of weapons. In using a building as a firing position, there are several considerations.

(1) The preparatory work should not disclose the intended use of the building to the enemy.

(2) Weapons must be sited well back from any opening so that neither weapons nor personnel are visible from the outside.

(3) Several firing positions should be available in order to obtain a wide field of fire. The shapes of the openings should not be changed for this purpose.

(4) Any openings other than the normal ones are very conspicuous unless they are close to the ground.

(5) There are no fixed designs for weapons platforms under these circumstances. Platforms must be improvised from materials immediately available. Sandbags should be used sparingly if there is any doubt about the strength of the floor.

Section XIII. Protective Shelters for Frozen Environment

1-48. SNOW HOLE

The snow hole (fig 1-63) is a simple, oneman emergency shelter for protection against a snow storm in open, snowcovered terrain. It can be made quickly, even without tools. Lying down in snow at least 1 meter (3.3 ft.) deep, the soldier pushes with his feet, digs with his hands, and repeatedly turns over, forming a hole the length of his body and as wide as his shoulders. At a depth of at least 1 meter (3.3 ft.), the soldier digs in sideways below the surface, filling the original ditch with the snow that has been dug out until only a small opening remains.

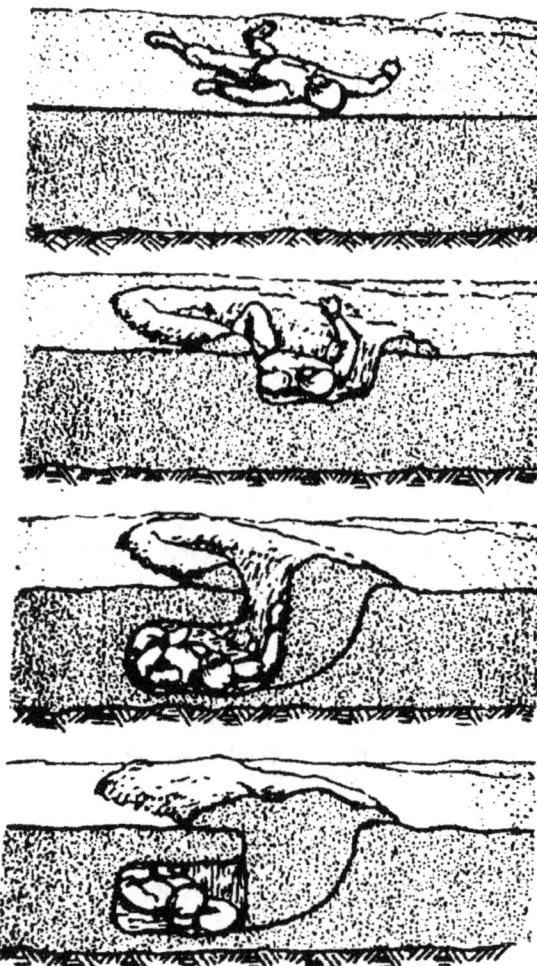

Figure 1-63. Snow hole.

This opening may be entirely closed, depending on the enemy situation and the temperature; the smaller the hole, the warmer the shelter.

1-49. SNOW CAVE

Snow caves (fig 1-64) are made by burrowing into a snowdrift and fashioning a room of desirable

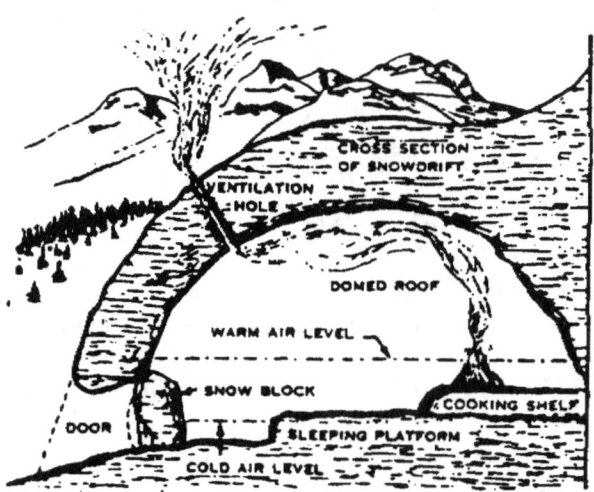

Figure 1-64. Snow cave.

size. This type of shelter gives good protection from freezing weather and a maximum amount of concealment. The entrance should slope upward for the best protection against the penetration of cold air. Snow caves may be built large enough for several men if the consistency of the snow is such that it will not cave in. Two entrances can be used while the snow is being taken out of the cave; one entrance is refilled with snow when the cave is completed.

1-50. SNOWPIT

The snowpit (fig 1-65) is dug vertically into the snow with intrenching tools. It is large enough for two or three men. Skis, poles, sticks, branches, shelter halves, and snow are used as roofing. The inside depth of the pit depends upon the depth of the snow, but should be deep enough for kneeling, sitting, and reclining positions. The roof should slope toward one end of the pit. If the snow is not

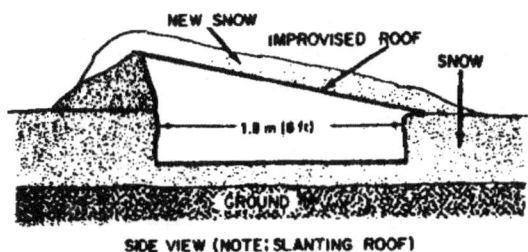

SIDE VIEW (NOTE: SLANTING ROOF)

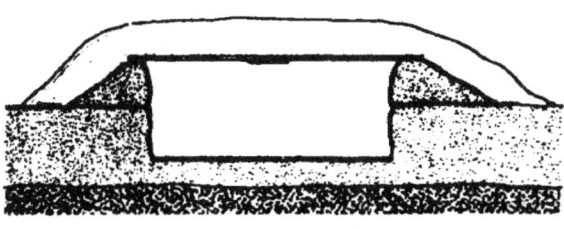

END VIEW

Figure 1-65. Snow pit in shallow snow.

deep enough, the sides of the pit can be made higher by adding snow walls.

1-51. SNOWHOUSE

The size and roof of a snowhouse are similar to those of a snowpit. The walls consist of snowblocks and may be built to the height of a man. Snow piled on the outside seals the cracks and camouflages the house (fig 1-66).

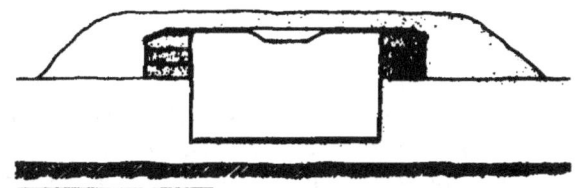

Figure 1-66. Snowhouse with iceblock walls.

Section XIV. Construction Techniques for Frozen Environment

1-52. GENERAL

Among engineering materials that have to be handled, modified, removed, used as a base for building on or traveling over, and used as construction materials; snow, ice, and frozen ground are unique in their appearance and disappearance. They are also unique in the rapid changes of their physical properties within short periods of time due to metamorphism, change of temperature, change of state, and of course, relatively large deformations following subjection to load.

1-53. MATERIAL

Fortifications constructed from snow, ice, and frozen ground have the following merits:

a. The wide distribution and cheapness of the material for constructing the fortifications and the presence the materials at the building site, thus eliminating their transportation.

b. The extensive possibility of substituting snow, ice, and frozen ground during winter for the usual building materials.

c. The relative speed of construction with snow, ice and frozen ground, especially the solidification speed of soils exposed to freezing.

d. The simplicity and speed of repairing structures of snow, ice, and frozen ground if damaged.

e. The great strength of structures made from frozen ground.

f. The complete safety from fire.

1-54. SNOW AS CONSTRUCTION MATERIAL

a. Suitability. Dry fresh fluffy snow is not suitable for expedient construction. Reworked snow, such as piles at road edge after clearing equipment passage, densifies and begins to harden within hours after disturbance even at very low temperatures. Artificial compacting, wind compacting, and compacting after a brief thaw make snow even more suitable for expedient shelter and protective structures.

b. Construction.

(1) A uniform snow cover with a minimum thickness of 25 cm (10 in.) in a given area is sufficient for shelter and revetment construction. Blocks of uniform size, typically 20 x 30 x 40 cm (8 x 12 x 16 in.) depending upon degree of hardness and density, can be cut from the snow pack with shovels or better with long knives (machetes) or carpenter's saws. Best practice for constructing cold weather shelters is that adopted from natives of polar regions (fig 1-67). It must be remembered that thicker walls render better protection. Systematic overlapping block-over-seam insures stable construction. "Caulking" seams with loose snow insures snug draft-free structures. Igloo shelters in cold regions have been known to survive a whole winter. An Eskimo-style shelter easily withstands above-freezing inside temperatures, thus providing comfortable protection for personnel against wind chill and low temperatures.

(2) Snow fortifications can be built during either freezing or thawing weather, if the thaw is not so long or intense that significant snow melt occurs. Mild thaw or temperatures of 1° or 2°C. are even more favorable than freezing weather, because the snow is then very plastic, conglomerates readily, and assumes any shape without disintegration. Of course, freezing weather is also necessary for snow construction in order to achieve solid freezing and strength. If water is available at low temperatures, expedient protective structures could be built by wetting down snow and shaping it into desired forms with shovels.

1-55. ICE AS CONSTRUCTION MATERIAL

a. Methods. Ice structures can be built in three ways:

(1) Layer-by-layer freezing by repeated watering.

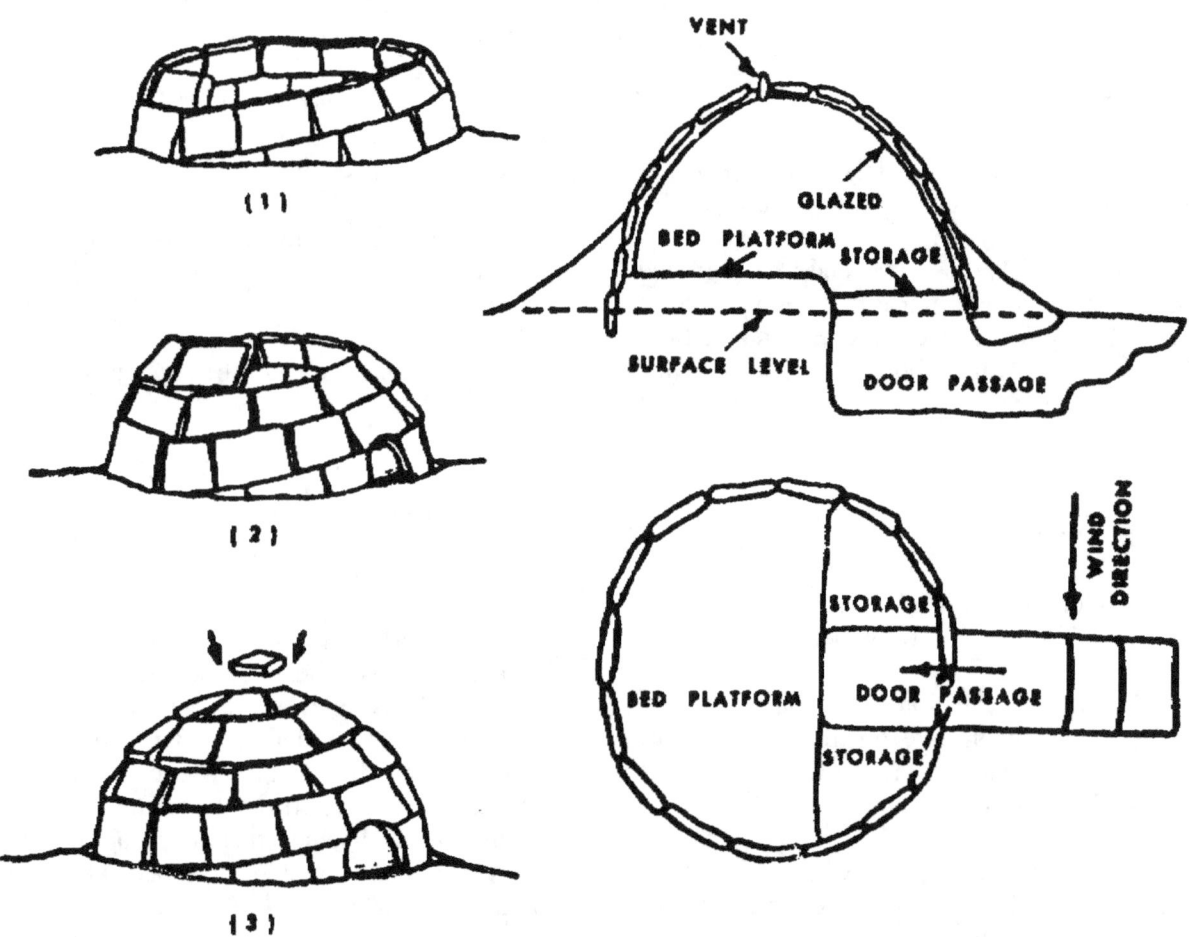

Figure 1-67. Construction of Eskimo style snowhouse.

(2) Freeing of ice fragments into layers by adding water.

(3) Laying of ice blocks.

b. Construction.

(1) Layer-by-layer freezing by water produces the strongest ice and is very cheap compared to other methods, but it requires much more time. The main condition for an effective freezing of ice layers by sprinkling is the right application of water according to the weather condition. Under working conditions, it can be assumed that about 0.5 cm (.2 in.) of ice is frozen per day for each degree below 0°C. Layer-by-layer freezing by watering is effective only at air temperatures below -5°C. At higher temperatures, the freezing should be discontinued. The most favorable temperature for this method is -10° to -15°C. with a moderate wind.

(2) Freezing of ice fragments into layers by adding water is very effective and the most frequently used method for building ice structures. The ice fragments are prepared on nearby plots or on the nearest river or water reservoir. The layer should be 20 to 30 cm (8 to 12 in.) thick and packed as densely as possible. The ice fragments should not be crushed as that would cause a weakening of the ice construction. If the weather is favorable (-10° to -15°C. with wind), a 50 cm (20 in.) thick ice layer can be frozen in a day.

(3) Laying of ice blocks is the quickest method but is much more expensive requiring the transportation of the ice blocks from the nearest river or water reservoir to the site. Ice blocks are laid like bricks; the blocks are overlapped. It is desirable to have the ice blocks uniform in size, especially of equal thickness. Before each new layer of ice blocks is laid, the preceding layer must be wet to achieve good adfreezing. Each layer of ice blocks must be allowed to freeze before placing the next.

1-56. FROZEN GROUND

a. Suitability. Frozen ground is three to five times stronger than ice; its strength increases with lower temperature. It has much better resistance to impact and explosion than to steadily acting load, an especially valuable feature for fortification purposes.

b. Methods. Construction using frozen ground is done by --

(1) Freezing chunks of frozen ground in layers.

(2) Laying prepared blocks of frozen ground.

(3) Preparing blocks of frozen ground from a mixture of water and aggregate (icecrete). Most suitable is a material consisting of gravel-sand-silt aggregate wetted to saturation and poured similar to Portland cement concrete. After freezing, such a material has the properties of concrete. These methods are analogous to the construction methods using ice.

1-57. PERMANANCE OF STRUCTURES FROM SNOW, ICE, AND FROZEN GROUND

a. Structures in subarctic regions. It is obvious that with the onset of warm weather, structures made of snow, ice, and frozen ground will disintegrate. A snow structure in early spring loses its camouflage. To extend its life, if needed, it should be covered with locally available material such as moss or forest litter. Depending upon the weather and layer thickness, the useful life of such a structure may be extended for more than a week.

b. Structures in arctic regions. In regions of shallow seasonal thaw underlined by permafrost, structures from snow, ice, and especially permafrost may be made permanent. For this purpose, the structure should be covered with the same material as the local permafrost. Typically, in tundra regions, the permafrost is covered by a shallow layer of thick vegetation, the so-called tundra mat which protects the permafrost from melting during the summer. The careful removal of the tundra mat and the construction of the structure on bare ground, and then covering all exposed surfaces with tundra mat material, protects the structure against summer disintegration. Special measures should be taken to minimize disturbance of the area around the structure during construction. Any disturbance of the area around the structure should be repaired. Careful preparation of such an expedient protective structure makes it permanent if needed.

1-58. RESISTANCE TO IMPACT AND EXPLOSION

a. To evaluate snow, ice, and frozen ground as materials for fortification, it is necessary to know the resistance of these materials to impact and explosion.

b. A rifle bullet rapidly loses its penetrating power, depending on the density of the snow. Snow packed in layers deflects the bullet at each layer. Loose snow spread over a defensive position will help smother ricochets.

c. Loose snow greatly reduces the explosive and fragmentation effects of shells. The depth, type of snow, and ammunition type are naturally the main consideration. The use of a delayed action fuse will generally cause the shell to penetrate the snow blanket and explode underneath, smothering and reducing the effect of the fragmentation. One meter (3.3 ft.) of snow will provide some protection against most light artillery fire. A superquick fuse setting will increase the effect of artillery fire, while

airburst will cause still more damage to surface targets.

d. Results of resistance tests of the impact of a bullet or explosion on samples of different frozen soils and icecrete at –4° C. are shown in table 1-12. On the basis of these test results the following general conclusions can be made:

(1) Construction from ice, frozen ground, and icecrete have a good resistance to the penetration of bullets and splinters. Because of their friability, which varies with different soils and increases with low temperatures, their resistance to explosion is less. This is especially true for ice, which should not be used for fortifications but only for obstacles.

(2) Fortifications made from frozen ground and icecrete should have an anti-spalling cover. Additionally, it is desirable to reinforce these materials with branches, straw, coniferous needles, and so forth. Wooden sheathing can be used as an anti-spalling cover. This sheathing is necessary during the construction and should be left as an anti-spalling cover after finishing the work. The reinforcement significantly increases the resistance of ice and frozen ground to impact and explosion. This reinforcement should be laid continuously rather than in layers. If reinforcement is made in layers, the impact of

Table 1-12. Resistance to Impact and Explosion of Frozen Soils and Icecrete
Test Temperature −4°C.

Type of sample	Effect of ordinary bullets fired from a machinegun at a distance of 100m			Effect of explosion using TNT charge of 04. kg (.9 lbs) in a vertical position
	5 rounds	10 rounds	20 rounds	
1. Ice, reinforced by spruce branches with antispalling cover of boards.	Crater 30 cm (12 in.) dia. 10 cm (4 in.) depth	Crater 45 cm (18 in.) dia. 25 cm (10 in.) depth	Crater 25 cm (10 in.) dia. 41 cm (16 in.) depth	Completely demolished.
2. Frozen clayey soil, reinforced by spruce branches with anti-spalling cover of boards.		No crater formed. Single bullet penetration 19-20 cm (7.5-7.9 in.)		A general split of 12 cm (5 in.) in re-inforcement. Crater 45 cm (18 in.) diameter. Sample not breached.
3. Icecrete, with antispalling cover of boards.	Crater 25 cm (10 in.) dia. 7 cm (2.75 in.) depth	Crater 30x18 cm (12x7½ in.) oval 10 cm (4 in.)	General Shattering of sample surface 10-11 cm (4-4½ in.) deep	Completely demolished.

1-70

explosion will split the material along the layer of reinforcement. Such reinforcement does not strengthen, but weakens the construction.

1-59. NATURAL OBSTACLES

a. Snow-covered and icy slopes. A steep slope is an obstacle to troops and vehicles even under normal conditions. When covered by deep snow or ice, it becomes much harder to surmount. The bogging-down action and the loss of traction caused by deep snow frequently create obstacles out of slopes which might be overcome easily, otherwise.

b. Windfalls. Occasionally, strong winds knock down many trees in a wooded area. These fallen trees are known as windfalls. They are very effective obstacles when covered with snow, especially to personnel wearing skis or snowshoes.

c. Avalanches. An avalanche makes an excellent obstacle for blocking passes and roads. Since it occurs in mountainous country where there are few natural avenues of approach, an avalanche can have a far-reaching influence over combat operations. The problem with those avalanches which occur naturally is that, unless their timing and location are just right, they may be of help to the enemy. It is possible to predict in advance where an avalanche can and probably will occur. Then by the use of recoilless rifle or artillery fire, bombs, or explosives, it is possible to induce the avalanche to slide at the desired time. This type of avalanche is an artificial obstacle in the technical sense. Generally, it will be of more value than the natural type.

1-60. ARTIFICIAL OBSTACLES

a. Barbed wire. There are many types of artificial obstacles used under summer conditions which are appropriate for winter use. Barbed wire normally employed makes an effective obstacle in soft, shallow snow. Triple concertina is especially effective since it is easy to install in addition to being difficult to cross. As the snow becomes deeper and more compact, a point is reached where it is possible to cross the barbed wire on top

of the snow. One type of barbed wire obstacle built to overcome this problem is known as the Lapland fence.

b. Lapland fence. The Lapland fence uses a floating type of anchor point or one which is not sunk into the ground. Poles are used to form a tripod. The tripod is mounted on a triangular base of wood. Six strands of wire are strung along the enemy side of the fence, four strands along the friendly side, and four strands along the base. As the snow becomes deeper, the tripods are raised out of the snow with poles or by other means to rest the obstacle on top of newly fallen snow. The base of the tripod and the base wires give enough bearing surface to prevent the fence from sinking into the snow.

c. Knife, rests. Knife rests are portable barbed wire fences, usually constructed prior to the snowfall. The fences are constructed by tying two wood poles at their center, forming an X. A similar X is made out of two other poles and then the two X's are lashed at each end of a 3 meter (10 ft) to 3.5 meter (11.7 ft) pole. This forms a framework to which barbed wire is fastened on all four sides. The obstacles can be stored until needed and easily transported to the desired location.

d. Concertina wire. Concertina wire is another quick way to improve on snow- covered obstacles. The concertina comes in 15 meter (50 ft.) sections which can be anchored quickly to the top of existing obstacles.

e. Abatis. The abatis is similar to a windfall. Trees are felled at an angle of about 45° to the enemy's direction of approach. The trees should be left attached to the stump to retard removal. Along trails, roads, and slopes, abatis can cause much trouble for skiers and vehicles.

f. Iced road grades. A useful obstacle can be made by pouring water on road grades. The ice that forms will seriously hamper vehicular traffic.

g. Ice demolition. In creating water obstacles to the enemy during winter conditions it becomes expedient to place charges below the ice and under water. To place charges under water, make boreholes in the ice with axes, chisels, ice augers, or shaped charges, then place the main charge below the ice. A charge of 36.3 kg (80 lb) of M3 demolition blocks, through 1.37 meters (4 1/2 ft) of ice, produces a crater 12 meters (40 ft) in diameter. To create a minefield in ice, sink boreholes about 3 meters (10 ft) apart in staggered rows. Suspend charge below the ice by means of cords with sticks bridging the top of the holes. The charges should be set least 60 cm (2 ft) below the bottom of the (fig 1-68). The size of the charge depends on the thickness of ice. Activate the firing devices on two or three charges in each underwater minefield, one on each end and one in the middle. The rest of the charges will detonate sympathetically. Blowing a field like this creates an obstacle to enemy vehicles for approximately 24 hours at -24°F.

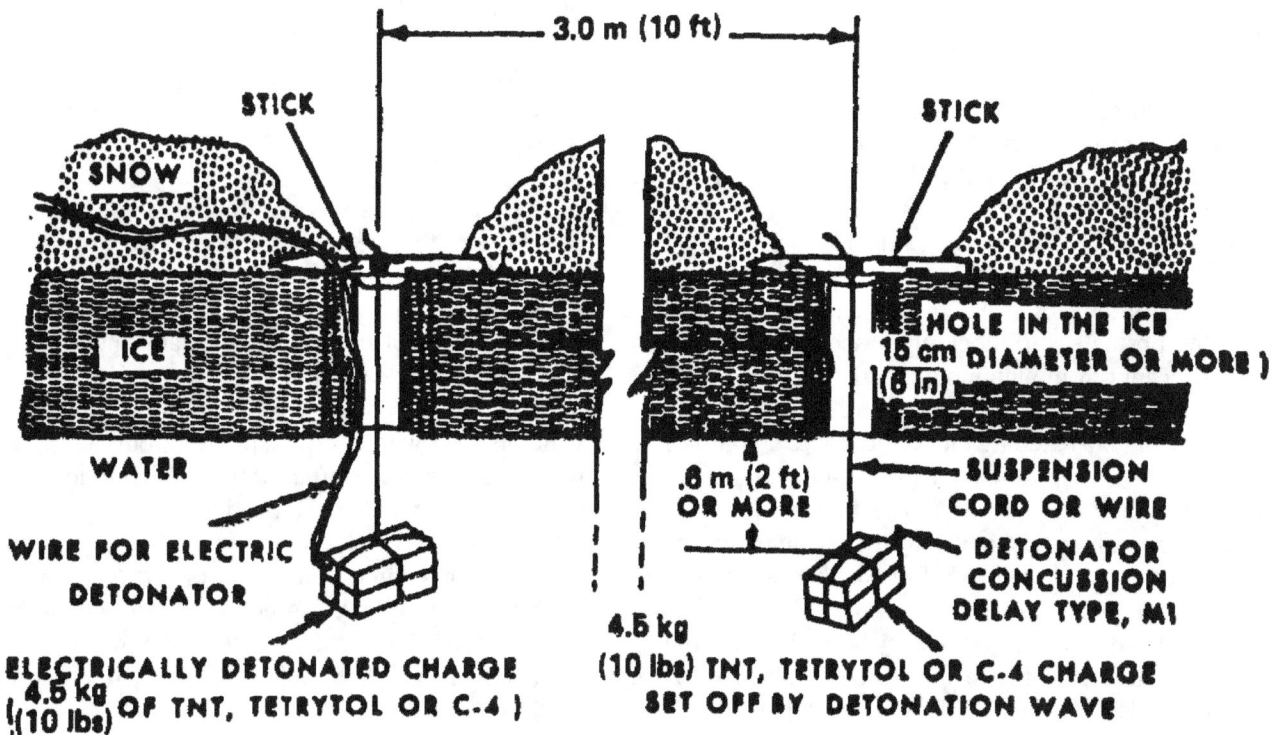

Figure 1-68. Method of Placing charges under ice.

SELF TEST

Requirement. Upon completion of the text assignment, solve the following self test questions and exercises:

Note: The following exercises are study aids. The figures following each question refer to the paragraph containing information related to the question. Write your answer in the space provided below each question. When you have finished answering all questions for this lesson, compare your answers with those given for this lesson in the back of this booklet. Review the lesson as necessary.

1. Plans for fortifications are usually based on what phasing of construction? (Para 1-1c)

2. What units normally construct hasty shelters and emplacements? (Para 1-2)

3. What are the three steps in the progressive development of the fortification? (Para 1-3d)

4. In the development of a fortification, what is the best protection against conventional weapons? (Para 1-4a)

5. Although shell craters offer immediate cover and concealment and can be quickly made into a hasty position, they have one marked advantage. What is the disadvantage? (Para 1-12 (1))

6. When immediate shelter from heavy enemy fire is required and existing defilade firing positions are not available what type of emplacement is used? (Para 1-12 (2))

7. Icecrete, formed by mixing dirt and water, is effective as an arctic building material. What minimum thickness will resist penetration of small arms fire? (Para 1-12a (4))

8. Craters, skirmisher's trenches, and prone emplacements can be developed into what basic defensive position? (Para 1-12a (1)(2)(3))

9. What is the primary means of protection against a nuclear explosion? (Para 1-1d)

10. For the full frontal berm overhead cover rifle position, at what angle should the firing aperture be cut? (Para 1-12c (2))

11. What depth of soil will the overhead cover for foxholes (fabric) support? (Para 1-12d (1))

12. What are the purposes of the cushion layer and the burster layer of the heavy overhead cover? (Para 1-37a (2)(4))

13. Why is a minimum depth of 18" of soil cover stipulated? (Para 1-32e)

14. What is the purpose of a standoff? (Para 1-34)

15. What engineer battalion is equipped to construct artillery firebases in areas where ground travel is prohibited? (Para 1-23)

16. What are the major tasks in Phase I, II and III of firebase construction? (Para 1-24)

17. What would be the effect of moisture on the resistance of soil cover to the penetration of rounds? (Note 2, Table 1-6)

18. Why is a light overhead cover needed for positions in wooded areas? (Para 1-38)

19. What characteristic of the design of the walls of the air transportable underground assault bunker (prefab) make it easier for the bunker to be pulled from the ground for relocation? (Para 1-45a)

20. What type of walls does the plywood perimeter bunker have? (Para 1-46)

LESSON 2

TRENCHES AND FIELDWORKS

CREDIT HOURS.. 3

TEXT ASSIGNMENT... Attached memorandum.

LESSON OBJECTIVES

Upon completion of this lesson, you should be able, in the indicated topic areas, to --

1. **Trench Types.** Describe the construction of the crawl trench, the fighting trench, and the standard trench.

2. **Traces.** Describe the octagonal and zigzag traces and know the advantages of each type of trace in trench layout.

3. **Trench Drainage.** Describe construction of trenches to keep out surface runoff, dispose of rainfall and seepage, and reroute natural drainage channels.

4. **Trench Overhead Cover.** Describe the construction of light and heavy overhead cover.

5. **Trench Revetment.** Discuss construction of the facing type, brushwood hurdle, continuous brush, pole and dimensioned timber, and metal types of revetments.

6. **Revetments and Breastworks.** Discuss the use of sandbags, sod blocks, and expedients. Describe the construction of breastworks.

7. **Defenses in Tropical Areas.** Discuss considerations necessary when constructing defenses in tropical areas.

8. **Tunneled Defenses.** Discuss soil, terrain, timbering, entrances, and ventilation of tunneled defenses.

ATTACHED MEMORANDUM

Section I. Trenches

2-1. PURPOSE

a. **Defensive area.** Trenches are excavated as fighting positions and to connect individual foxholes, weapons emplacements, and shelters in the progressive development of a defensive area. They provide protection and concealment for personnel moving between fighting positions or in and out of the area. Trenches should be included in the overall layout plan for the defense of a position. The excavation of trenches involves considerable time, effort, and materials and is only justified when an area will be occupied for an extended period. Trenches are usually open excavations but sections may be covered to provide additional protection if the overhead cover does not interfere with the fire mission of the occupying personnel. Trenches are difficult to camouflage and are easily detected, especially from the air.

b. Development. Trenches are developed progressively as is the case for other fighting positions. As they are improved, they are dug deeper, from a minimum of 60 cm (2 ft) to approximately 1.7 meters (5 1/2 ft). As a general rule, there is a tendency to excavate deeper for other than fighting trenches to provide more protection or to allow more headroom. Some trenches may also have to be widened to accommodate more traffic, including stretchers. It is usually necessary to revet trenches that are more than 1.5 meters (5 ft) deep in any type of soil. In the deeper trenches some engineer advice or assistance may be necessary in providing adequate drainage.

2-2. CONSTRUCTION

a. Crawl trench. The crawl trench is used to conceal movement into or within a position, and to provide a minimum of protection. Crawl trenches should be 60 to 75 cm (24 to 30 in.) deep and about 60 cm (24 in.) wide. This trench is the narrowest practicable for most purposes and of the least width that can be dug without difficulty. It should be zigzagged or winding. The spoil is placed on the parapets, normally on each side of the trench. If the trench runs across a forward slope, it is better to place all the spoil on the enemy side to make a higher parapet.

b. Fighting trench. In developing a trench system, the outline of the trench is marked out on the ground if time permits; if the digging is to be done at night, the ground is taped. The berm line is indicated about 45 cm (18 in.) from the front edge of the trench. The trench is dug by men working in the same direction (not facing each other or back to back), and far enough apart so that they do not interfere with each other.

(1) First step. The trench is dug to a depth of 90 cm (3 ft.) below ground level (1, fig 2-1). At this point both men are able to fire in either direction, in a kneeling or crouching position. In ordinary soil this step can be completed in approximately 2 hours. The sides of the trench are

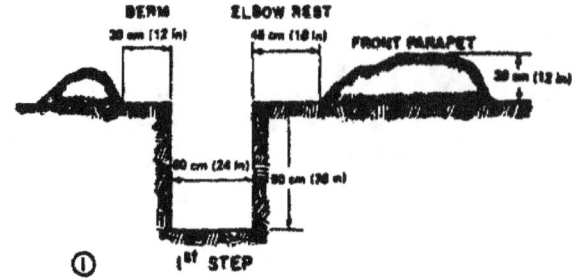

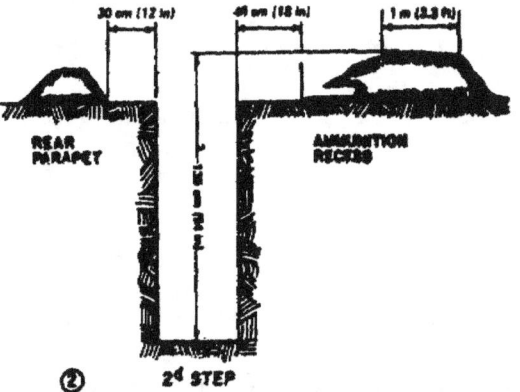

Figure 2-1. Development of a fighting trench.

kept vertical, or as steep as possible. If the soil is not stable, the sides require revetting immediately. Spoil is placed on each side of the trench in alternate shovelfuls beyond the berm lines until each parapet is about 30 cm (12 in.) high and at least 45 cm (18 in.) wide on the back parapet. The remaining spoil is placed on the front parapet until it is at least 150 cm (5 ft.) wide (fig 2-1).

(2) Second step. The second step consists of deepening the trench until it is approximately 1.35 meters (4 1/2 ft.) deep from the level of the trench parapet (2, fig 2-1). Normally, the front parapets are 30 cm (12 in.) high and the dirt settles 5 to 10 cm (2 to 4 in.). Parapets are then shaped and camouflaged.

(3) Front parapet. The front parapet must be made according to the lay of the ground and the requirements of the weapon. A front parapet is often unnecessary on a steep forward slope. At most sites a front parapet improves the field of fire and should be constructed as follows:

   (a) **Height.** A convenient height for the front parapet for firing purposes is 23 to 30 cm (9 to 12 in.) when the ground is level. It should be higher to fire uphill and the crest should be irregular to aid concealment. The height shown in figure 2-1 is average.

   (b) **Width.** A reasonably bulletproof parapet should be 1 meter in width. Since it is sloped in front and rear, the total width on the bottom will be approximately 2 meters (6.5 ft.).

   (c) **Berms.** The berm on the front of the trench forms an elbow rest which is usually about 45 cm (18 in.) wide. If an M60 machinegun on a bipod is to be fired, the firing platform should be 90 cm (36 in.) from front to rear.

   (4) **Rear parapet.** The rear parapet is made of spoil that is not required for the front parapet. If the spoil is available the rear parapet should be higher than the front parapet to prevent silhouetting of soldiers' heads when firing. The rear parapet may be up to 45 cm (18 in.) high and should be at least 45 cm (18 in.) wide at the top, sloped steeply in front. Parapets may be omitted to aid concealment or when ground provides background and protection to the firer's rear.

   (5) **Concealment.** Parapets are finished off by replacing turf or topsoil. The trench and parapets are covered with any available camouflage material, arranged to permit firing.

   (6) **Drainage.** A sump is dug at the lowest point to prevent the floor of the trench from becoming wet and muddy.

   c. **Standard trench.** The standard trench is developed from the fighting trench by lowering it to a depth of 1.7 meters (5 1/2 ft.). It may be constructed with fighting bay (fig 2-2) or with a fighting step (fig 2-3). Fighting positions are constructed on both sides of the trench to provide alternate positions to fight to the rear, to provide step off areas for foot traffic in the trench, and to provide protection against enfilade fire. The trench provides

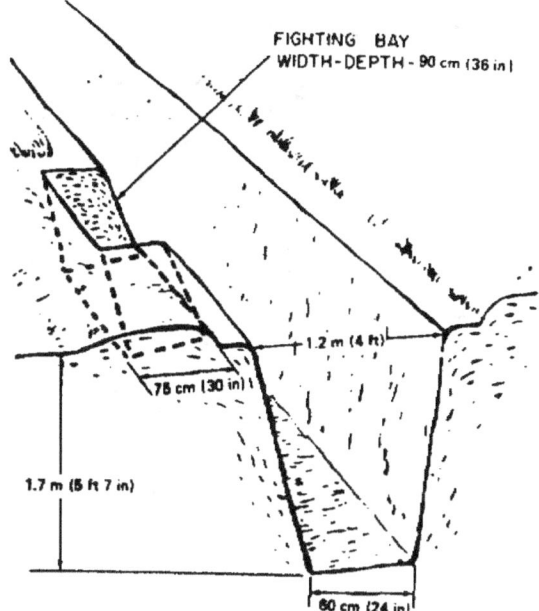

Figure 2-2. Standard trench with fighting bay.

more protection than the fighting trench due to its depth. Additional protection in the form of overhead cover may also be provided. This trench is primarily a fighting position, but it can also be used for communications, supply, evacuation, and troop movements.

   d. **Traces.** Each trench is constructed to the length required and follows one of the traces described below to simplify construction. Special combinations and modifications may be developed.

   (1) **Octagonal trace.** The octagonal trace (1, fig 2-4) is excellent for fighting trenches in most situations. The octagonal trace has the following advantages:

   (a) It affords easy communication.

   (b) It affords excellent protection against enfilade fire.

   (c) It facilitates oblique fire along the front.

   (d) It is economical to construct, both in labor and material.

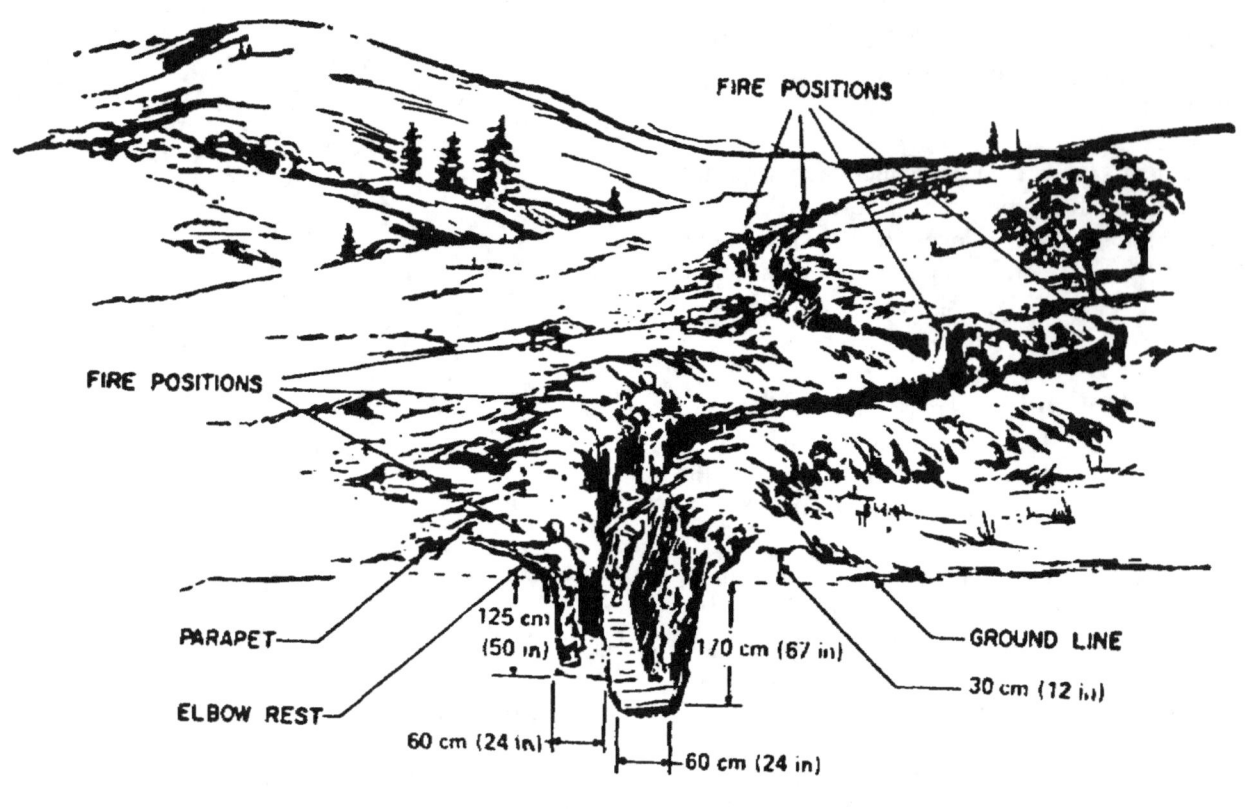

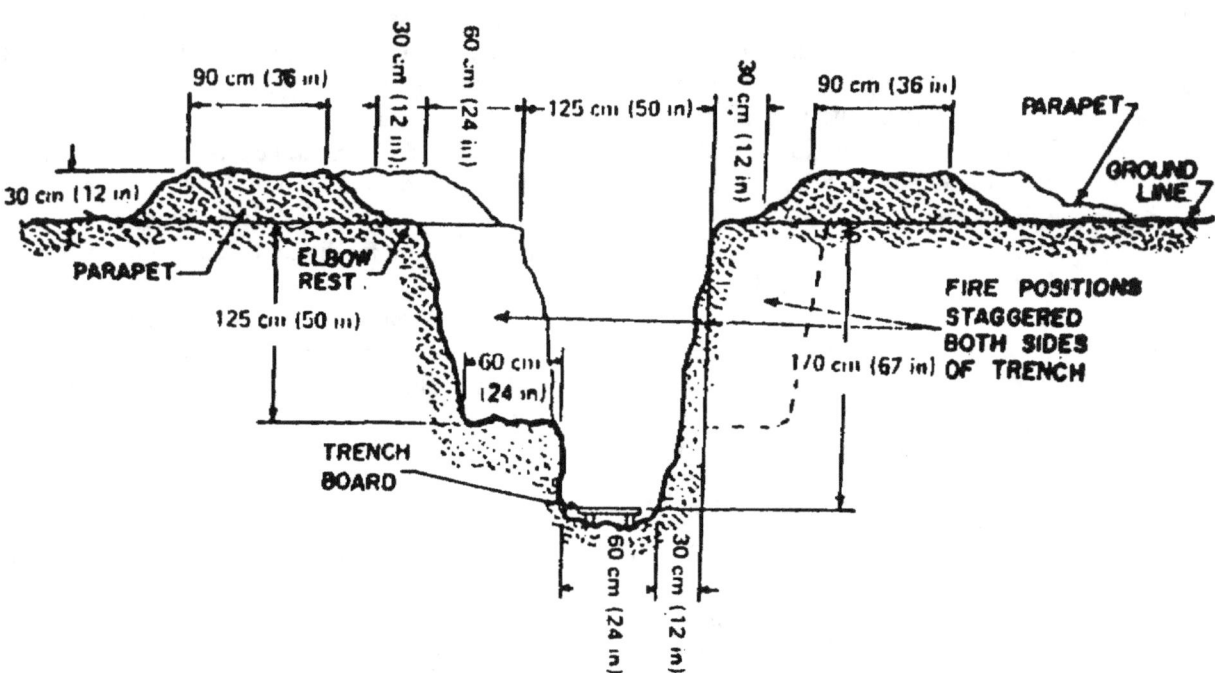

Figure 2-3. Standard trench with fighting step.

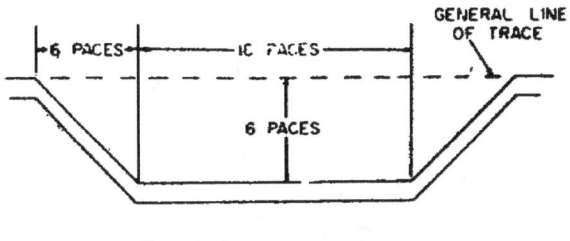

① OCTAGONAL TRACE

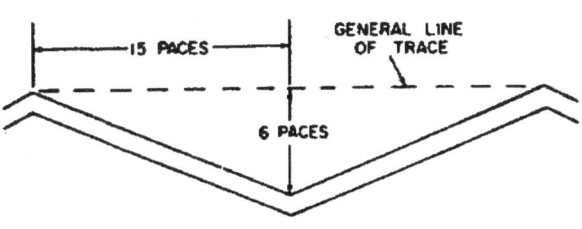

② ZIGZAG TRACE

Figure 2-4. Standard trench traces.

(e) It can be provided with a continuous fire step. Its chief disadvantage is that its layout lacks simplicity of detail.

(2) **Zigzag trace.** The zigzag trace (2, fig 2-4) can provide protection from enfilade fire and shell bursts by the employment of short tangents, and by the occupation of alternate tangents. The zigzag trace has the following advantages:

(a) It is the simplest and easiest to trace, construct, revet, and maintain.

(b) It may be readily adapted to the terrain.

(c) It permits both frontal and flanking fire.

(d) This trace has no specific disadvantages.

e. **Trench boards.** If the sumps are choked with mud, they will cease to function. When this happens, alternatives include some forms of flooring. Trench boards (fig 2-5) are the most practical. Timber planks, metal mats, or saplings wired together may also be used.

2-3. DRAINAGE.

a. **Siting.** Emplacements, shelters, and trenches are sited to take advantage of the natural drainage

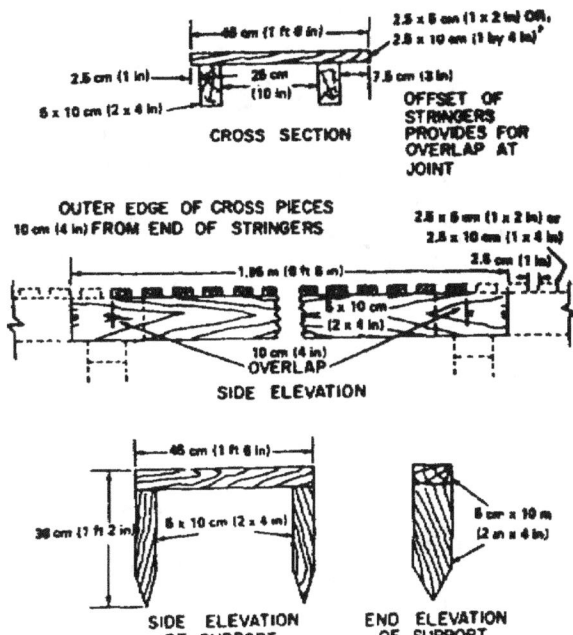

Figure 2-5. Trench board and support.

pattern of the ground. They are constructed to provide for--

(1) Exclusion of surface runoff.

(2) Disposal of direct rainfall or seepage.

(3) Bypassing or rerouting natural drainage channels if they are intersected by the emplacement or shelter.

b. **Surface runoff.** Proper siting, as illustrated in figure 2-6, can lessen the problem of surface runoff by locating the emplacement, shelter, or trench in an area not subject to excessive runoff. Surface water may be excluded by excavating interceptor ditches upslope from the emplacement or shelter. It is much easier to prevent surface water from flowing in than to remove it after it is in the excavation. Fortifications should be sited so as to direct the water to natural drainage lines. If this is not possible, the water is conducted across the trench through open flumes developed for the purpose or under the trench using a combination of trench drains and culverts. An application of the open flume method for use with trenches is shown in figure 2-7. A typical undertrench drain is shown in figure 2-8.

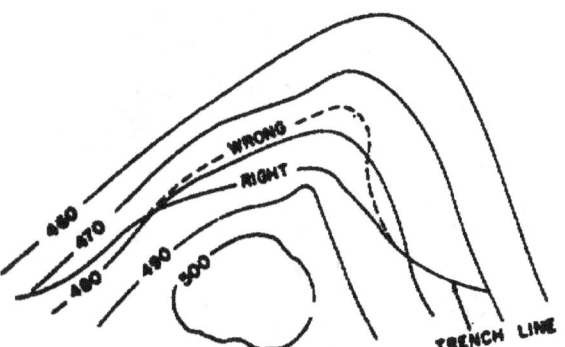

Figure 2-6. Siting to lessen problem of runoff disposal.

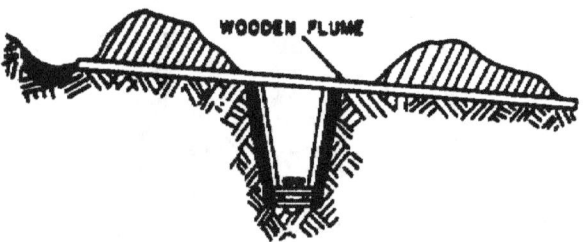

Figure 2-7. Use of open flume to direct water across ditch.

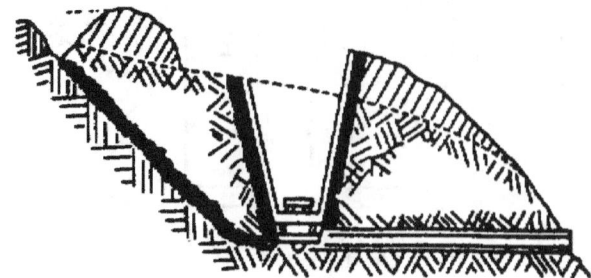

Figure 2-8. Use of undertrench drains.

c. Direct rainfall or seepage. Water collecting within an emplacement or shelter is carried to central points by providing longitudinal slopes in the bottom of the excavation. A very gradual slope of 1 percent is desirable. In trenches the slope is best provided for by fitting the trench to the terrain in such a way that the original surface has a moderate slope, as shown on the contoured layout in figure 2-9. When permitted by the tactical situation, excavation of trenches should commence at the lowest level and progress upward in order to avoid collecting water in the bottom of a partially

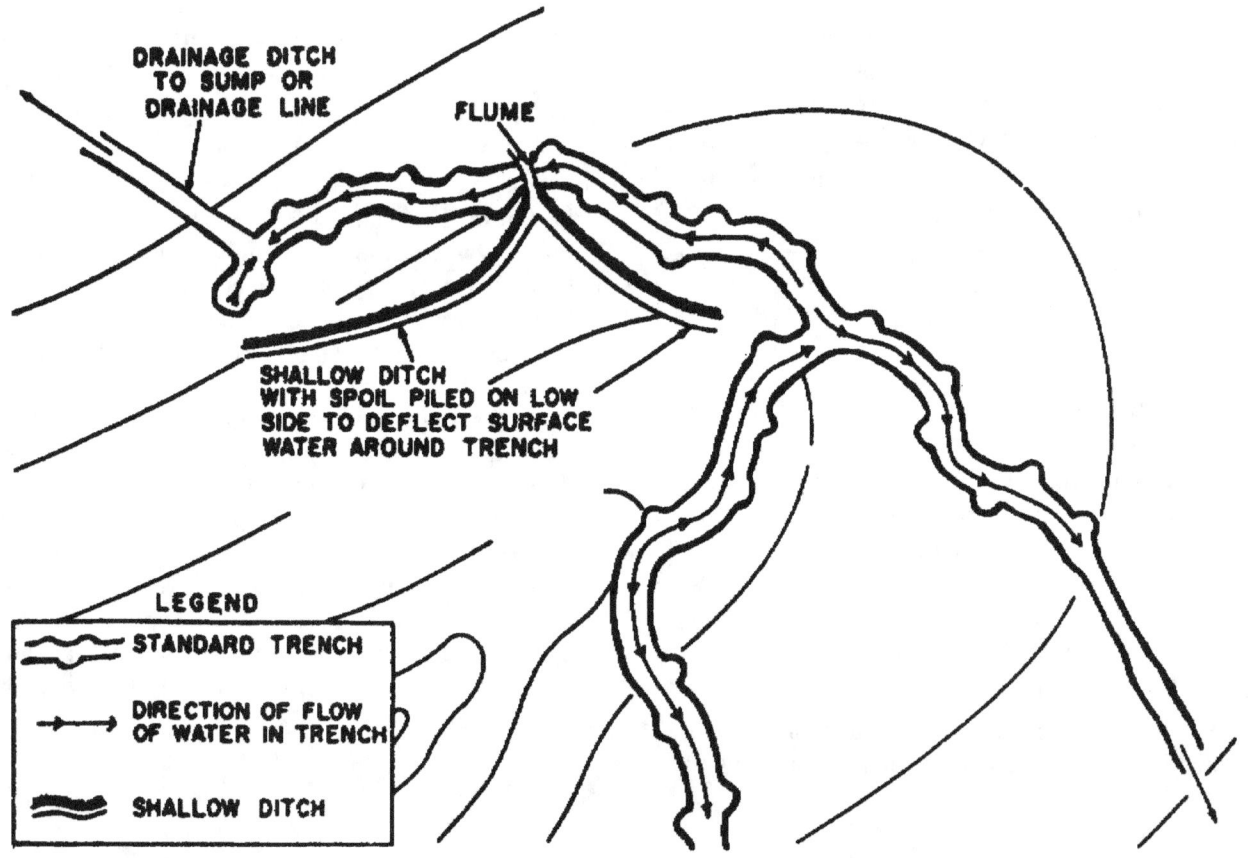

Figure 2-9. Method of siting trench to provide longitudinal drainage.

completed trench. The central collecting points may be either natural drainage lines or sumps below the bottom of the excavation as shown in figure 2-10. Such sumps are located at points where the water will percolate through permeable soil or can be piped, pumped, or bailed out.

Figure 2-10. Drainage sump in bottom of excavation.

2-4. OVERHEAD COVER

a. Light cover. Expedient overhead cover may be supported as shown in figure 2-11. Logs 15 to 20 cm (6 to 8 in.) in diameter should be used to support light earth cover. Saplings laid in a laminated pattern to a depth of 15 to 20 cm (6 to 8 in.) may be used as a substitute for the logs. The total thickness of the logs or saplings and the earth cover should be a minimum of 45 cm (18 in.)

b. Heavy cover. If heavy overhead cover is used in the construction of trenches, it should be installed in 6- to 12-meter (20 to 40 ft.) sections and in conjunction with the cover of emplacements and shelters connected by the trenches. Support for heavy overhead cover is provided by post-cap-stringer type structures as shown in figures 2-12 and 2-13. Trenches must be widened and deepened to accommodate these structures in accordance with information contained in the above illustrations. Bills of materials are shown in tables 2-1 and 2-2.

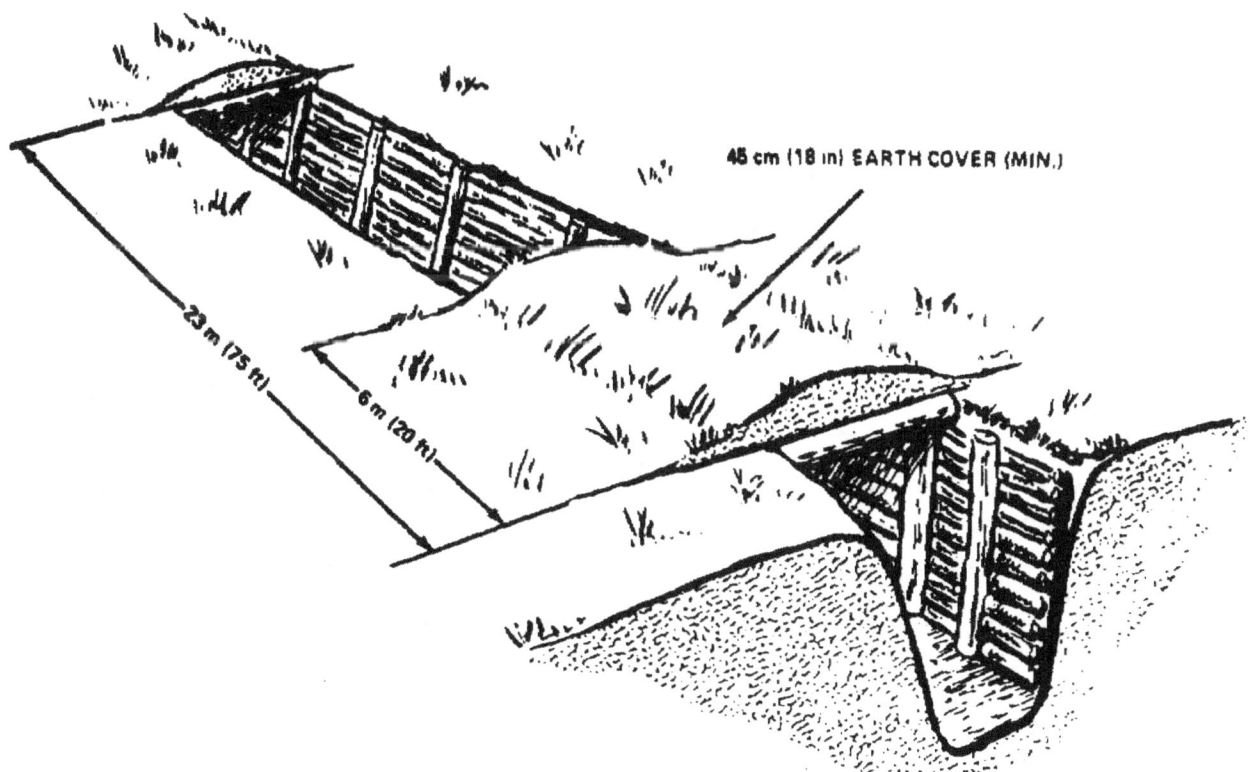

Figure 2-11. Revetted fighting trench with cover.

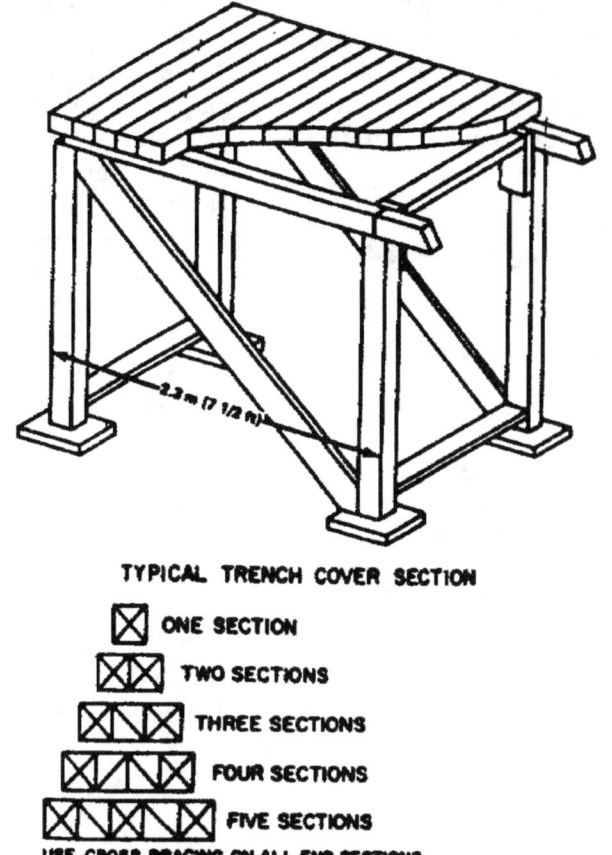

TYPICAL TRENCH COVER SECTION

⊠ ONE SECTION

⊠⊠ TWO SECTIONS

⊠⊠⊠ THREE SECTIONS

⊠⊠⊠⊠ FOUR SECTIONS

⊠⊠⊠⊠⊠ FIVE SECTIONS

USE CROSS BRACING ON ALL END SECTIONS.
MORE THAN FIVE SECTIONS USED (9 m (30 ft) OR GREATER)
CROSS BRACE CENTER SECTION.

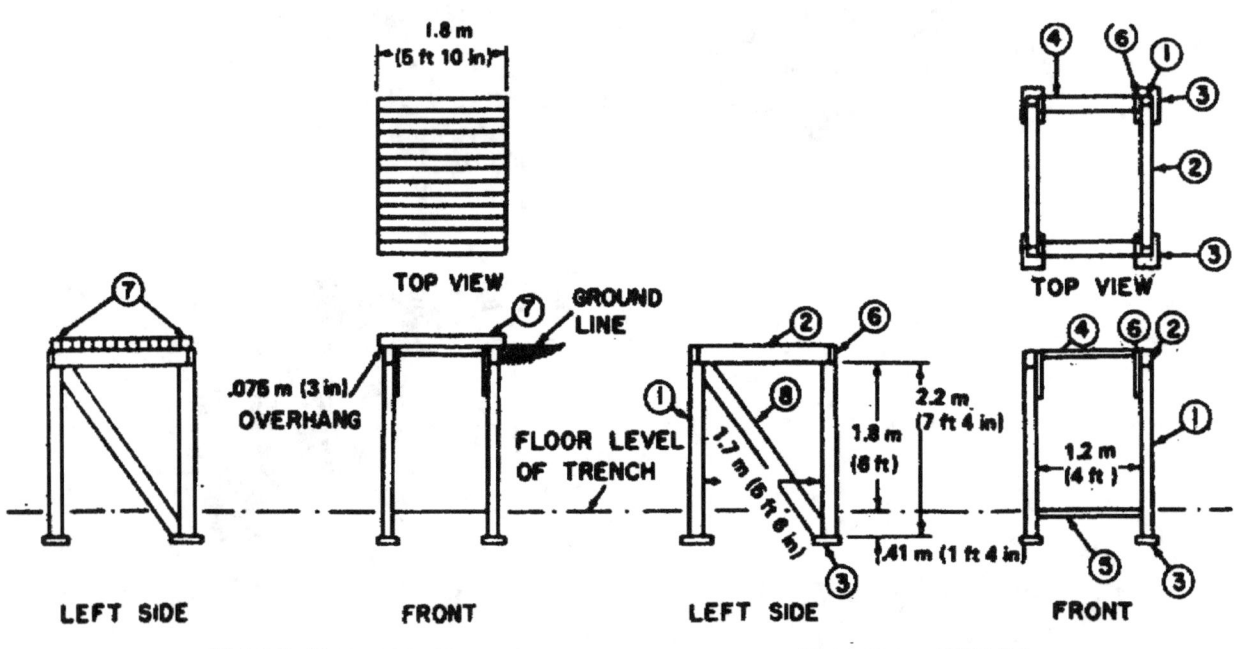

Figure 2-12. Trench cover section, dimensioned timber.

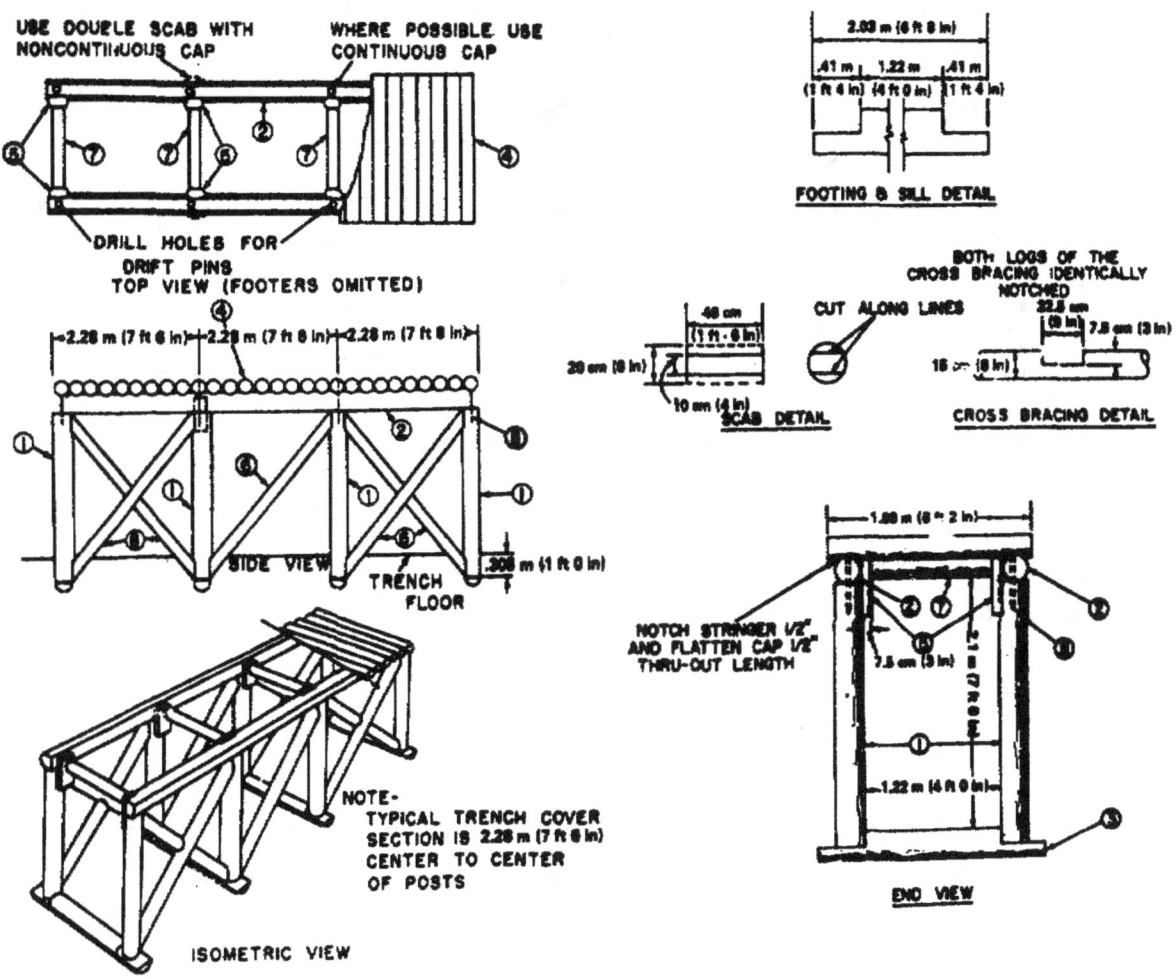

Figure 2-13. Trench section, log construction.

2-5. REVETMENT

a. **Wall sloping.** The necessity for revetment may sometimes be avoided or postponed by sloping the walls of the excavation. In most soils a slope of 1:3 or 1:4 is sufficient. This method may have to be used temporarily if the soil is loose and revetting materials are not available. Wall sloping can seriously reduce the protection due to the increased width of the trench at ground level. In any case where wall sloping is used, the walls should be dug vertical first and then sloped. Multiply the height of the wall as in figure 2-14 by the slope to be used 1:4 (l/4). This gives the amount the wall must be cut back at ground level. Then, cut out a section about 30 cm (12 in.) wide for a guide, as shown.

b. **Facing type revetment.** Facing revetment serves mainly to protect revetted surfaces from the effects of weather and damage caused by occupation. It is used when soils are stable enough to sustain their own weight. This revetment (fig 2-15) consists of the revetting or facing material and the supports which hold the revetting material in place. The facing material may be much thinner than that used in a retaining wall. For this reason facing type revetments are preferable since less excavation is required. The top of the facing should be set below ground level so the revetting is not damaged by tanks crossing the emplacement.

(1) **Materials for facing.** The facing may be constructed of brushwood hurdles,

Table 2-1. Bill of Materials, Trench Cover Section, Post, Cap, and Stringer, Construction Dimensioned Timber.

No.	Nomenclature	Size	Basic section as shown	Additional sections when used in series "X"
1	Post	20cm x 20cm x 2.2m (8"x 8"x 7'4")	4	2
2	Cap	20cm x 25cm x 1.85m (8"x 10"x 6'2")	2	2
3	Footing	5cm x 20cm x .40m (2"x 8" x 1'4")	16	8
4	Top spreader	7.5 cm x 20cm x 1.05m (3"x 8"x 3'6")	2	1
5	Bottom spreader	7.5 cm x 20cm x 1.2m (3"x 8" x 4'0")	2	1
6	Scab	7.5cm x 20cm x .6m (3"x 8"x 2'0")	4	2
7	Stringer*	15cm x 20cm x 1.75m (6"x 8"x 5'10")	13	13
8	Bracing	7.5cm x 20 cm x 2.85m (3"x 8"x 9'6")	2**	2**
9	Driftpin	1.91cm x 40cm (¾" x 16")	8	4
10	Driftpin	1.25cm x 30cm (½" x 12")	26	24
11	Nails	60d	20 lb	15 lb

*Laminated wood roof, designed in accordance with table 3-4 may be substituted if desired.
**Change to 4 when cross bracing is required. See bracing details.

Suggested Construction Procedure

1. Dig holes for footers.
2. Place footers in holes making them as level as possible.
3. Nail posts to footers.
4. Place caps on top of posts and secure with driftpins (bore one-half-inch holes for pins).
5. Nail scabs in place.
6. Nail top and bottom spreaders in place.
7. Nail side braces in place.
8. Put stringers on top of caps and secure with one-half-inch driftpins.
9. Use typical overhead cover.

Table 2-2. Bill of Materials, Trench Cover Section, Post, Cap, and Stringer, Construction Log.

No.	Nomenclature	Size	Basic section as shown	Additional sections when used in series
1	Post	30cm x 2.2m (12" log x 7'4")	4	2
2	Cap	30cm x 2.25m (12" log x 7'6")*	2	2
3	Sill	30cm x 1.9m (12" log x 6'4")	2	1
4	Stringer***	25cm x 1.9m (10" log x 6'4")	8	8
5	Scab	7.5cm x 20cm x .45m (3"x 8"x 1'6")**	4	2
6	Bracing	15cm x 2.85m (6" log x 9'6")	4	4
7	Top spreader	15cm x 1.05m (6" log x 3'6")	2	1
8	Driftpins	1.25cm x .4m (½" x 16")	46	34
9	Nails	60d	20 lb	18 lb

*Or larger multiples thereof.
**Scab should be dimension timber as indicated, whenever such material is available. When only logs are available the scab should be split out of the center of an 8" log.
***Laminated wood roof, designed in accordance with table 3-4, may be substituted if desired.

Construction Notes

1. Dig trenches for sills.
2. Place sills and level up.
3. Fasten posts to sills with one-half-inch driftpins.
4. Place caps on posts, secure with driftpins.
5. Nail scabs in place.
6. Nail in top spreaders.
7. Nail cross bracing in place.
8. Place stringers on top of caps and secure with one-half-inch driftpins.
9. Use typical overhead cover.

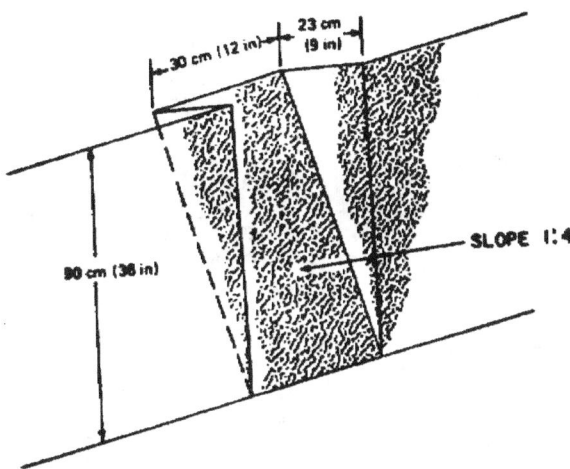

Figure 2-14. Method of sloping earth walls.

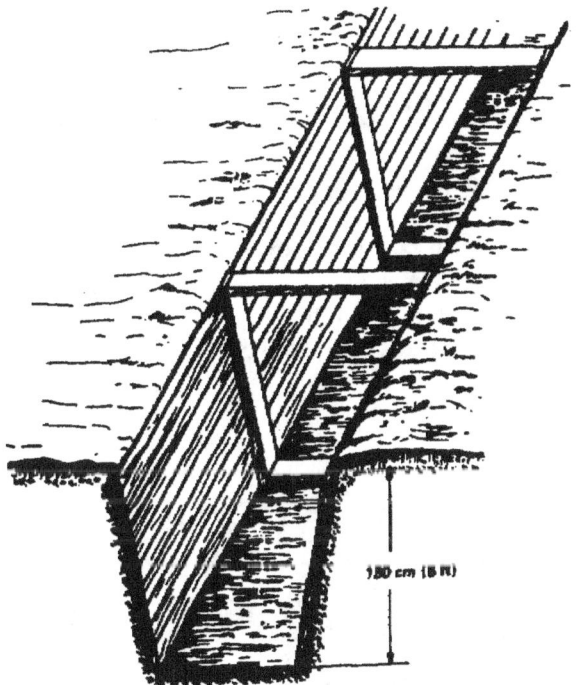

Figure 2-15. Facing revetment supported by frames.

continuous brush, pole and dimensioned timbers, corrugated metal, or burlap and chicken wire. The method of constructing each type is described below.

(2) **Methods of support.** The facing may be supported by --

(a) **Timber frames.** Frames of dimensioned timber are constructed to fit the bottom and sides of the position, and hold the facing material apart over the excavated width.

(b) **Pickets.** Pickets are driven into the ground on the position side of the facing material and held tightly against the facing as shown in figure 2-16 by bracing the pickets apart across the width of

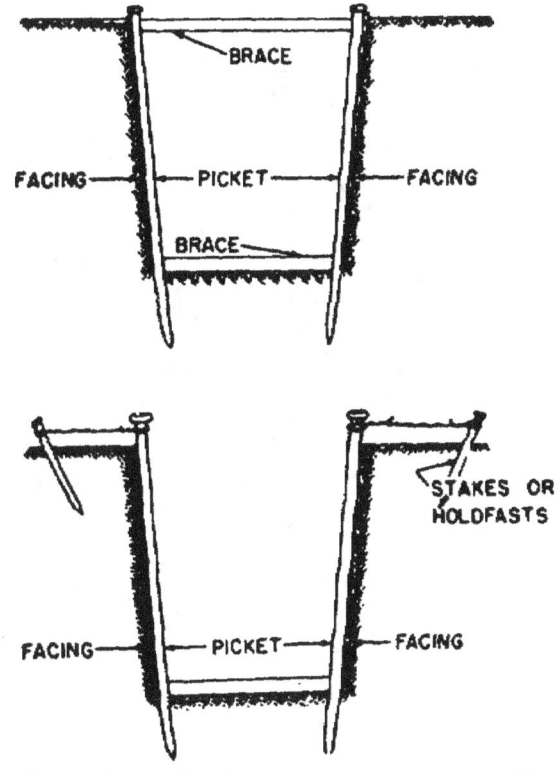

Figure 2-16. Facing revetment supported by pickets.

the position and anchoring the tops of the pickets by means of stakes driven into the ground and tiebacks.

(3) **Facing type revetments.** Facing type revetments may be supported either by timber frames or pickets. The size of pickets required, and their spacing, are determined by the soil and the type of facing materials used. Wooden pickets should not be smaller than 7.5 cm (3 in.) in diameter or in the smallest dimension. The maximum spacing between pickets should be about 2 meters (6.5 ft.). The standard pickets used to support barbed wire entanglements are excellent for use in revetting. Pickets are driven at least 45 cm (18 in.) into the floor of the position.

2-11

Where the tops of the pickets are to be anchored, an anchor stake or holdfast is driven into the top of the bank opposite each picket and the top of the picket is racked to it as shown in figure 2-17. The distance between the anchor stake and the facing is at least

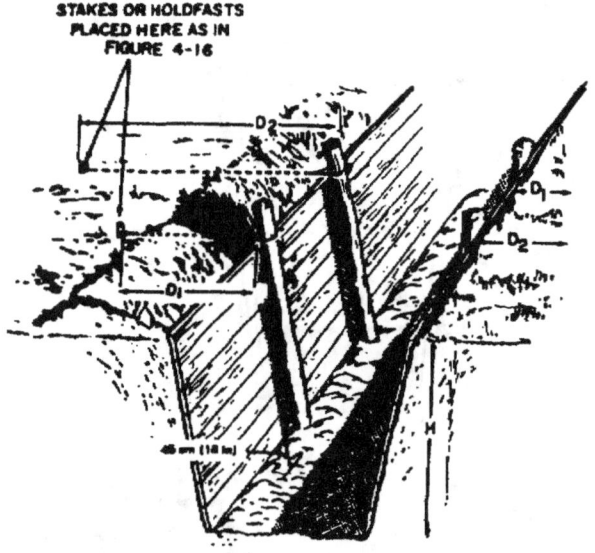

D_1 IS EQUAL TO OR GREATER THAN H
D_2 IS EQUAL TO H+0.61 METER

Figure 2-17. Method of anchoring pickets.

equal to the height of the revetted face, with alternate anchors staggered and at least 60 cm (24 in.) farther back. Several strands of wire holding the pickets against the emplacement walls must be straight and taut. A groove or channel is cut in the parapet to pass the wire through.

c. Brushwood hurdle. A brushwood hurdle is a woven revetment unit usually 2 meters (6.5 ft.) long and of the required height. As shown in figure 2-18, pieces of brushwood about 2.5 cm (1 in.) in diameter are woven on a framework of sharpened pickets driven into the ground at 50 cm (20 in.) intervals. When completed, the 2-meter (6.5 ft.) lengths are carried to the position, where the pickets are driven in place and the tops of the pickets are tied back to stakes or holdfasts. The ends of the hurdles are then wired together.

d. Continuous brush. As shown in figure 2-19, a continuous brush revetment, which is constructed in place. Sharpened pickets, 7.5 cm

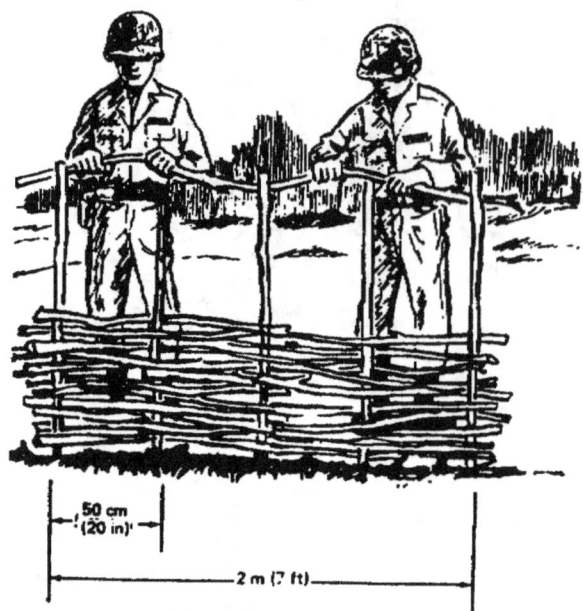

Figure 2-18. Making a brushwood hurdle.

(3 in.) in diameter, are driven into the bottom of the trench at 1-pace intervals and about 10 cm (4 in.) from the earth face to be revetted. The space behind the pickets is packed with small straight brushwood laid horizontally and the tops of the pickets are anchored to stakes or holdfasts.

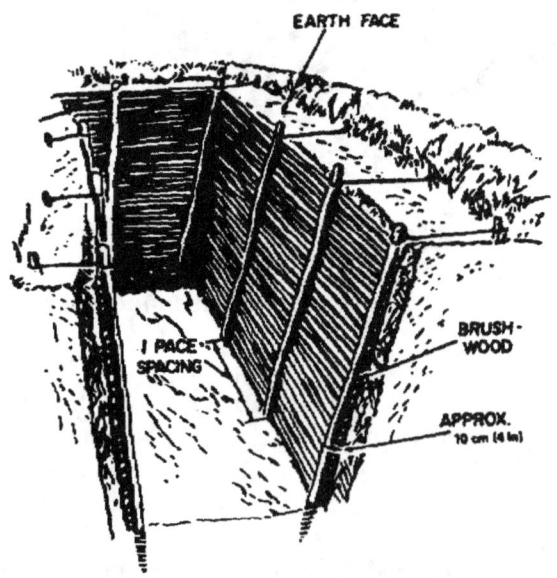

Figure 2-19. Continuous brush revetment.

2-12

e. Pole and dimensioned timber. A pole revetment (fig 2-20) is similar to the continuous brush revetment except a layer of small horizontal round poles, cut to the length of the wall to be revetted, is used instead of brushwood. Instead of poles, boards or planks are used if available; they have the added advantage of being more quickly installed. Pickets are held in place by holdfasts or struts.

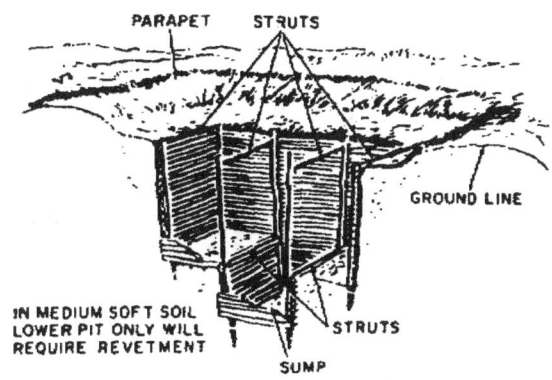

Figure 2-20. Timber revetment using small poles.

f. Metal. A revetment of corrugated metal sheets, ((1), figure 2-21) or pierced steel plank may be installed rapidly and is strong and durable. It is well adapted to emplacement construction because the edges and ends of sheets or planks can be lapped as required to produce a revetment of a given height and length. All metal surfaces must be smeared with mud to eliminate possible reflection of thermal radiation and to aid in camouflage. Burlap and chicken wire revetments are installed as shown in ((2), figure 2-21). When damaged, corrugated metal forms dangerous sharp edges. Prompt attention should be given to the repair of damaged revetments to prevent injuries to personnel or damage to equipment.

2-6. REPAIR AND MAINTENANCE OF TRENCHES

a. Maintenance.

(1) Drainage. It is important to keep the drainage system working properly. If water is allowed to stand in the bottom of a trench, the revetment will eventually be undermined and

Figure 2-21. Types of metal revetment.

become useless. Sumps and drains must be kept clear of silt and refuse. Trench boards should be lifted periodically so that the mud can be cleaned out from beneath them.

(2) Berms. Berms must be kept clear and of sufficient width to prevent soil from the parapets falling into the trench.

(3) Revetted trenches. When wire and pickets are used to support revetment material, the pickets may become loose, especially after rain. Improvised braces may be wedged across the trench at or near floor level, between two opposite pickets. Anchor wires may be tightened by further twisting. Anchor pickets may have to be driven in farther to hold the tightened wires.

(4) **Sandbag revetments.** Periodic inspections must be made of sandbags. Any bags that are split or damaged should be replaced.

b. **Repair.**

(1) **Top of trench.** If the walls are crumbling at the top, making the trench wider at ground level, an elbow rest should be cut out of the full width of the berm and about 30 cm (12 in.) deep, or until firm soil is reached. Sandbags or sods are then used to build up the damaged area ((1), figure 2-22).

(2) **Bottom of trench.** If the trench walls are wearing away at the bottom, place a plank on edge, or shift brushwood as shown in ((2), figure 2-22). The plank is held against the trench wall with short pickets driven into the trench floor. If planks are used on both sides of the trench, they are held in position with a piece of timber cut to the right length and wedged between the planks at floor level. Earth is placed in back of the planks.

(3) **Collapsed wall.** If an entire wall appears to be collapsing, the trench must be completely revetted or the walls sloped (fig 2-14) so they will stand. If the walls are permitted to cave in, the trench usually must be widened at ground level which reduces its protective value. Cave-ins should be prevented as far as possible by revetting the trench in time or by one of the remedial measures described above.

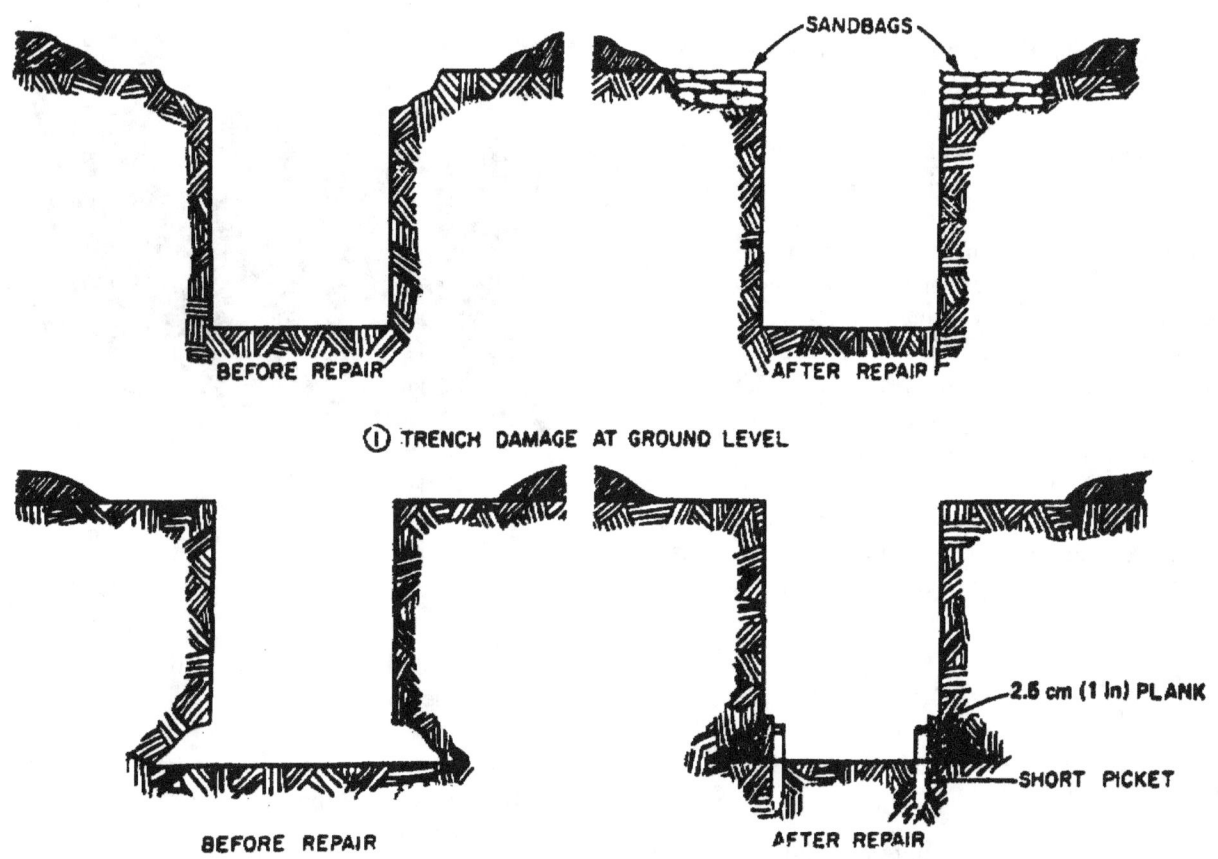

① TRENCH DAMAGE AT GROUND LEVEL

② DAMAGE NEAR FLOOR LEVEL

Figure 2-22. Trench repair.

2-7. REVETMENTS

a. Use of sandbags. Walls are built of sandbags or sod in much the same way as bricks are used. Sandbags are also useful for temporary retaining wall type revetments, especially where silent installation is essential. The three types of sandbags in use are the cotton osnaburg, the polypropylene, and the acrylic. All are used in the same manner. The polypropylene bag will last approximately seven months, twice as long as the cotton osnaburg bag. The acrylic sandbag which is replacing the osnaburg and the polypropylene is rot and weather resistant. The bag under all climate conditions has a life of at least 2 years, with no visible deterioration. It is readily stacked to form a sandbag revetment or breastwork with no slippage of individual bags within the stack. Holes in a bag caused by a bullet or a fragment do not enlarge due to continued weakening or unravelling of the bag material around the hole or holes. The bag is lusterless olive drab in color. The useful life of sandbags can be prolonged by filling them with a mixture of dry earth and portland cement, normally in the ratio of 1 part of cement to 10 parts of dry earth. The cement sets as the bags take on moisture. A ratio of 1 to 6 should be used for a sand-gravel mixture. The filled bags may be dipped in a cement-water slurry as an alternative method. Each sandbag should be pounded with a flat object, such as a 5 by 10 cm (2 by 4 in.) board, to make the wall more stable.

(1) Construction. As a rule sandbags are used for revetting only when the soil is very loose and requires a retaining wall to support it or for the repair of damaged trenches. A sandbag revetment will not stand with a vertical face. The face must have a slope of 1:4 and the base must be on firm ground and dug at a slope of 4:1. The sandbag wall should lean against the earth if it is to hold in place (fig. 2-23).

(a) The bags are uniformly filled about three-fourths full with earth or with a dry soil-cement mixture and the choke cords are tied.

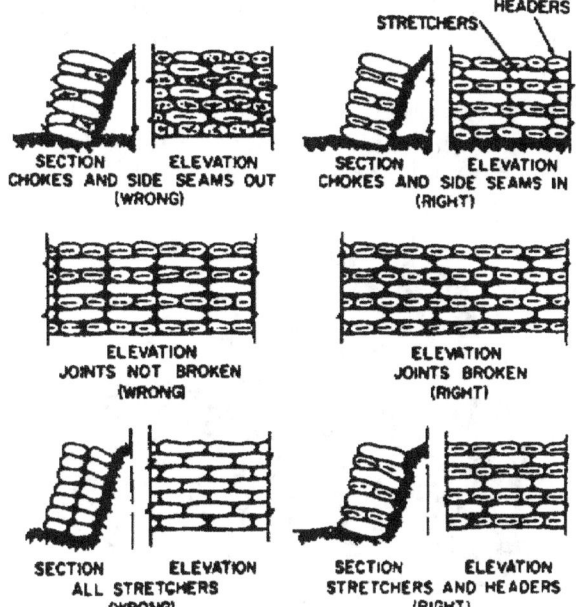

Figure 2-23. Retaining wall revetment.

(b) The bottom corners of the bags are tucked in after filling.

(c) As the revetment is built, the revetted face is made to conform to this slope by backfilling or additional excavation.

(d) Sandbags are laid so that the planes between the layers have the same pitch as the foundation, i.e., at right angels to the slope of the revetment.

(e) The bottom row of the revetment is constructed with all bags placed as headers (fig 2-23). The wall is then constructed using alternate rows of stretchers and headers with the joints broken between courses. The top row of the revetment wall consists of headers.

(f) All bags are placed so that side seams on stretchers and choked ends on headers are turned toward the revetted face.

(2) Common faults. The common faults in sandbag revetments are illustrated in figure 2-23.

(3) Expedient means of filling sandbags. Often the requirement for filled sandbags far exceeds the capabilities of men using shovels to fill sandbags. A high speed combat intrenching machine can be used to fill sandbags if local soil is to be used as the filler. The bag is filled by holding it under the discharge conveyor as the intrenching machine is run forward at a slow speed (fig. 2-24).

Figure 2-24. Use of combat intrencher to fill sandbags.

This method will produce filled sandbags at a rate of one every four to five seconds. The spillage can be used to fill sandbags also since it is often loose and easily shoveled. If the sandbags are to be filled from a stockpile of sand or other material, the work can be made easier and the bags filled faster by using the funnel as shown in figure 2-25. The funnel can be constructed using either lumber or steel.

b. Sod blocks. Thick sod with good root systems provides a satisfactory revetting material.

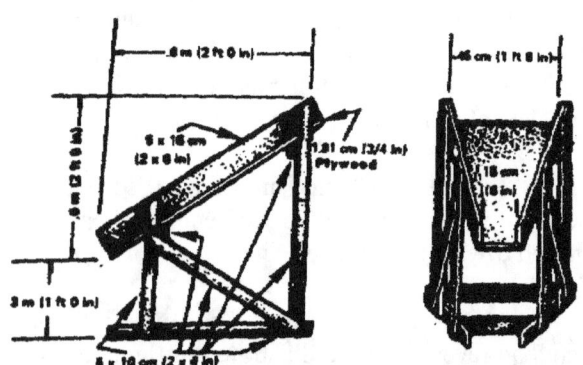

Figure 2-25. Expedient funnel for filling sandbags.

Sod blocks cut into sections about 23 by 46 cm (9 by 18 in.) are laid flat, using the alternate stretcher-header method described above for use with sandbags. Sod is laid grass-to-grass and soil-to-soil, except for the top layer which should be laid with the grass upward, to provide natural camouflage. As each layer of sod is completed, wooden pegs are driven through the layers to prevent sliding until the roots grow from layer to layer. Two pegs are driven through each 23 by 46 cm (9 by 18 in.) sod. Sod revetment is laid at a slope of about 1 horizontal to 3 vertical.

c. Expedients. In cold weather blocks of ice may be used to construct retaining wall type revetments. They are stacked in the same manner as sandbags or sod. Water is applied to bind them together by freezing. Other expedients include earth-filled packing cases or ammunition boxes. Empty boxes or packing cases are placed in position and nailed to the lids of the layer below; the boxes and filled with earth or rock and the lids fastened in place. This procedure is repeated for each row. The tops of the revetment are tied to pickets to prevent overturning.

2-8. BREASTWORKS

Breastworks may be substituted for trenches, weapons emplacements, etc., when soil conditions or a high water table makes excavation to the required depth impossible. Under these circumstances earth must be built up above ground level to form protective walls. This work requires more time and effort than digging trenches of comparable depth. Breastwork defenses are not as good protection against airbursts as excavated positions. They also have serious disadvantages against blast and nuclear radiation.

a. Construction. When breastworks are constructed for fire positions and weapons emplacements their dimensions should conform to the excavated positions. A front breastwork should be bulletproof, i.e., of approximately 1 meter (3.3 ft.) minimum thickness. The outer face should be sloped gently; not steeper than 1:2 (fig 2-26). The inner face

2-16

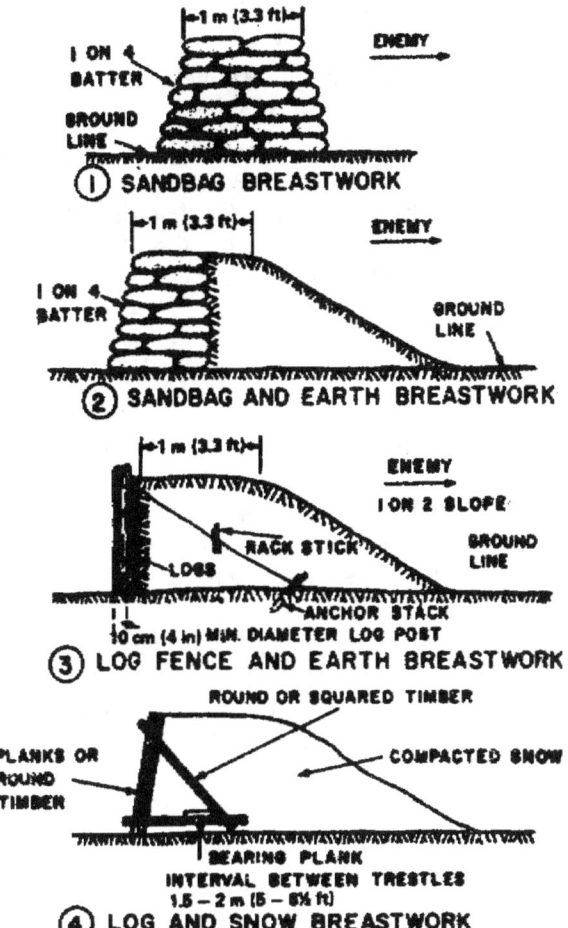

Figure 2-26. Varied types of breastworks.

should be sloped 1:4 and revetted. A rear breastwork may be similar to the front.

b. Snow breastworks. Snow breastworks can be constructed as shown in ((4), figure 2-26).

2-9. SNOW DEFENSES

a. Snow as protective material. Snow must be packed to be effective against small arms fire. Drifted snow is usually well compacted by the wind. Loose snow has only about half the value of packed snow in resisting penetration, but shells and grenades bursting on impact are largely ineffective in loose snow because the fragmentation is blanketed. The thickness of snow required for protection against small arms and shell splinters is as follows:

Newly fallen snow........ At least 4 meters
(13 ft)

Firmly frozen snow   At least 2.5-3 meters
(8-10 ft.)
Packed snow..................At least 2 meters
(6 1/2 ft.)
Ice................................At least 30 cm (12 in.)

b. Trenches. In deep snow, trenches and weapons emplacements may be excavated in the snow to approximately normal dimensions. Unless the snow is well packed and frozen, revetment will be required, ((4), figure 2-26). In shallow snow, not deep enough to permit excavation to the required depth, snow breastworks must be constructed. These should be of compacted snow, at least 2 meters (6 1/2 ft.) thick and revetted.

2-10. DEFENSES IN TROPICAL AREAS

a. Advantages.

(1) Concealment is comparatively easy.

(2) Timber is readily available.

b. Tools. A variety of cutting tools are required to --

(1) Clear fields of fire.

(2) Cut tree roots during excavation.

(3) Cut timber for overhead cover.

c. Equipment. When large cleared areas are necessary bulldozers with winches or dozers with land clearing blades are required for grubbing trees. Bulldozers can clear from 10,000 to 12,000 square meters (11,960 to 14,350 sq. yd.) of heavy jungle is 8 hours. Dozers with land clearing blades can clear 15,000 to 25,000 square meters (17,940 to 29,900 sq. yd.) of heavy jungle in the same length of time.

d. Drainage. Good drainage is required for all excavations and should be considered in the initial siting of the position. Trenches, shelters, and emplacements are floored as soon as possible. Stone, brushwood covered with bamboo matting may be used.

e. Overhead cover. Waterproof material such as building paper should be included in the overhead cover for shelters or trenches and should overlap the sides of the structure about 60 cm (2 ft.). Material used as overhead cover must be well supported and sloped so water will run off.

2-11. DUMMY EARTHWORKS

a. **Dummy trenches.** Dummy trenches are dug to conceal the true extent of a defended area or locality. Dummy trenches should be dug about 45 cm (18 in.) deep, with brushwood laid in the bottom, ((1), fig 2-27). The brushwood has the effect of

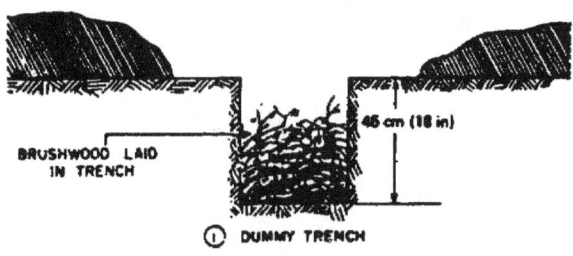

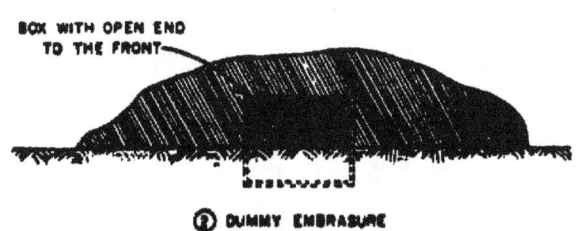

Figure 2-27. Dummy earthworks.

producing an internal shadow similar to that cast by a deep trench. Parapets must be similar to those of other trenches in the position. False parapets should also be concealed.

b. **Dummy emplacements.** The most noticeable feature of a roofed emplacement is the deep internal show of its embrasure. This appears to the enemy from the ground as a black patch of regular shape. Usually, it will appear rectangular if the roof is flat. A rectangular embrasure can be simulated by means of a box placed in the ground, with open end to the front, and covered with earth ((2), fig 2-27). Some attempt at concealment and occasional signs of occupation will add realism.

2-12. TUNNELED DEFENSES

a. **Considerations.** Tunnels are not used frequently in the defense of an area due to the time, effort, and technicalities involved; however, they have been used to good advantage. Tunneled defenses can be used when the length of time an area must be defended justifies the effort and the ground lends itself to this purpose.

b. **Soil.** The possibility of tunneling also depends to a great extent on the nature of the soil, which can be determined by borings or similar means. Tunneling in hard rock is so slow that it is generally impractical. Tunnels in clay or other soft soils are also impractical since they must be lined throughout or they will soon collapse. Construction of tunneled defenses is usually limited to –

(1) Hilly terrain - steep hillsides.

(2) Favorable soil, including hard chalk, soft sandstone, and other types of hard soil or soft rock.

c. **Tunnel examples.** A sketch of tunnels is shown in figure 2-28. In this tunnel system, the soil was generally very hard and only the entrances were timbered. The speed of excavation, using handtools, varied according to the soil, seldom exceeding 7.5 meters

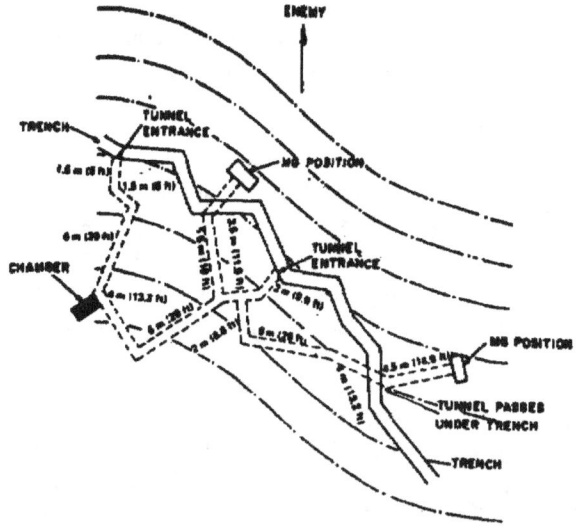

Figure 2-28. Tunneled defenses.

(25 ft.) per day. In patches of hard rock, as little as 1 meter (3.3 ft.) was excavated in a day (24 hr.). The use of powertools did not alter the speed of excavation significantly. The work was done by engineer units assisted by infantry personnel.

d. Construction. Tunnels of the type shown (fig 2-28) are excavated about 9 meters (30 ft.) below ground level. They may be horizontal or nearly so.

(1) Entrances. The entrances must be strengthened against collapse under shell fire and ground shock from nuclear weapons. The first 5 meters (16.5 ft.) from each entrance should be framed with timber supports using 10 cm x 10 cm (4 in. x 4 in.) or comparable timbers.

(2) Size. Untimbered tunnels should be about 1 meter (3.3 ft.) wide and 1.5 to 2 meters (5 to 6.5 ft.) high.

(3) Chambers. Chambers may be constructed in rock or extremely hard soil without timber supports. If timber is not used the chamber (fig 2-28) should not be more than 2 meters (6.5 ft.) wide. If timbers are used the width may be increased to 3 meters (10 ft.). The chamber should be the same height as the tunnel and up to 4 meters (13 ft.) long.

(4) Grenade trap. Grenade traps should be constructed at the bottom of straight lengths where they slope. It can be done by cutting a recess about 1 meter (3.3 ft.) deep in the wall facing the inclining floor of the tunnel.

(5) Disposal of soil. A considerable quantity of spoil from the excavated area must be disposed of and concealed. The volume of spoil is usually estimated as one-third greater than the volume of the tunnel. Approximately 100 tons of spoil were removed from the tunnel system shown in figure 2-28.

(6) Concealment. Tunnel entrances must be concealed from enemy observation and it may be necessary to transport spoil by hand through a trench. Cold air rising from a tunnel entrance may give away the position.

e. Precautions.

(1) Picks and shovels. There is always danger that tunnel entrances will be blocked, trapping the occupants. Picks and shovels must be kept in each tunnel so men trapped can dig their way out.

(2) Entrances. At least two entrances are necessary for ventilation purposes; whenever possible one or more emergency exits should be provided. These may be small tunnels whose entrances are normally closed and concealed; a tunnel may be dug from inside the system to within a few feet of the surface so a breakthrough can be made if necessary.

SELF TEST

Requirement. Upon completion of the text assignment, solve the following self test questions and exercises.

Note: The following exercises are study aids. The figures following each question refer to the paragraph containing information related to the question. Write your answer in the space provided below each question. When you have finished answering all questions for this lesson, compare your answers with those given for this lesson in the back of this booklet. Review the lesson as necessary.

1. What are the two purposes for the construction of trenches? (Para 2-1a)

2. Would you say that trenches are easy or difficult to camouflage? (Para 2-1a)

3. What is the purpose of the crawl trench? (Para 4-2a)

4. What depth and width should a crawl trench be? (Para 2-2a)

5. How far is the berm line located in front of the fighting trench? (Para 2-2b)

6. To what initial depth is the fighting trench dug? (Para 2-2b(1))

7. How is the front parapet of a fighting trench constructed in order to help prevent its detection? (Para 2-2b(3)(a))

8. If spoil is available, why should the rear parapet of a fighting trench be higher than the front parapet? (Para 2-2b(4))

9. When can parapets of fighting trenches be omitted? (Para 2-2b(4))

10. How is the floor of the fighting trench prevented from becoming wet and muddy? (Para 2-2b(6))

11. The necessity for revetment of walls may sometimes be avoided by what procedure? (Para 2-5a)

12. In most soils, what slope is sufficient to avoid revetment? (Para 2-5a)

13. What is a serious disadvantage of having sloping walls of trenches? (Para 2-5a)

14. What is the purpose of facing type revetment of trenches? (Para 2-5b)

15. What condition or type of soil permits the use of facing revetment? (Para 2-5b)

16. What methods of support are used to keep the revetment in place? (Para 2-5b(2))

17. Sandbags can be used for revetting and the repair of trenches. How full must the sandbags be? (Para 2-7a (1)(a))

18. How should sandbags be placed with reference to side seams or stretchers and choked ends on headers? (Para 2-7a(1)(f))

19. What two pieces of equipment can be used to expedite the filling of sandbags? (Para 2-7a(3))

20. Dummy trenches are dug to conceal from the air or ground, the true extent of the defended area. How deep should they be dug and what means taken to make them effective? (Para 2-11a))

LESSON 3

OBSTACLE EMPLOYMENT

CREDIT HOURS... 3

TEXT ASSIGNMENT... Attached memorandum.

MATERIALS REQUIRED... None.

LESSON OBJECTIVES

Upon completion of this lesson you should be able, in the indicated topic areas, to:

1. **Natural Obstacles.** Describe the four characteristics of a well situated natural obstacle to include capability of improvement, defilade from enemy observation, and best location for defensive fires.

2. **Tactical Obstacles.** Describe the four types of tactical obstacles - antitank, antivehicle, antipersonnel, and beach and river line.

3. **Principles of Employment.** Discuss the principles of employment of obstacles to include coordination with the tactical plan, covering by observation and fire, employment with natural and other artificial obstacles, and employment in depth.

4. **Ditches.** Describe the types of ditches, their characteristics, and construction.

5. **Log Hurdles and Cribs.** Describe purposes and construction of log hurdles and cribs.

6. **Steel and Concrete Obstacles.** Describe the purposes and construction of steel and concrete obstacles.

7. **Expedients.** Discuss types of expedient roadblocks and their construction.

8. **Beach and River Line Obstacles.** Discuss purposes and construction of obstacles to include beach obstacles, antiboat obstacles, and antipersonnel obstacles.

ATTACHED MEMORANDUM

Section I. Principles

3-1. BASIC CONSIDERATIONS

a. Definition. An obstacle is any terrain feature, condition of soil, climate, or man-made object other than firepower, that is used to stop, delay, or divert enemy movement.

b. Purposes. Obstacles should be included in the overall defense plan to restrict the movement of enemy forces, delay them, or require them to regroup.

c. Tactical obstacles. The following obstacles are commonly referred to as tactical types:

(1) Antitank obstacles intended to impede or stop the movement of tracked vehicles across country or on roads;

(2) Antipersonnel obstacles constructed to slow up, confuse or divert enemy foot troops when they attempt to overrun or infiltrate a defended position or locality;

(3) Antivehicle obstacles including roadblocks, crates and other means that are used to stop or delay enemy wheeled vehicles so they can be brought under aimed fire.

(4) Beach and river line obstacles that delay, obstruct or divert enemy amphibious operations.

d. Observation. Tactical obstacles must be under observation and covered by fire for maximum benefit. An obstacle which is not covered by observed fire may be ineffective or at best lead to a false sense of security.

e. Offensive use of tactical obstacles. Obstacles are used to anchor a flank or flanks of an advancing unit. They may also be used behind enemy lines to delay, disorganize, and harass troop movements and communications, especially when an enemy force is withdrawing. The wide intervals between dispersed units of company size or larger should be blocked by a combination of obstacles and firepower.

f. Nontactical obstacles. Obstacles falling in this category may be of the same general design as obstacles constructed under tactical conditions, but the same considerations of siting and concealment do not apply. Nontactical obstacles may be used --

(1) For the protection of important installations against infiltration or sabotage.

(2) In civil policing operations to check the movement of rioters or to isolate a section of a town or city.

(3) For administrative purposes.

3-2. CHARACTERISTICS OF NATURAL OBSTACLES

Desirable characteristics of a natural obstacle are ease of conversion into a more effective obstacle with a minimum of effort, materials, and time; defilade from enemy observation; location where observation and defensive fires can prevent enemy breaching; and difficulty of bypassing. The most effective natural obstacles against tanks are steep slopes, unfrozen swamps, and broad, deep streams. Rice paddies, lava fields, and similar areas can also be formidable obstacles. Usually time labor, and materials can be saved by improving natural obstacles rather than constructing artificial ones to serve the same purpose.

a. Steep slopes. Varying degrees of steepness are required to stop different types of vehicles. Tanks can negotiate slopes as steep as 60 percent. However, trees, unfavorable soil conditions, large rocks and boulders can make slopes of less than 60 percent impassable, even though this would not be true if the same natural features were encountered on level ground. The movement of infantry is also slowed down by steep slopes since movement is slower and the troops tire more rapidly.

b. Escarpments. A steep face of rock is a formidable obstacle to both vehicles and personnel if it is over 1 1/2 meters (5 ft) in height.

c. Ravines, gullies, and ditches. Ravines, gullies, and ditches are generally obstacles to wheeled vehicles. If they are over 5 meters (16 1/2 ft) in width, and approximately 2 meters (6 1/2 ft) in depth and the banks are nearly vertical, they are usually effective against tracked vehicles.

d. Rivers, streams, and canals. The major obstacle value of rivers, streams, and canals is that they must be crossed by special means, either deepwater fording, surface or aerial. The width, depth, velocity of the water, and bank and bottom conditions determine the ease of crossing a water obstacle by deepwater fording and floating equipment. However, a river over 150 meters (500 ft) wide and over 1 1/2 meters (5 ft) deep is a major obstacle, limited only by the presence of bridges, favorable sites for amphibious vehicles, and fording sites. The obstacle value of fordable rivers, streams, and canals is significant when the stability of the banks and bottoms is considered. Although a few vehicles may be able to ford a water obstacle, the poor condition of the banks and bottom may prevent further use of the ford without time-consuming improvement of the crossing site. Stream velocity may likewise limit the use of a ford and enhance its value as an obstacle.

c. **Frozen streams.** Antitank obstacles (fig 3-1) can be improved in frozen streams by cutting an opening about 3 to 4 meters (10 to 13 ft) wide in the ice and forcing the cut blocks of ice under the solid surface so the blocks will be carried downstream by the current. The openings are then closed with a light frame covered with cloth, brush, or tar paper with about 10 cm (4 in.) covering of snow. The

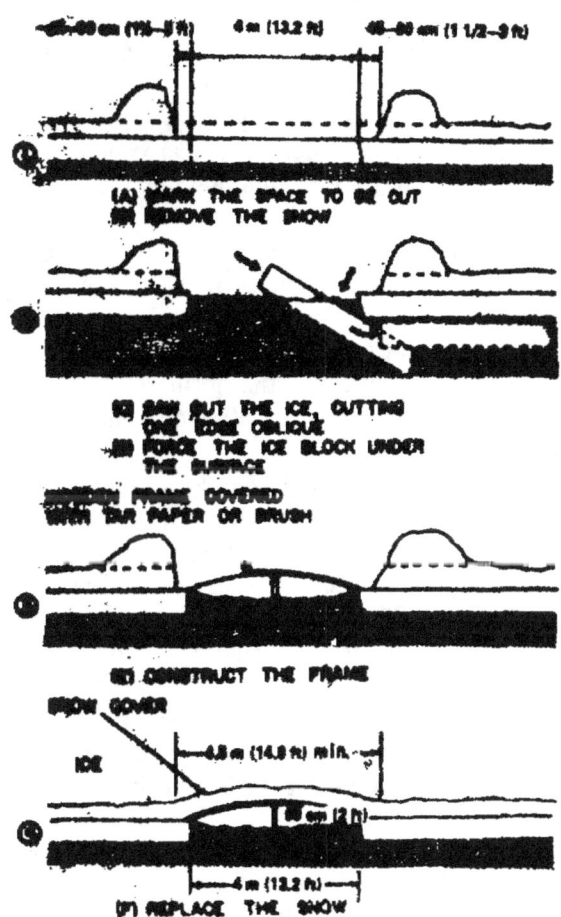

Figure 3-1. Antitank trap in ice.

effectiveness of this type of obstacle depends on keeping the water in the channel from freezing. A well made trap will be effective for an extended period of time if it is inspected frequently to maintain the snow cover. If the ice freezes solid in the area of the trap, the procedure outlined above must be repeated.

f. **Lakes.** Lakes are usually unfordable and if unbridged, must be bypassed unless they are frozen solid enough to support vehicles and personnel.

g. **Swamps and marshes.** The principal obstacle value of swamps and marshes is the canalization of vehicular movement onto causeways thereby exposing the columns to air or artillery attacks. Swamps and marshes over 1 meter (3.3 ft) in depth may be better obstacles than rivers, since causeways are usually more difficult to construct than bridges. The physical effort required for foot troops to cross swamps and marshes is an important factor in their usefulness as an obstacle. All roads and causeways through swamps and marshes should be extensively cratered, mined, or blocked by abatis.

h. **Forests.** Forests have the effect of canalizing movement, since the roads, trails, and fire breaks through them provide the only means for rapid movement. The obstacle value of a forest is dependent on tree size and density, soil condition, slope, and depth. If the trees are at least 20 cm (8 in.) in diameter and sufficiently close together, they will seriously obstruct or stop the movement of tanks. Even though the trees are seldom close enough together to stop tanks, they may prevent tank movement when they are pushed over and tangled. Much smaller trees (10 cm (4 in.) in diameter) will slow and sometimes stop tanks on 20 percent slopes. Tree stumps that are 45 cm (18 in.) in diameter or larger are obstacles to tank movement. Forest undergrowth in the temperate zone is not usually dense enough to seriously obstruct foot movement, but such movement will be slowed significantly by steep slopes, adverse soil conditions, and fallen trees and branches. The most effective way of increasing the obstacle value of forests is to:

(1) Construct abatis or craters.

(2) Place mines along the roads, trails, and firebreaks.

(3) Construct log cribs, hurdles, and post obstacles if the necessary materials are available.

i. Jungle obstacles. Tropical jungles are important obstacles to the movement of vehicles and personnel. The ground between the trees is usually covered by interwoven vines, bushes, plants, or rotting vegetation. The ground is often swampy or marsh. The tangled undergrowth and overhead foliage limits the visibility and there are few if any paths or trails except those that permit limited foot traffic. Vehicles can seldom operate satisfactorily unless routes are prepared or extensively improved. Foot troops are required to cut trails through the dense undergrowth or move with extreme difficulty. Since the jungle is an effective obstacle to movement, any road or trails that exists should be blocked and the stream fords and amphibian vehicle entry and exit sites should be mined. If the streams and rivers provide the best routes, obstacles should be constructed to slow up or prevent the use of floating equipment. The following obstacles are effective against foot movement in the jungle:

(1) Punji jungle trap. Punji traps (fig 3-2) are most effective when they merge with or resemble natural jungle obstacles. In the defense, they may be

Figure 3-2. Punji jungle trap.

used either as barricades around camps or as barriers to impede the advance of an assault. In the offense, they may be constructed behind enemy lines to stop or hinder any retreat. Enemy patrols can be disbanded by skillful use of these traps in connection with covering snipers. A pit 1.5 to 2 meters (5 to 6 1/2 ft) deep, about the same length and one meter (3.3 ft) wide is dug in the middle of a jungle trail or at a stream crossing. A number of long, sharp punjis (bamboo spikes sharpened to a needle point) are placed upright in this pit, with the fire-hardened points slightly below ground level (fig 3-2). The pit is concealed by a flimsy lid consisting of a bamboo lattice covered with a few bamboo creepers and camouflaged with mud or leaves to blend with the surrounding area. Anyone falling into the pit is instantly impelled on the spikes.

(2) Slit trench. A slit trench can be so placed that enemy troops will be likely to use it. Like the cover of the punji pit, the bottom of this trench is false, and underneath it are sharp punjis, which will impale anyone jumping into the trench.

j. Snow. Snow is considered deep for purposes of foot or vehicle movement when the average depth above ground elevation is 1 meter (3.3 ft). Snow at this depth and even deeper is not unusual in the Arctic and the northernmost regions of the temperate zone. It is found at these depths also in mountainous regions. Deep snow and the accompanying ice and intense cold combine to make obstacles to movement of both foot troops and vehicles. It also blankets terrain features such as boulders, rocky areas, ditches, small streams and fallen trees so as to effectively impede movement. The obstacle value of snow can be increased by-

(1) Erecting snow fences or breaks so that the prevailing winds will accelerate the accumulation of snow into drifts to form obstacles of packed snow.

(2) Building snow walls (fig 3-3) as obstacles against armor. The snow must be packed hard for this purpose. Walls of this type are most effective when they are sited on an upgrade.

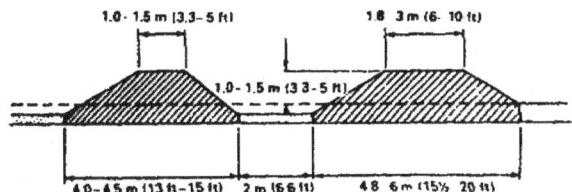

Figure 3-3. Antivehicular obstacle of packed snow.

k. Deserts. The obstacle value of deserts is that specially equipped vehicles and specially trained personnel are required to operate successfully in this

environment. Minefields are comparatively easy to install and relocate in the desert and the prevalent winds quickly cover up the usual signs of mine installation.

l. Built-up areas. The natural obstacle of built-up areas can be increased by cratering streets, demolishing walls, overturning or derailing street or railroad cars, and constructing roadblocks from steel rails, beams, and rubble. When combined with mines and barbed wire, such obstacles are effective against vehicles and personnel.

Section II. Artificial Land Obstacles

3-3. BASIC CONSIDERATIONS

a. Definition. An artificial obstacle is any object constructed to hinder movement. Artificial obstacles include minefields, antitank ditches, contaminated areas, hedgehogs, road craters, demolished bridges, and barbed wire. They may be constructed entirely on land or partially under water as in the case of beach and river line obstacles.

b. Use. Major types of artificial obstacles are discussed separately in subsequent chapters; however, they are normally used in conjunction with natural obstacles and in combinations of two or more types of artificial obstacles. When artificial obstacles are used in barriers, a variety of them should be used, when practicable, to increase effectiveness and as an aid to surprise and deception. Obstacles can be divided into three groups according to their uses. Seldom does an obstacle fall clearly into one of these three groups. More often than not an obstacle may be used for two or three purposes. The arbitrary classification of obstacles merely clarifies their primary uses.

(1) Protective. Protective obstacles are those obstacles used to provide security. Obstacles of this type are usually artificial and include such items as wire, minefields, and various warning devices. They are intended primarily to prevent the enemy from

making a surprise assault from areas close to a position.

(2) Defensive. Defensive obstacles are obstacles used to delay the enemy force in areas where it can be engaged with heavy, intense defensive fire. They may be either natural or artificial. A defended roadblock or an obstacle in front of a defensive position which stops or delays the enemy force once it is in range of defensive weapons are examples of this type. Defensive obstacles should be covered by appropriate fire, kept under observation, and should be employed in conjunction with protective obstacles.

(3) Tactical. Tactical obstacles are obstacles used to break up enemy attack formations and canalize the enemy force into areas where it is blocked by defensive obstacles or can be brought under intensive defensive fires. Tactical obstacles delay, harass, or demoralize the enemy by forcing him to employ dangerous to exhaustive breaching measures.

3-4. PRINCIPLES OF EMPLOYMENT

a. Coordination with tactical plan. Obstacles should be coordinated with the tactical plan.
All obstacles should contribute to the success of this plan, and all units concerned should know the location of and understand the purpose and type of obstacles employed.

In addition, all concerned should know when the obstacles are to be executed, and how long they are to be defended. Only by coordination with all elements can an integrated plan be prepared that will use all defensive measures to their best advantage against the enemy.

b.   Covering by observation and fire.

(1)   Observation. If accurate fire is to be delivered on an obstacle or obstacle system, it must be under observation. The observation and defense of obstacles for close-in defense is the responsibility of the unit occupying the ground. However, when an obstacle system covers a large area, observation is normally the responsibility of roving patrols, an outpost system, aerial observation, of tactical air. Their final defense is a mission for mobile forces that can be brought quickly to any point of the system. At times it is not feasible to have an obstacle under direct observation. When this is the case, warning devices or alarm systems such as tripflares, boobytraps, or electronic sensors in connection with noisemakers should be used.

(2)   Fire. Covering an obstacle by fire usually means the difference between causing the enemy only small delay and annoyance and forcing him into a costly engagement.

(a) Both antivehicular and antipersonnel obstacles should be covered by both antivehicular and antipersonnel fire. Fire that covers antipersonnel obstacles should not only be capable of discouraging breaching, bypass, or capture by personnel but should also be capable of stopping any vehicles that may be used in the assault. Also, antivehicular obstacles must be covered by fire that will not only destroy vehicles but will prevent troops from breaching the obstacles and clearing a path for the vehicles.

(b) Obstacles are best covered by direct-fire weapons, but when this is not feasible, observed artillery fire and tactical air should be used. Artillery covering obstacles should be prepared to deliver fire that is effective against both personnel and vehicles. When it is impossible to cover obstacles by fire, they should be contaminated or

heavily boobytrapped to cause the enemy to employ dangerous and exhaustive breaching measures.

c.   Employment in conjunction with natural and other artificial obstacles. It is fundamental that an obstacle system should usually be as difficult to bypass as it is to breach except when the obstacle is intended to divert or deflect the enemy rather than to delay or stop him. Artificial obstacles must be sited to take full advantage of natural and other artificial obstacles, so as to keep logistic and construction requirements to a minimum. Natural obstacles are improved and exploited to the fullest extent.

d.   Employment in depth. Obstacles do not seriously hamper the enemy's movement until they overload or heavily tax his breaching capabilities. This cannot be accomplished unless obstacles are employed in depth. With the exception of contaminated areas it is usually prohibitive in time and materials to construct a large deep area of continuous obstacles. The same end is accomplished by constructing successive lines of obstacles, one behind the other, as time and conditions permit. These successive lines require the enemy force to continually deploy and regroup, thus dissipating, canalizing, and dividing its effort until friendly forces can destroy it or force its withdrawal.

e.   Camouflage and concealment.

(1)   Camouflage. Obstacles should be camouflaged or employed in such a way that they come as a surprise to the enemy. When the enemy has no prior knowledge of an obstacle, he has to reduce it without benefit or prior planning. If the obstacle is defended the defender has the advantage of the enemy's first reaction, which is usually confusion, and the enemy may be caught without the men and material to breach the obstacle.

(2)   Siting. Proper siting is often the easiest solution to obstacle camouflage problem. Large obstacle systems cannot be concealed by siting alone, but when proper advantage is taken of the terrain and the obstacles are located in folds of the ground, around blind curves in roads, or just over the tops of hills, they can be made inconspicuous from the enemy's ground observation. To help camouflage obstacles from aerial observation, regular geometric layouts of obstacles and barrier systems should be avoided and phony obstacles used to confuse the enemy as to the exact location and extent of the system.

(3) **Concealment.** The best way to conceal an obstacle usually is to postpone its execution or construction as long as possible, without interfering with its readiness when needed. This cannot be done when large barrier systems are involved but is possible when preparing obstacles to block narrow avenues of approach, such as roads or bridges. Obstacles created by demolitions lend themselves readily to this procedure. When their use is contemplated they should be completely prepared for firing at the last minute.

f. Provision for lanes and gaps. When obstacles are employed around a defensive position or area, lanes or gaps through the system are left and concealed. These lanes are provided so patrols, counter attacks, and friendly troops on other missions may move through the system without difficulty. Under normal circumstances the lanes or gaps necessary to mount a general offensive through the obstacle system are not provided during construction, but prepared later when the need for them arises. It is important there be a sufficient number of lanes to allow for alternate use and that they be concealed and changed periodically to insure they are not discovered by the enemy. Prior plans must exist to insure all lanes or gaps can be blocked quickly when enemy action is expected. Lanes and gaps should be covered by fire to preclude the possibility of the enemy rushing through them before they can be closed.

g. Affording no advantages to the enemy. Enemy forces may use certain obstacles to an advantage as they are breached or assaulted. Antitank ditches should be constructed so they are useless to the enemy as fighting trenches. Log cribs should be located so the enemy cannot deliver effective fire on defending weapons while using the crib as a breastwork. Obstacles should be located so

the enemy cannot use hand grenades against the defenders from cover or concealment provided by the obstacles. Barbed wire, mines, and boobytraps should be used extensively to deny use of any cover or concealment that might be provided to the enemy by natural or reinforcing obstacles. Care should be taken to guard against the inadvertent placing of an obstacle which might later hinder friendly maneuver.

3-5. MINEFIELDS

Minefields are not only an obstacle to the advance of the enemy, but unlike obstacles of a passive nature, they can also inflict significant casualties; therefore minefields are considered the best form of artificial obstacle. The installation of minefields changes favorable terrain to unfavorable terrain and materially enhances the strength of the defense.

3-6. CALTROPS

a. Description. A caltrop (fig 3-4) has four sharpened prongs oriented so that one prong will always be vertical regardless of how the caltrop lands. The prongs are .25 cm (3/32 in.) in diameter and 3.8 cm (1.5 in.) long.

b. Uses. Caltrops are employed as antipersonnel obstacles either by themselves or in conjunction with barbed wire. When emplaced with a density of 38 per meter (3.3 ft) of barrier front, an effectiveness equivalent to triple standard concertina is achieved. Caltrops are designed to cause injury by penetrating the footgear of a man who steps

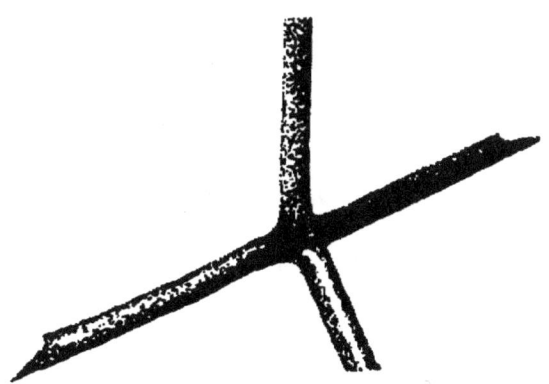

Figure 3-4. Caltrop.

on one. Serious injury will result if a man quickly falls to the ground to avoid small arms or artillery fire. Caltrops can be dispensed by hand, from the rear of a truck, or from fixed and rotary winged aircraft.

3-7. BARBED WIRE ENTANGLEMENTS

Obstacles constructed from barbed wire are simple, flexible and effective against personnel. They may also be used to impede the movement of vehicles.

3-8. ANTIVEHICULAR OBSTACLES

In defensive positions, antivehicular obstacles are used to obstruct gaps between natural obstacles or they can be placed in a continuous line of considerable length in open terrain. Antivehicular obstacles are usually employed in conjunction with wire entanglements, minefields, and other obstacles. Under some conditions they may be continuous in areas just inland of beaches.

Section III. Antivehicular Obstacles

3-9. DEFENSE

Antivehicular obstacles should not be continuous across the front of a position, but should have gaps which can be kept under observation and fire and at which flares and other warning devices can be kept in operational condition. Such gaps tend to canalize vehicular movement. With observation and effective covering fire placed on these gaps, an attack with vehicles can be stopped. If enemy forces are equipped with short gap bridging, the effectiveness of antivehicular obstacles under 20 meters in width is materially decreased. A narrow ditch will halt a unit so equipped only until this organic bridging can be brought into use.

3-10. SITING

Antivehicular obstacles are sited to take advantage of trees, brush, or folds in the ground for concealment and surprise effect. If they can be sited to permit flooding with water, the obstacle becomes more effective and helps to deny its use to the enemy as a protected firing position for infantry. In some situations, antivehicular obstacles may also be sited for close-in protection in front or to the rear of the main line of resistance and as adjuncts to other obstacles. In such locations, vehicles may be separated from their infantry support and are vulnerable to antivehicular weapons.

3-11. DITCHES

a. **Types** (fig 3-5).

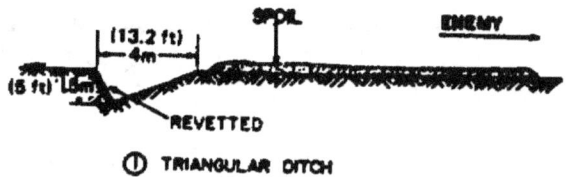

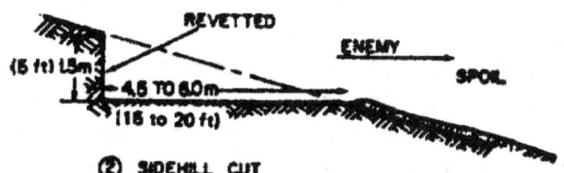

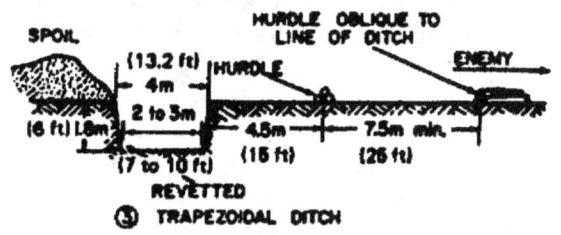

Figure 3-5. Antivehicular ditches.

(1) **Triangular ditches.** These are relatively easy to build, but a vehicle stopped in a ditch of this type can usually back out and try another route.

(2) **Sidehill cuts.** Sidehill cuts are variations of the triangular ditch adapted to sidehill locations, and have the same advantages and limitations.

(3) Trapezoidal ditches. These require about double the construction time of triangular type ditches, but they are more effective obstacles. In a trapezoidal ditch, as the center of gravity of the vehicle crosses the edge, and if the ditch depth exceeds the height of the vehicle wheels or treads, vehicles are trapped. Sections of ditch longer than 100 meters (328 ft) are not normally camouflages. In winter a trapezoidal ditch may be camouflaged by snow to resemble a standard trench (fig 3-6).

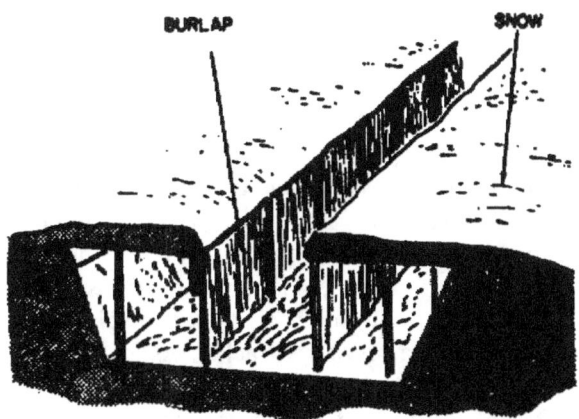

Figure 3-6. Antivehicular ditch camouflaged to resemble a trench.

b. Construction procedures.

(1) Excavation. Ditches are excavated by earthmoving equipment, by explosives as described in FM 5-25, or by handtools. To be effective, ditches made by explosives must be dressed to true surfaces by excavating equipment or handtools. Triangular and sidehill-cut ditches are constructed rapidly by a combination of explosives and motorized graders and angle-dozers.

The actual time required varies widely in different types of soils. If available and if it can be used at the site of the ditching, the standard 1/4-yard (.57 m³) shovel is used in ditch excavation. Estimating factors for construction time in average soil are shown in table 3-1.

(2) Revetting. The face of the ditch, or both faces in the case of a trapezoidal ditch, should be revetted as soon as possible after it has been dug. Facing type revetting is used almost exclusively, with pole type or brushwood hurdles preferred because of their durability. It is particularly important that the top of the revetment be about 20 cm (8 in.) below the top of the ditch and that the anchor stakes and tieback wires be buried under 30 cm (12 in.) of earth.

3-12. CRATERS

a. Use. Crater type obstacles are used for blocking roads, trails, or defiles, preferably at points where the terrain prevents bypassing the obstacle or where terrain suitable for bypassing can be mined and covered by antivehicular fire. Craters should be improved wherever possible by steepening the sides, flooding or mining.

b. Preparation. As in the case of bridge demolitions, craters are formed by explosive charges placed in advance and prepared for later detonation. The weights of charges, depths, and arrangement are given in detail in FM 5-25. The methods normally employed include-

(1) Placement of charges in a culvert

Table 3-1. Estimating Data on Ditch Construction (Average Soil)

Method of construction	Dimensions of ditch		Crew size	Construction rate	
	Depth (meters)	Width at top (meters)		(meters /hr)	(ft /hr)
Handtools	2m (6½ ft)	4m (13 ft)	Platoon [1]	4 (triangular)	13
				2 (trapezoidal)	6.5
Explosives [3]	3m (10 ft)	9m (30 ft)	Squad [2]	7.5	25
Earthmoving equipment (¼ yd shovel, w/2 operators and 8-10 hand laborers).	2m (6½ ft)	4m (13 ft)	Platoon [1]	7 (triangular)	23
				3 (trapezoidal)	10

[1] 40 men.
[2] 13 men.
[3] 36 pounds of ammonium nitrate per meter of length of crater.

under the road and concealed and wired for detonation from a safe distance.

(2) If a culvert is not available at the point selected, charges are placed in the bottoms of holes excavated in the road. Truck-mounted earth augers, if available, are used for digging the holes. The charges are placed and wired for detonation at a safe distance. The holes are backfilled in such a way that they are not readily noticed. The use of ADM to produce craters is covered in FM 5-26.

3-13. LOG OBSTACLES AND CRIBS

a. **Hurdles.** Log hurdles can be formed of 25- to 45-cm (10- to 18-in.) logs as shown in figure 3-7 may be used to add to the obstacle effect of a crater, or other type of roadblock. The hurdles force vehicles to reduce speed as they approach the obstacles or they may act as an additional means of trapping vehicles in the vicinity of antitank ditches. Each hurdle consists of one 45 cm (18 in.) or three 25 cm (10 in.) logs firmly staked in place on a roadway or on ground suitable for use as a bypass. A hurdle of this size stops or damages most types of wheeled vehicles. Tanks can cross them at reduced speeds on reasonably level ground but are stopped by hurdles on uphill grades which approximate the critical grade of the vehicle. To stop a tank on such a slope, the size and location of the pole or log hurdle must be such that the ground line of the tank will be tilted to a slope of 1 to 1. The poles must be firmly tied between strong stakes at not more than .5 meter (5 ft) intervals. To determine the height of the hurdle required, a stick 3.5 meters (11.5 ft) long is held at an angle of 45° above horizontal, with one end of the ground downhill from the hurdle location. The distance between the downhill end of the stick and the ground is how high to construct the log hurdle. The hurdle should be sited on the steepest part of the slope and as near the top as possible.

b. **Cribs.** Rectangular or triangular log cribs (fig 3-8 through 3-10) are used effectively as roadblocks where standing timber is available and where such an obstacle cannot be bypassed readily. Unless substantially built, obstacles of this type are not effective against heavy tracked vehicles. Cribs are strengthened by filling them with earth; and preferably the earth is obtained by digging a shallow ditch in front of the obstacle. Log

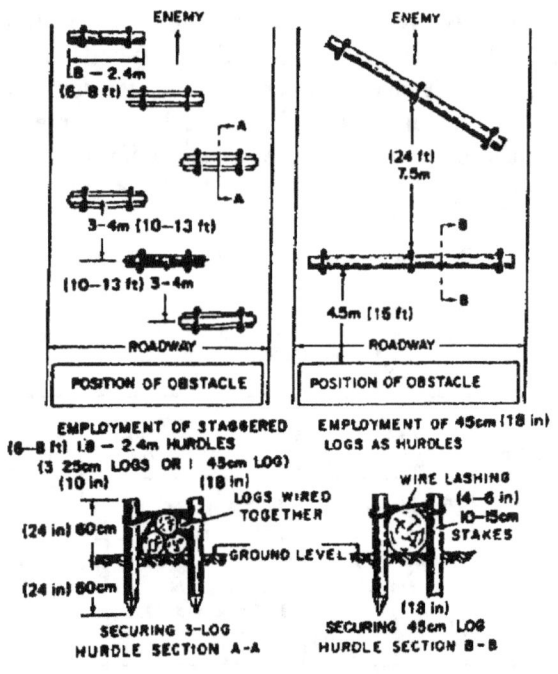

Figure 3-7. Types of log hurdles.

Figure 3-8. Rectangular log crib used as a roadblock.

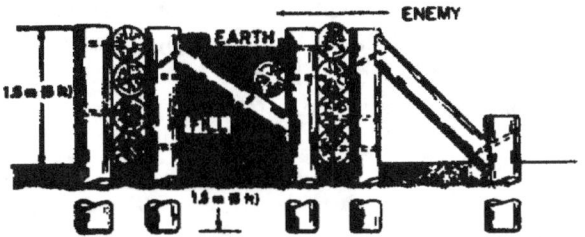

CROSS SECTION

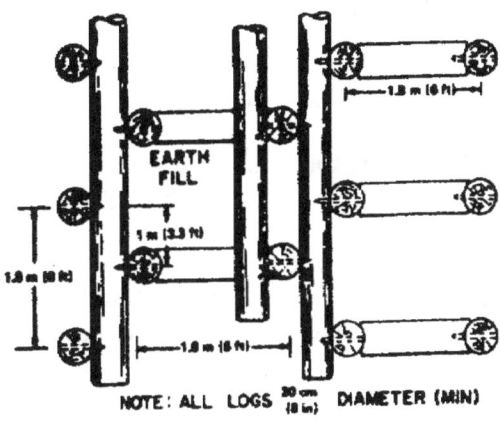

NOTE: ALL LOGS 30 cm (8 in) DIAMETER (MIN)

PLAN

Figure 3-9. Details of log crib used as a roadblock.

INTERIOR OF CRIB SHOULD BE FILLED WITH EARTH

LOGS 30 cm (8 in) DIAMETER (MIN)

Figure 3-10. Triangular log crib used as a roadblock.

hurdles in front of a log crib force vehicles to reduce speed and add to the effectiveness of the roadblock. An engineer platoon equipped with platoon tools can build 6 meter (20 ft) of this obstacle in 4 to 8 hours.

3-14. POSTS

a. **Use.** Posts are among the most effective antivehicular obstacles because each post presents a breaching problem to the attacker. There is no fast method of breaching a belt of posts. Normally, the attacker will seek to bypass such an obstacle. Post obstacle belts may be constructed using either steel, log, or concrete posts.

b. **Steel posts.** These posts usually are sections of rail, heavy pipe or structural members. Due to their small cross-sectional area, steel posts are installed over footings to prevent their being driven into the earth by the weight of a tank.

c. **Log posts.** These posts should be hardwood with a minimum diameter of 40 cm (15.8 in.). Footings are used under log posts only where the soil has exceptionally poor load-bearing characteristics. Figure 3-11 depicts a belt of log post obstacles.

d. **Concrete posts.** Precast concrete posts may be emplaced either vertically or angled in the direction of the enemy line of approach using lengths, spacing, and arrangements

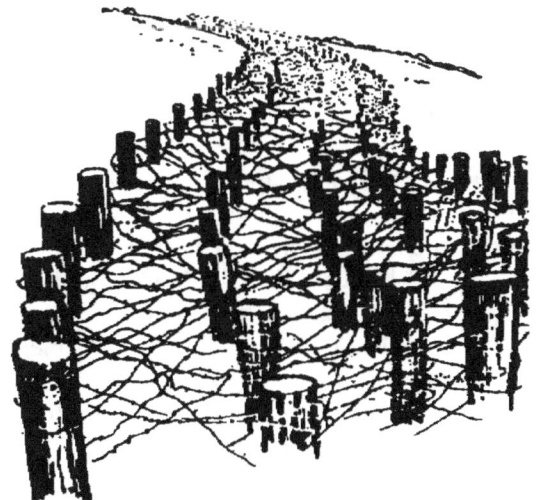

Figure 3-11. Belt of log post obstacles.

as described for wood or steel post obstacles.

(1) Concrete posts should be square in cross section and 3 meters (10 ft.) or more in length. They can be precast readily in horizontal open-top boxes with plank bottoms and removable sides and ends. Two lifting rings are set in the top surface at the quarter points of the length, for loading and unloading, and a similar ring is positioned at the top end for raising it into position. A chisel-shaped point can be formed easily at the bottom end if the concrete posts are to be driven in with pile-driving equipment. Lengthwise reinforcement is provided several centimeters inside the surface near each corner of the square post with a traverse wrapping of wire at each cm (12 in.) of length. Round reinforcing bars of 1.25 cm (l/2 in.) diameter are adequate for the longitudinal reinforcement. Reinforcement can be improvised by using 4 to 6 strands of barbed wire at each corner, attached to the form ends and racked tightly, preferably to almost the breaking strength of the wire. After curing for 1 week or more under wet burlap, such posts are installed in the same manner as described for wood posts or steel posts. If pile-driving equipment is to be used, a steam or air hammer may be required for driving heavy posts of this type depending on the type of soil.

(2) Round concrete posts may be improvised from corrugated metal pipe of small sizes filled with concrete. Because of the time required to funnel concrete into pipe held vertically and because of the expenditure of the pipe, this method is less efficient than the use of square precast concrete posts.

e. Placing.

(1) All posts are buried 1.5 meters (5 ft.) in the ground either vertically or at a slight angle toward the enemy, and project above ground level between 75 and 120 cm (30 and 48 in.). The height should vary from post to post. The minimum acceptable density for posts is 200 per 100 meters (328 ft.) of front. The spacing should be irregular, with at least 1 meters (3.3 ft.) and not more than 2 meters (6.6 ft.) between posts.

(2) Posts are equally useful whether employed in long belts or in short sections as

roadblocks. By predigging holes, lining them with pipe, and covering them for later rapid installation of posts, the road may be kept open for use until the roadblock is needed. The rate of construction of such roadblocks is approximately as follows, based on a 6-meter (20 ft.) road width:

(a) Using pile-driving equipment, 2 NCOs and 16 men: 4 to 6 hours.

(b) Using power earth auger or demolitions (shaped charges), 1 NCO and 8 men: 2 to 2 l/2 hours.

(c) Using handtools, one combat engineer platoon: 3 to 5 hours.

(3) Use of spirals of wire with posts. The effect of post type obstacles can be improved, and the obstacles made more difficult to breach, by weaving spirals of barbed wire among the posts as shown in figure 3-11. The belt illustrated is an antipersonnel as well as an antivehicular obstacle.

3-15. ABATIS

a. Use. Tree felled as shown in figure 3-12 can be used to block a road or defile. To

Figure 3-12. Abatis used as a roadblock.

stop tracked vehicles the trees should be at least 60 cm (24 in.) or more in diameter and at least 6 meters (20 ft) tall. To effectively block a road through a heavily wooded area, an abatis, at least 75 meters (250 ft) deep is required.

b. Construction. Abatis may be constructed using handtools, by the use of explosives alone, or by a combination of notching and explosives as shown in figure 3-13. Using only handtools, one engineer platoon can build 75 meters (250 ft) of abatis in 8 hours. Information on the use of explosives for the construction of abatis is contained in FM 5-25. Bushy-top trees with heavy branches and thick foliage should be used for abatis wherever possible since the branches reduce the movement of the vehicle and the foliage sets up a screen. The trees should be felled as shown in figure 3-12 so that the trunk remains attached to the stump. To insure that the trunk remains attached, no cut is made on the side of the tree toward which it is to fall, the tree is strained to fall in the required direction, and the butt is cut two-thirds through on the opposite side. The effectiveness of an abatis is increased by interlacing barbed wire in the branches of the trees.

Figure 3-13. Preparing explosive charges for abatis construction.

3-16. STEEL OBSTACLES

a. Hedgehogs. Steel hedgehogs as shown in figure 3-14 are relatively lightweight for the obstacle effect they provide, and they are quickly installed or removed. They are designed to revolve under wheeled vehicles and puncture them or to belly up tracked vehicles. Unless kept under observation and covered with fire, the enemy can readily move them aside. They are well adapted for use in vegetation high enough to afford complete or partial concealment. Exposed parts should be painted to blend with the background. Hedgehogs are made up in rear areas, using three angles about 10 cm by 10 cm by 1 cm (4 in. by 4 in. by 4 in.), 120 cm (4 ft.) long, and 1 cm (.4 in.) steel plate about 50 cm (20 in.) square. A hedgehog of this size weighs about 75 kg (160 lb.). Hedgehogs are used in rows, with at least 150 hedgehogs to each 100 meters (328 ft.) of front which is to be protected in this manner.

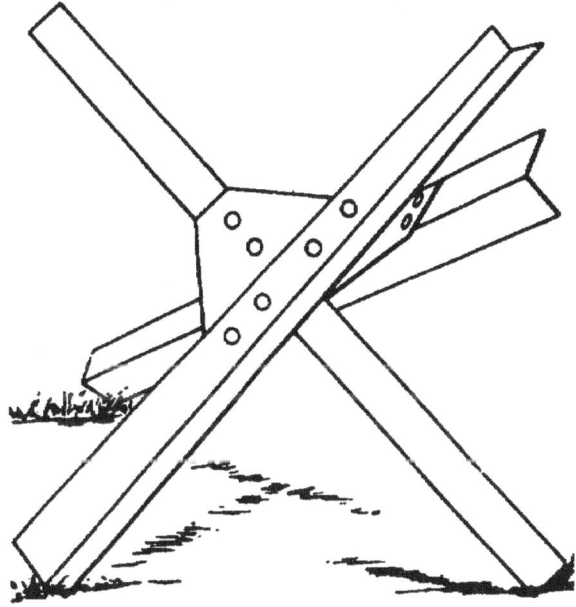

Figure 3-14. Steel hedgehog.

b. Tetrahedrons. Steel tetrahedrons shown in figure 3-15 are employed in a manner similar to that of hedgehogs. They are usually made of 10 cm by 10 cm by 1.5 cm (4 in by 4 in. by .6 in.) angles, the base and sides in the shape of equilateral triangles, 1.5 meters (5 ft.) on a side. Their finished height is approximately 1.2 meters (4 ft.).

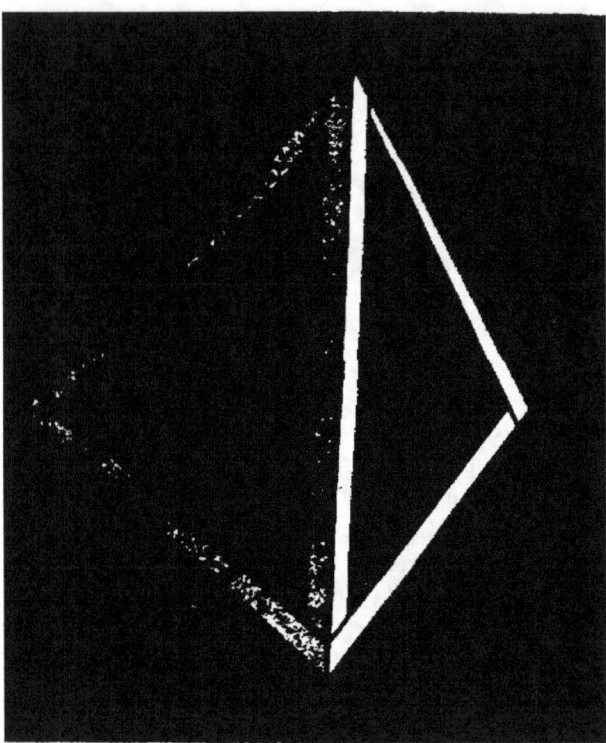

Figure 3-15. Steel tetrahedron.

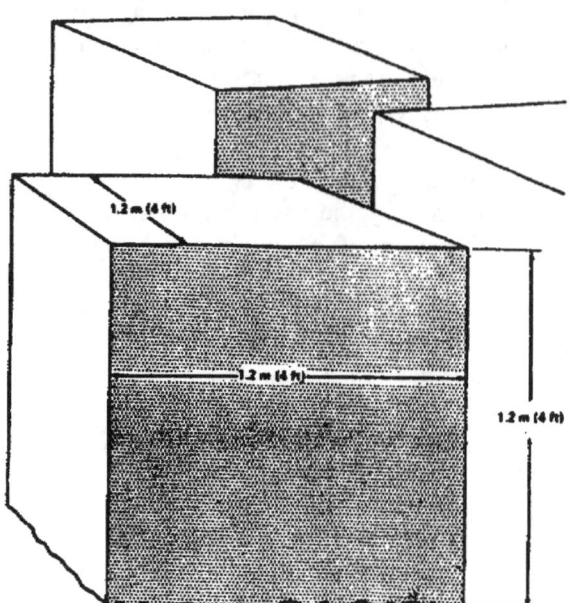

Figure 3-16. Concrete cubes.

3-17. CONCRETE OBSTACLES

a. **Cubes.** Cubes are concrete obstacles of approximately cubical shape, set in irregular rows. A typical size and arrangement is shown in figure 3-16. Because of the weights involved and the simplicity of erecting forms for cubes, these obstacles are best cast in place if the situation permits. A cube of the size shown in figure 3-16 requires about 1.8 cubic meters (2.4 cu yd.) of concrete and weighs slightly less than 4 1/2 metric tons (5 tons).

b. **Cylinders.** Concrete obstacles of cylindrical shape are usually smaller than cubes and are light enough to be precast. Their use is similar to that of cubes, and they may be preferable in situations in which precast obstacles are the type required. Cylinders may be precast in forms made of lightweight sheet metal which need not be removed. A cylinder of the size shown in figure 3-17 requires 1 cubic meter (1.3 cu yd.) of concrete and weighs a little less than 3 tons.

c. **Tetrahedrons.** Concrete tetrahedrons are pyramids with base and sides of equilateral triangles, 1.5 meters (5 ft.) on a side. They are

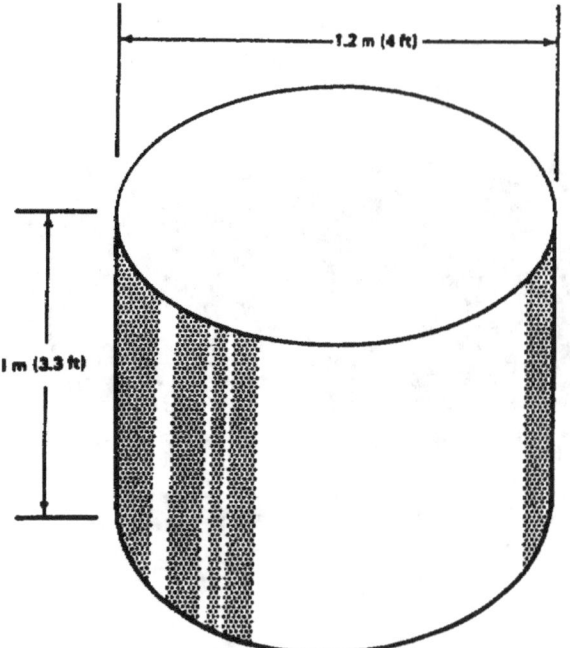

Figure 3-17. Concrete cylinder.

set in irregular rows as shown in figure 3-18. A tetrahedron of this size has a vertical height of about 1.2 meters (4 ft.), requires 0.9 cubic meter (1.05 cu yd) of concrete, and weighs about 1 metric ton (1.1 tons). They may be precast in trough-shaped forms between triangular divisions, with a

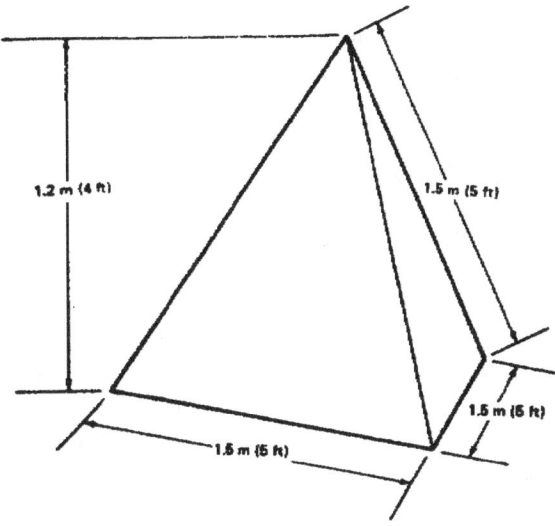

Figure 3-18. Concrete tetrahedron.

lifting ring embedded in the center of the top surface of each tetrahedron.

3-18. EXPEDIENTS

a. Roadblocks may be improvised from farm carts, automobiles, and trucks, which are loaded with rock, concrete, or other heavy material. When placed in position their wheels should be damaged or removed, and the vehicles should be anchored firmly.

b. Vehicles can be moved to close a gap that has been left to keep the road open.

c. A roadblock which may be effective in some situations is constructed quickly by the method shown in figure 3-19. A heavy tree at one side of a

Figure 3-19. Wire-rope roadblock.

road is cut almost through and its trunk is attached by a wire rope to a tree across the road in such a way that if a passing vehicle strikes the rope the tree will fall and damage the vehicle or pin it in place.

3-19. USE OF SCREENS AND DUMMY OBSTACLES

a. Purpose. Wherever possible, antivehicular obstacles, particularly roadblocks, should be concealed by screens for the following reasons:

(1) To conceal the true nature of the obstacle.

(2) To prevent fire from being directed at the most vulnerable part.

(3) To confuse the crew of the vehicle. Screens should also be erected in front of dummy obstacles and at sites where no obstacle exists, causing delay and expenditure of valuable ammunition. The enemy force will not know with any certainty what form of obstacle or defense opposes it or whether any real obstacle exists. If the force stops to investigate, the defense will have an opportunity to destroy it; if it goes ahead, it runs the risk of running into mines or of being held on an obstacle under fire.

b. Siting. Screens should be sited not more than 3 meters (10 ft.) from the obstacles which they are concealing. If a vehicle goes through a screen at this distance, it will encounter the obstacle before it can halt. Therefore it will not be in position to fire at the obstacle. Screens must not obscure the fields of fire of the defenders.

c. Construction. A form of screen suitable for concealing a roadblock consists of two horizontal strips of canvas, garnished netting, or blankets, the lower part suspended from wires about 120 cm (4 ft.) from the ground, and the upper part at a height of 2 to 2.5 meters (6 1/2 to 8 ft.). The upper part should overlap the lower part by 15 to 33 cm (6 to 13 in.).

d. Dummy obstacles. Dummy obstacles should be used extensively to confuse and delay tanks and cause them to waste ammunition. They should be made carefully in order to present a realistic appearance. They can be made of plaster, wood, or asbestos sheets. Wooden obstacles can be used to represent steel obstacles.

Antitank and antipersonnel mines should be interspersed extensively between dummy obstacles.

Section IV. Beach and River Line Obstacles

3-20. RESPONSIBILITY

In unilateral Army shore-to-shore amphibious operations, Army forces are responsible for the installation and removal of beach and underwater obstacles. In joint Army-Navy amphibious operations, Navy forces are normally responsible for removal of obstacles on a hostile shore seaward from the high waterline. The underwater demolition teams (UDT) of the Navy have the responsibility of removing obstacles from the high waterline to the 3-fathom (5.54 meters (18.2 ft.)) line. Beyond that point Navy minesweepers clear boat and shipping lanes. The responsibility for installation of beach and underwater obstacles in friendly territory is assigned by the commander of the forces involved.

3-21. OCEAN BEACH DEFENSES

An assault across an ocean normally involves a ship-to-shore assault in which the enemy requires adequate anchorages for assault shipping and shore for beaching large landing craft. Where the overwater distance is short, however, or where the enemy can develop a nearby base in neutral or unoccupied territory, shore-to-shore operations are practicable using smaller craft capable of landing troops and vehicles at almost any point. Against either of these types of operation, antiboat and antipersonnel obstacles at wading depths are desirable in most situations. Antipersonnel obstacles so located, however, are not effective against large landing craft if the latter can beach at the waterline or can sidecarry floating causeways and use them to get ashore.

a. **Beach obstacles.** Beach obstacles are designed to force landing craft to unload at low tide several hundred yards seaward of the high watermark. Thus, on beaches with gradual slopes assaulting infantry must cross a wide expanse of

obstacle-studded beach covered by heavy defensive fire before reaching the high watermark. At high tide, beach and underwater obstacles should be covered by just enough water so they cannot be seen by personnel in landing craft. When landing craft strike the obstacles they are disabled and the assaulting troops are forced to disembark in deep water.

b. **Antiboat obstacles.** Antiboat obstacles are constructed at varying heights so they are about 30 to 60 cm (2 to 4 ft.) below the surface of the water at high tide, echeloned in depth in various arrangements of which those shown in figure 3-20 are typical.

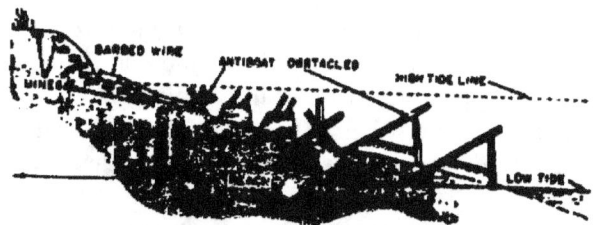

Figure 3-20. Antiboat obstacles in beach defense.

3-22. RIVER LINE DEFENSES

All possible means of crossing are studied, including assault boats, footbridges, fixed and floating vehicular bridges, and the use or rehabilitation of existing bridges. In addition to antiboat and antipersonnel obstacles, the defender considers the use of obstacles to hamper the enemy's bridging activities and his installation of booms and other protective devices to protect bridges.

3-23. EFFECTIVE OBSTACLES

a. **Siting.** The basic requirements for artificial obstacles and their employment apply equally to beach and river line obstacles. Of particular importance are the requirements

3-16

that artificial obstacles be used to exploit natural obstacles, that they be inconspicuous, be kept under surveillance, and be capable of being covered by fire. Gaps and lanes are provided and are marked or referenced for the use of friendly troops. Antiboat obstacles selected for use should be of a type which will be effective against boats which can operate in the surf, current, and various wind conditions to be expected. They are sited for maximum obstacle effect at the tide stage at which an assault is probable and for maximum effectiveness against amphibious tracked and wheeled vehicles.

b. Beach slopes. Due to tide and current action, beaches and river lines tend to fall into two general types-those with steep slopes into deep water, and those with gradually sloping bottoms for a considerable distance offshore. Each type has advantages and disadvantages for the defense. The steep slope prevents debarkation until boats reach the beach, but it renders placing underwater obstacles more difficult. The gentle slope facilitates placing obstacles but it also allows the attacking troops to disembark while still afloat.

(1) Steep. For beaches with steeply sloping bottoms, provision should be made for stopping landing craft offshore in deep water. The obstacles may include mines of various types anchored just below the waterline, floating log booms anchored or tied to shore, which may have mines attached, and heavy chains or wire rope stretched between pile dolphins. Preferably such obstacles should be submerged so as to be out of sight but tide variations may make this impracticable. In such cases a compromise must be made between minimum visibility and maximum practicable effectiveness. Where possible, provision is made for adjusting the height of log booms and the like, to conform with water level fluctuations.

(2) Gradual. For beaches with gradually sloping bottoms, the defense attempts to prevent landing craft from reaching the beach or from reaching wading or fording depth for personnel and vehicles. In addition to obstacles of the types described above, in water of wading depth the bottom is covered thoroughly with underwater wire

entanglements of all types. These must be anchored in place very securely to prevent damage from surf or currents and so both enemy and friendly fire will tend to form tangles rather than to clear lanes. In such entanglements, channels provided for passage of friendly small boats may be closed rapidly by the use of anchored concertinas or weighted spirals.

c. Employment in depth. Beach obstacles are typically established in bands in depth, as follows:

(1) Antiboat obstacles. These are located from wading depth at low tide to wading depth at high tide.

(2) Barbed wire entanglements. These are placed from wading depth at high tide, inshore across the width of the beach.

(3) Antivehicular and antipersonnel obstacles. These are installed beginning at low waterline and extending inshore across the width of the beach. Mines or other obstacles are normally installed at the beach exit.

(4) Antivehicular ditches. These are dug beginning at the inshore edge of the beach, where concealment is possible.

(5) Other obstacles. These are located inshore of the beach area, in the same manner as obstacles for land defense.

3-24. LOCATION

Some of the types of land obstacles described previously can be used as antiboat obstacles for some types of boats in water depths for which they are adapted and in which they can be sited and anchored. The tide range determines the water depths for which it is practicable to position obstacles on the bottom above the low waterline. Outside this line, heavy obstacles may be sunk from boats or lowered by cranes operating from the beach or afloat in small landing craft. Posts of timber, steel, or concrete are effective antiboat obstacles, readily placed except in rocky or coral bottoms. Posts preferably are emplaced or driven with a slope or batter toward deep water. Wooden obstacles of other types should be filled with rock or otherwise anchored in position. Antiboat obstacles may be connected with wire rope or may have barbed wire or other types of obstacles anchored between them. In rivers or other locations where the water level is constant or the tide range is minor or negligible, standard cased antitank mines tied to posts or other obstacles under the surface provide effective obstacles.

3-25. TIMBER OBSTACLES

Unpeeled round logs provide the types of antiboat obstacles described and shown, but sawed timbers may be used if more readily available. In addition to the uses of wooden posts described in paragraph 3-14, timber obstacles of the following types are used effectively under various conditions:

a. **Rock-filled cribs and pillars.** Rock-filled timber cribs (fig. 3-21) are normally 2 to 3 meters (6 1/2 to 10 ft.) long by 1 meter (3.3 ft.) wide, and have stability at heights up to 2 meters (6 1/2 ft.). The logs are driftpinned at the corners. Cribs may be installed on a beach at low water or may be dragged or lowered into water before completing the rock fill. For lower heights, smaller cribs, triangular in shape and known as pillars (fig. 3-22), are built with less material and effort. Both types may be connected by barbed wire, wire rope, or a combination of both.

b. **Tetrahedrons.** Timber tetrahedrons (fig 3-23) are pinned and wired to a triangular bottom frame which is weighted in place with rocks.

Figure 3-21. Rock-filled cribs.

Figure 3-22. Rock-filled pillars.

A post may be driven through the obstacle for improved anchorage. Tetrahedrons are normally spaced at intervals of 5 to 10 meters (16 1/2 to 33 ft.) and may be connected with wire rope or incorporated in a barbed wire fence.

Figure 3-23. Timber tetrahedrons.

3-18

c. Log scaffolding. In suitable water depths, log scaffolding, as shown in figure 3-24, is effective in impeding small boats. Wooden posts driven into the bottom are reinforced by diagonal braces extending inshore and have horizontal stringers attached to the offshore face.

Figure 3-24. Log scaffolding.

d. Braced wooden posts. This obstacle (fig. 3-40) may be built in relatively shallow water in which there is little or no tide range. The posts are driven approximately to water level in two rows. They are staggered so diagonal braces can extend from each rear post to two of the front posts to provide a structure of exceptional rigidity. The bottom ends of the braces may be fastened to the rear posts before the latter are fully driven and before the work is so deep as to require diving equipment. The front posts may be connected with wire rope or barbed wire to further improve the rigidity of the structure and to add to the obstacle effect. The efficiency of this obstacle is further enhanced by the liberal use of barbed wire tangles securely fastened to and between the posts.

e. Log tripods. Braced log tripods, constructed of logs at least 20 centimeters (8 in.) in diameter, as shown in figure 3-26, are effective antiboat obstacles. The obstacle is positioned with its longest leg facing the direction of expected

Figure 3-25. Braced wooden posts.

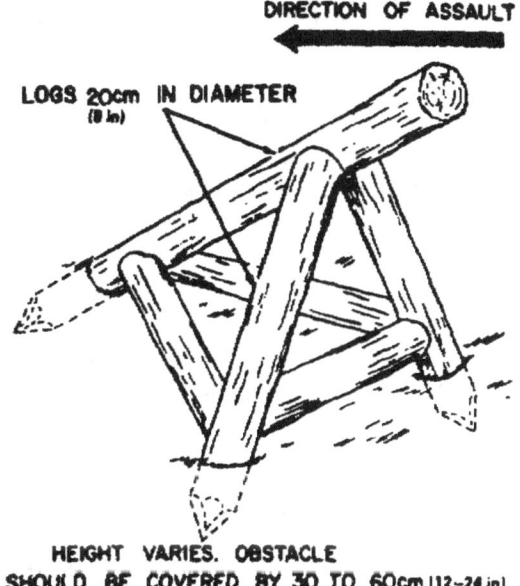

DIRECTION OF ASSAULT

LOGS 20cm IN DIAMETER (8 in)

HEIGHT VARIES. OBSTACLE SHOULD BE COVERED BY 30 TO 60cm (12-24 in) OF WATER AT HIGH TIDE.

Figure 3-26. Log tripod.

assault; this leg may be capped with a standard antitank mine or sharpened to a point. Constructed in varying sizes so they are covered by 30 to 60 cm (1 to 2 ft.) of water at high tide, these obstacles are placed on beaches from the low-tide mark back to about halfway to the high-tide line.

f. Log ramps. Log ramps are constructed as shown in figure 3-27. They are

Figure 3-27. Log ramps.

used to tear the bottoms out of assault craft riding up on them, and to upset such craft. They are effective obstacles with or without mines fastened to the high end of the ramp. Ramps may be placed either in an irregular pattern or in a continuous belt spaced at approximately 3-meter (10-ft.) intervals.

g. Nutcrackers. Nutcrackers are constructed as shown in figure 3-28. The .9- by .9- by .6-meter (3- by 3- by 2-ft.) base has a center well or recess large enough to house one or two antitank mines, depending on whether a one-way or two-way obstacle is desired. It also has a built-in socket for the bottom end of the activating rail or pole.

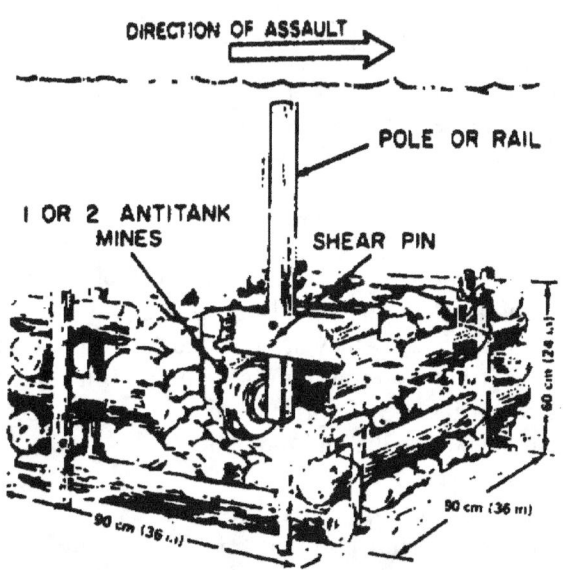

Figure 3-28. Nutcracker.

Shearpins, usually of one-half cm soft iron, hold the rail erect and prevent detonation of the mines by wave action. A landing craft striking the pole will break or bend the shearpin sufficiently to detonate the mines. Nutcrackers normally are employed in an irregular pattern interspersed with plain steel and log posts.

3-26. STEEL OBSTACLES

Steel beams, piles, and rails provide simple and effective antiboat obstacles of the post type. Steel rails can be driven in rocky or coral bottoms in which wood piles would be splintered. Steel obstacles of portable types are advantageous for underwater use because of the high unit weight of steel; they remain in position without anchorage against waves or currents. Steel obstacles intended for field fabrication for antiboat use are described in **a** and **b** below.

a. Scaffolding. On beaches having considerable tidal range, 5 cm (2 in.) steel pipe may be driven into the bottom and welded together to form a structure of the scaffolding type, as shown in figure 3-29. Floating mines may be attached below the normal water level, to be detonated if scraped by a vessel.

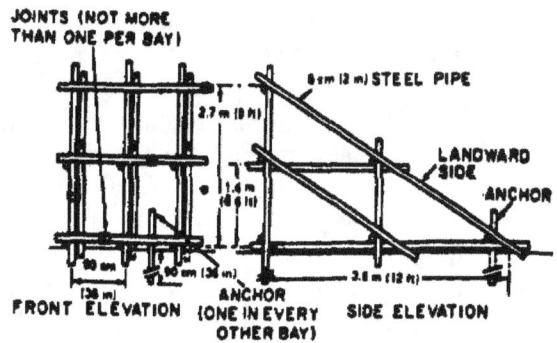

Figure 3-29. Steel scaffolding.

b. Hedgehogs. Steel hedgehogs of the type shown in figure 3-14 are fabricated in rear areas, shipped knocked down, and quickly assembled with bolted connections. The angles used are usually about 2 meters (6 1/2 ft.) long, making the obstacle about 1 meter (3.3 ft.) high. The hedgehog is emplaced without anchorage so that it revolves under a boat or amphibious vehicle, holes it, and anchors it as it sinks. Normally hedgehogs are installed in several rows, using about 150 hedgehogs to each 100 meters (328 ft.) of beach.

3-27. CONCRETE OBSTACLES

As with obstacles of other materials, all types of concrete obstacles previously described can be used as beach obstacles under certain conditions. Concrete obstacles of post type particularly are useful if heavy pile-driving equipment is available. Some types are improved for antiboat use by embedding rails in their tops to form horned scullies. The cylinder modified in this manner is shown in figures 3-30 and 3-31). By setting the rails at an angle of about 45° with the vertical, a fast-moving boat is holed and may be sunk as its momentum carries it down over the length of the horn. The horns may be improved by pointing them, using oxyacetylene cutting equipment.

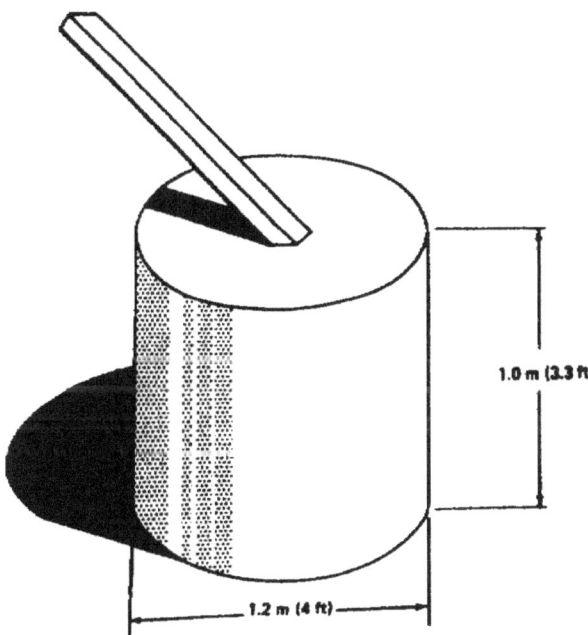

Figure 3-30. Horned scully bases on concrete cylinder.

3-28. BARBED WIRE BEACH OBSTACLES

Wire entanglements are used as antipersonnel obstacles but will stop light landing craft. They are

Figure 3-31. Horned scullies based on small dragon's teeth.

placed inshore of scaffolding or sunken obstacles and, if possible, are covered by machine gun fire. Entanglements normally are built at low tide. They require constant maintenance, particularly if placed in surf. Wire also is erected on beaches or riverbanks, often in connection with antitank and antipersonnel manifolds. Almost all of the types of wire obstacles described previously may be used in conjunction with other types of beach and underwater obstacles.

3-29. EXPEDIENT UNDERWATER OBSTACLES

The obstacles described in **a** and **b** below are made with native materials, some supplemented with barbed wire, and are difficult to reduce. Wherever possible, mines should be used with the obstacles to increase their effectiveness and to hinder removal by enemy underwater demolition teams.

a. Rock mounds. These consist simply of mounds of rock about 1-meter (3.3 ft.) high and 3.5-meters (11 1/2 ft.) square and staggered at intervals of 3 to 5 meters (10 to 16 1/2 ft.) on the outer edges of reefs or likely landing beaches.

b. Rocky walls (fig 3-32). Rocky walls are about 1 meter (3.3 ft.) high and 1 meter (3.3 ft.) wide, in sections or continuous lines. They should be mined and topped with concertinas. They should be sited so the top of the wire is just under the surface at high tide.

Figure 3-32. Rock walls.

SELF TEST

1. What is the purpose of employing obstacles? (Para 3-1a and b)

2. Give an example of a nontactical obstacle. (Para 3-1f)

3. Which of the following is the more effective natural obstacle against tracked vehicles -- an escarpment 1.6 meters high or a river 60 meters wide and 1.1 meters deep? (Para 3-2a, b)

4. In what type of terrain does the punji pit serve most effectively as an obstacle? (Para 3-2i(1)(2))

5. When should trip flares be used with obstacles? (Para 3-4b(1))

6. What may be used with barbed wire to make it a more effective antipersonnel obstacle? (Para 3-6b)

7. Which type of ditch is the most effective as an obstacle when it is camouflaged with snow: (Para 3-11a(3), fig. 3-6))

8. Where is the best location for a cratering charge intended to impede the advancement of enemy vehicles traveling on a road? (Para 3-12b)

9. From where should the earth be obtained to fill crib roadblocks? (Para 3-13b, fig. 3-8)

10. In what position should posts be placed to serve as an antivehicular obstacle? (Para 3-14e)

11. What type of tree is most effective as an abatis? (Para 3-15b)

12. What disadvantage do steel hedgehogs have as an obstacle? (Para 3-16a)

13. Which concrete obstacle is most frequently cast in place? (Para 3-17a)

14. What is the procedure which makes a truck a more effective roadblock? (Para 3-18a)

15. What will make dummy road obstacles more effective? (Para 3-19d)

16. In major amphibious assault operations, who is responsible for the removing of obstacles in boat lanes in 8 meters of water on ocean shorelines? (Para 3-20)

17. Where should beach obstacles cause the enemy to disembark? (Para 3-21a)

18. What obstacle is placed from wading depth at high tide to wading depth at low tide? (Para 3-21b)

19. What obstacle may have a post driven through it for better anchorage? (Para 3-25b, fig. 3-23)

20. The hedgehog, the log ramp, the rock pillar, and the rock wall are all obstacles. Which is an expedient under water obstacle? (Para 3-29b, fig. 3-32)

LESSON 4

BARBED WIRE ENTANGLEMENTS

CREDIT HOURS.. 3

TEXT ASSIGNMENT.. Attached memorandum.

MATERIALS REQUIRED.. None.

LESSON OBJECTIVES

Upon completion of this lesson on Barbed Wire Entanglements, you should be able to accomplish the following in the indicated topic areas:

1. **Purpose**. Describe the two purposes of the use of barbed wire entanglements.

2. **Siting and Layout**. State the 5 requirements for effective siting and layout of barbed wire entanglements.

3. **Classification -- by Use**. Describe the 3 classes of entanglements -- tactical, protective, and supplementary.

4. **Classification -- by Depth**. Describe the 3 types of entanglements -- belt, band, and zone.

5. **Barbed Tape**. State the advantages and disadvantages of barbed tape.

6. **Material and Labor Estimates**. Estimate the manhours and material needed to construct tactical, protective, and supplementary entanglements of a defensive position.

7. **Uses**. Describe the 7 uses of entanglements -- outpost area, battle position, artillery area, reserve area, antipersonnel obstacles, roadblocks, and to strengthen material obstacles.

8. **Pickets and Ties**. Describe types and uses of pickets and ties.

9. **Fences**. Describe fences to include four strand cattle fence, double apron fence, standard concertina fence, and triple standard concertina fence.

10. **Portable Barbed Wire Obstacles**. Describe the portable barbed wire obstacles and their uses.

ATTACHED MEMORANDUM

Section I. Materials

4-1. CONCEPT

a. Purpose. Barbed wire entanglements are artificial obstacles designed to impede the movement of foot troops and, in some cases, tracked and wheeled vehicles. The materials used in constructing barbed wire entanglements are relatively lightweight and inexpensive, considering the protection they afford.

Barbed wire entanglements can be breached by fire but are built rapidly, repaired, and reinforced.

b. Siting and layout. To be effective, barbed wire entanglements are sited and laid out to meet the following requirements:

(1) Under friendly observation, covered by fire, and where practicable, protected by antipersonnel mines, flame mines, tripflares, and warning devices.

(2) Concealed from enemy observation as far as practicable by incorporating terrain features such as reverse slopes, hedges, woods, paths and fence lines.

(3) Erected in irregular and non-geometrical traces.

(4) Employed in bands or zones wherever practicable.

(5) Coordinated with other elements of the defense.

c. Classification. Entanglements are classified according to their use, their depth, and whether fixed or portable.

(1) Use. Entanglements are classified by use as tactical, protective, or supplementary. The employment of these types in a defensive area is shown schematically in figure 4-1.

(a) Tactical. Tactical wire entanglements are sited parallel to and along the friendly side of the final protective line. They are used to break up enemy attack formations and to hold the enemy in areas covered by the most intense defensive fire. Tactical entanglements extend across the entire front of a position but are not necessarily continuous.

(b) Protective. Protective wire entanglements are located to prevent surprise assaults from points close to the defense area. As in the case of all antipersonnel obstacles, they are close enough to the defense area for day and night observation and far enough away to prevent the enemy from using hand grenades effectively from points just beyond the obstacle, normally 40 to 100 meters (131 to 328 ft.). Protective wire surrounds the individual units of a command, usually the platoons (fig 4-2). These entanglements should be connected to entanglements around other platoons by supplementary wire to enclose the entire defensive positions. Protective entanglements are erected around rear-area installations in the same manner and to serve the same purpose as protective

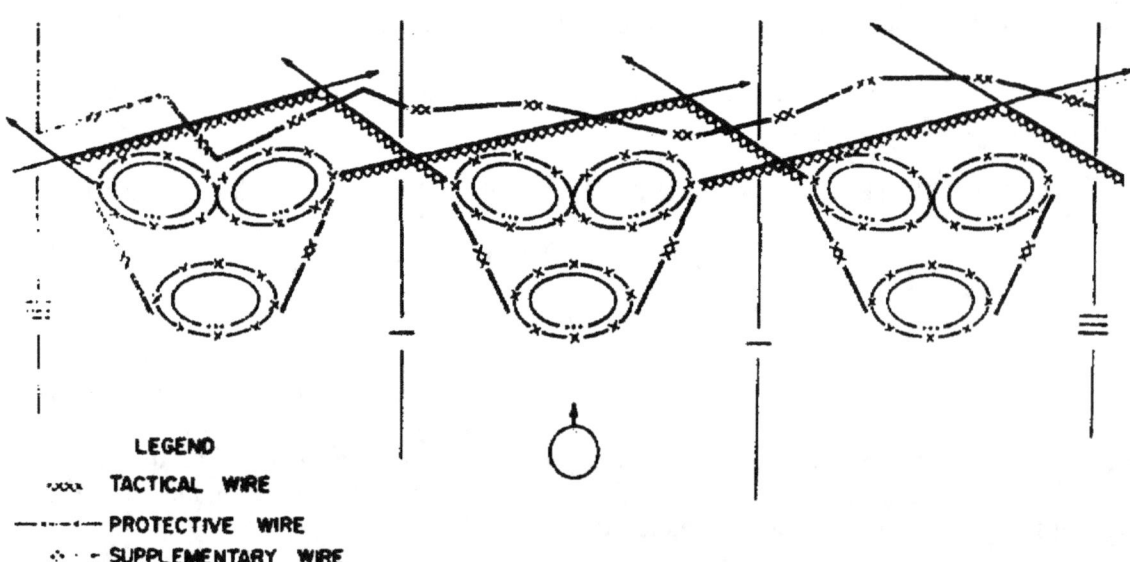

LEGEND

⟋⟍⟋ TACTICAL WIRE

—···— PROTECTIVE WIRE

⟐·⟐·⟐ SUPPLEMENTARY WIRE

Figure 4-1. Schematic layout of barbed wire entanglements in a defensive area.

4-2

Figure 4-2. Protective wire on top of overhead cover.

wire around defensive positions in forward areas. Protective wire also includes the entanglements which should be installed over the tops of installations provided with overhead cover (fig 4-2).

(c) Supplementary. Supplementary wire entanglements in front of the forward edge of the battle area are used to conceal the exact line of the tactical wire. To the rear of the FEBA, supplementary wire is used to enclose the entire defensive position by connecting the protective wire entanglements. Supplementary wire entanglements used to break up the line of tactical wire should be identical to the tactical wire entanglements and constructed simultaneously with them whenever possible.

(2) Depth. Entanglements are classified by depth as belts, bands, or zones.

(a) Belt. A belt is an entanglement one fence in depth.

(b) Band. A band consists of two or more belts in depth, with no interval between them. The belts may be fences of the same type, or the band may be composed of two or more fences of different types.

(c) Zone. A zone consists of two or more bands or belts in depth, with intervals between them.

(3) Equivalent effectiveness. Entanglement depths are also described or specified in terms of comparative effectiveness. Tactical wire entanglements should be equivalent in effectiveness to three belts of 4- and 2-pace double apron fence whenever possible. Protective wire may employ any type of entanglement provided its effectiveness is at least the equivalent of that of the 4- and 2-pace double apron fence. Supplementary wire should have an effectiveness equivalent to that of the type of wire it supplements. It should be equivalent to tactical wire or equivalent to the type of protective wire being used if it connects the outer perimeters of protective wire at the flanks and rear.

(4) Portability.

(a) Fixed entanglements are those types which must be erected in place and which cannot be moved unless completely disassembled.

(b) Portable entanglements are those types which can be moved without complete disassembly. Portable entanglements have been developed for one of the following reasons: To permit assembly in rear areas, with ease of transportation and rapid installation in forward positions. For the temporary closing of gaps or lanes which can be reopened quickly for patrols or counterattacking forces.

d. Lanes and gaps. Lanes and gaps are provided for the passage of patrols, working parties, and attacking or counterattacking forces. When not in use they are kept closed by the use of portable obstacles covered by fire. In barbed wire zones, lanes and gaps are staggered in a zigzag pattern.

e. Uses.

(1) Outpost area. Combat outposts should be surrounded with wire entanglements. These entanglements should be carefully sited to serve as both protective and tactical wire and must be covered by small arms fire. The wire obstacle should be supplemented by antipersonnel mines, warning devices, and booby traps.

(2) Battle position. In the battle area, each company defense position is normally surrounded by a wire entanglement which is connected laterally across the front to the entanglements surrounding the other units in the position.

(3) Artillery and reserve area. Wire entanglements are used in the outer protection of howitzer positions. Heavier weapons, and shelters or other installations in the reserve area, are similarly protected if justified by the situation.

(4) Antipersonnel obstacles. Barbed wire entanglements, tripflares, noisemakers, and antipersonnel mines are sited to warn against enemy patrol action or infiltration at night; to prevent the enemy from delivering a surprise attack from positions close to the defenders; and to hold, fix or delay the enemy in the most effective killing ground. Such obstacles should be near enough to defensive positions for adequate surveillance by the defenders by night and day and far enough away to prevent the enemy from using hand grenades against the defender from points just beyond the obstacles.

f. As roadblocks. A series of barbed wire concertinas as shown in figure 4-3 will stop wheeled vehicles. A series of these concertinas should be placed in blocks about 10 meters in depth. The ends of adjacent coils are wired together and the obstacle lightly anchored at the sides of the road. The block should be sited to achieve surprise.

g. To strengthen natural obstacles. Deep rivers, canals, swamps, and cliffs which form effective delaying obstacles to infantry, and thick hedgerows, fences, and woods, which are only partial obstacles, can be improved by lacing with

barbed wire, by the addition of parts of standard fences on one or both sides, or by entangling with loose wire.

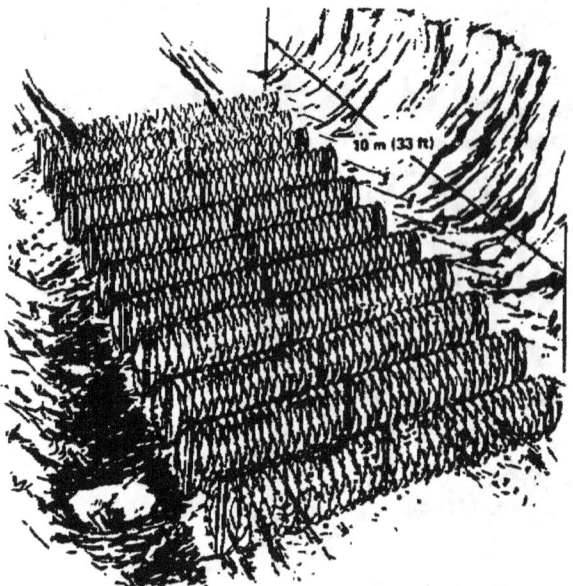

Figure 4-3. Concertina roadblock.

4-2. STANDARD BARBED WIRE

a. Description. Standard barbed wire is 2-strand twisted No. 12 steel wire with 4-point barbs at 10 cm (4 in.) spacing (fig 4-4).

b. Handling. In handling barbed wire, the standard barbed wire gauntlets shown in figure 4-4 heavy leather gloves are worn. They permit faster work and avoid cuts and scratches. As an added safety precaution, the wire should be grasped with the palm down.

c. Issue. Barbed wire is issued in reels (fig 4-5) containing about 400 meters (1312 ft.) of wire. The wire weighs 40.8 kg (90 lb.) and the reel 0.6 kg. In building a fence, two men carry one reel.

d. Bobbins. Bobbins (fig 4-6) holding about 30 meters (98 ft.) of wire are prepared, normally in rear areas, for use in building short lengths of fence and in repairing entanglements. In use, two men handle one bobbin. One unwinds the bobbin while the

Figure 4-4. Standard barbed wire.

Figure 4-5. Barbed wire reel.

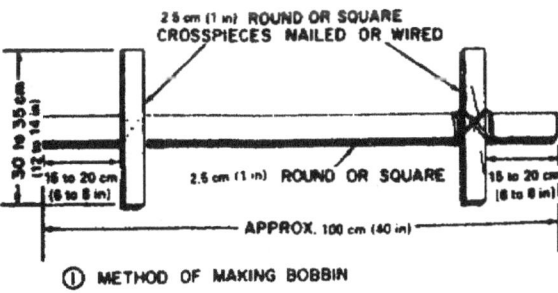

① METHOD OF MAKING BOBBIN

FREE END MARKED WITH WHITE TAPE
② COMPLETED BOBBIN

Figure 4-6. Barbed wire bobbin.

other installs the wire. Two or more men may make the bobbins as follows:

(1) The bobbin sticks are prepared.

(2) The reel is rigged on a improvised trestle or other support.

(3) One man unrolls and cuts 30-meter (98 ft.) lengths of wire. One end of each piece is fastened to the trestle.

(4) The wire is wound in figure-eight shape on the bobbin sticks.

(5) A piece of white tracing tape should be tied to the loose end of the wire to facilitate finding it.

4-3. BARBED STEEL TAPE

a. Characteristics.   The   physical characteristics of barbed tape (fig. 4-7) are as follows:

Width: 3/4 inch (1.91 cm)
Thickness: 0.222 (.056 cm)
Weight: 4.438 lb/50 meters (/164 Ft)
Width of barb: 7/16 inch (1.11 cm)
Interval between barbs: 1/2 inch (1.25 cm)
Breaking load: 500 lb. (1111 kg)

b. Handling. In handling barbed tape, heavy barbed tape gauntlets should be used instead of the standard gauntlets. Small metal clips on the palm and fingers prevent the barbs of the tape from cutting the leather (fig. 4-8). The light weight of the barbed tape and compactness, is much easier to handle, store, and transport than barbed wire.

c. Issue. Barbed tape is issued in 50-meter (164 ft.) reels weighing 2.4 kg. There are six reels to a cardboard carrying case.

d. Barbed tape dispenser. A dispenser (fig. 4-8) is required to install barbed tape. It consists of a frame to hold the 50-meter (164 ft.) reel of barbed tape and two sets of rollers. The reel is inserted on the spindle and the tape is threaded through the two sets of parallel rollers. The outside set of rollers are then turned 90° in a clockwise direction. The hinged arm of the frame is then closed and

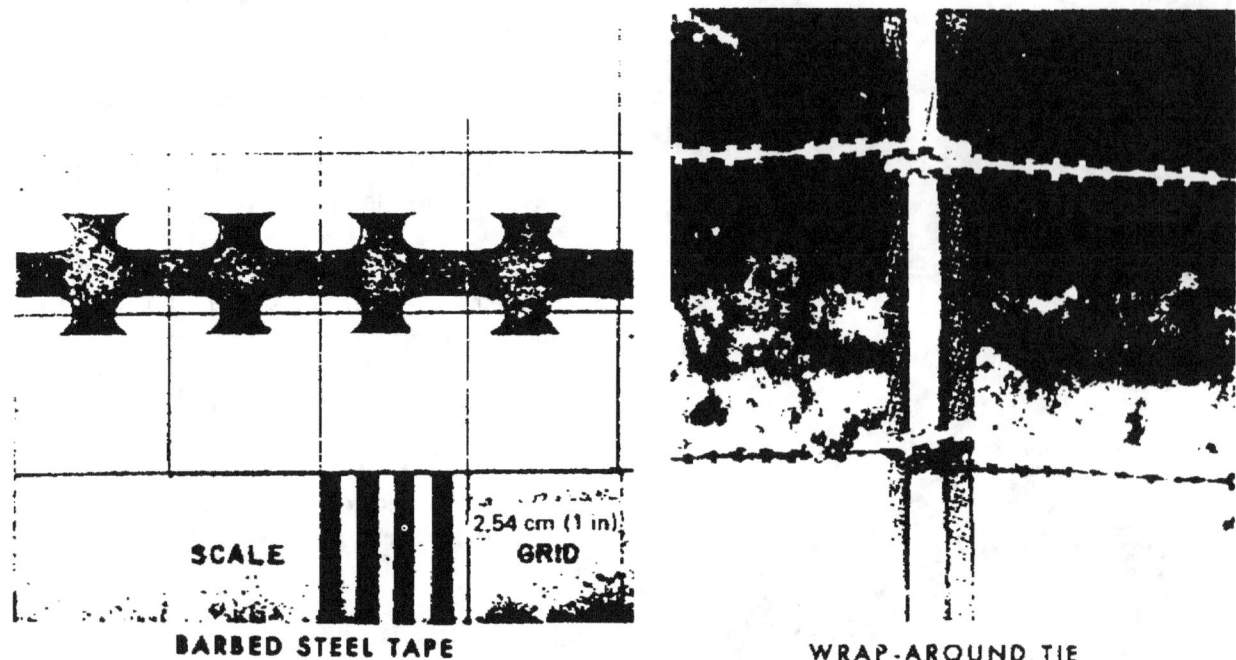

Figure 4-7. Barbed steel tape.

Two significant characteristics shown above which are important to field users are the weight and the breaking load. A comparison of pertinent characteristics of barbed tape and barbed wire is shown below.

Characteristic	Barbed tape	Barbed wire
Weight (400 meters)	16kg (35.5 lb)	48 kg (104.5 lb)
Breaking Load	168 kg (370.0 lb)	489 kg (1075.0 lb)
Barb interval	1.25 cm (½ in.)	10 cm (4 in.)
Size (3000 meters) (9,900 ft)	47.3 x 49 x 44.4 cm (18⅝ x 19 1/ x 17 ½ in.)	68.6 x 68.6 x 58.4 cm (27 x 27 x 23 in.)
Cube	1.02 m³ (3.6 ft³)	2.75 m³ (9.7 ft³)

locked in place by the frame of the rotating rollers. As the tape unwinds from the reel, the two sets of rollers oriented 90° to each other impart a twist to the tape. To be effective the barbed tape must be twisted as it is installed.

e. Uses. Barbed tape can be used in place of standard barbed wire in most all cases except when it is to be repeatedly recovered and reused. The most effective fence that can be constructed using barbed tape is the double-apron fence.

(1) The principal advantages of barbed tape are its size and weight. For equal lengths, barbed tape occupies a third of the space and weighs a third as

much as standard barbed wire. A double-apron fence constructed with barbed tape is more difficult to breach by crawling through than one constructed with standard barbed wire because the barbs of the barbed tape are closer together. Because of the flat configuration, it is more difficult to cut barbed tape with wire cutters.

(2) At the present time, the major disadvantage of barbed tape is the breaking strength. Standard barbed wire is twice as strong. Installation of barbed tape requires a dispenser. A major problem could arise if the dispenser is not available. The tape is not recoverable to its original condition. However, it may be recovered on bobbins in the

4-6

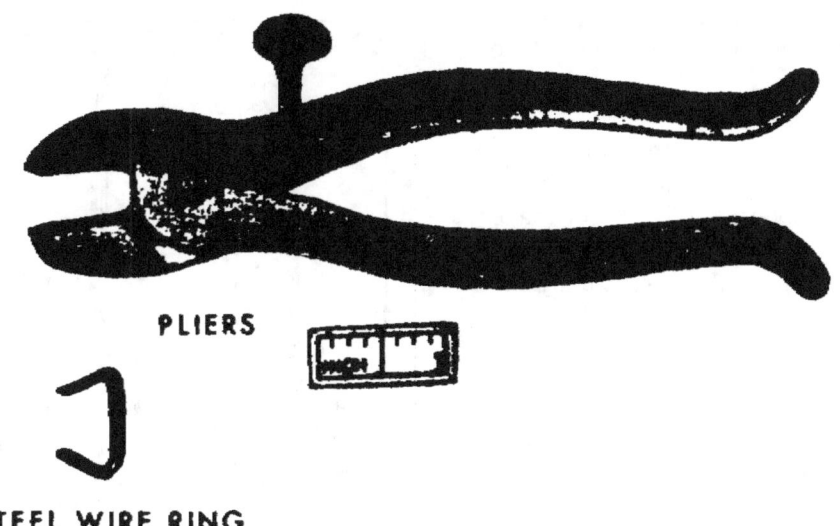

PLIERS

STEEL WIRE RING

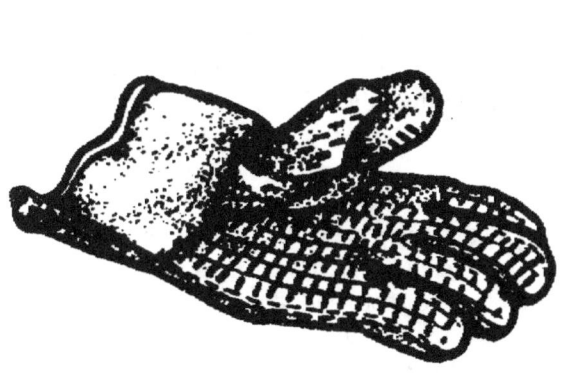

BARBED TAPE - WIRE GAUNTLETS.

BARBED TAPE DISPENSER
WITH 50 - METER REEL OF TAPE.

Figure 4-8. Barbed tape equipment.

twisted condition. Barbed tape is more easily cut by shell fragments than standard barbed wire. Barbed tape can also be cut with a bayonet.

f. **Double-apron fence**. The standard double-apron fence is one of the best obstacles that can be made with barbed tape; and the effectiveness of this obstacle is increased by –

(1) Raising the top wire to preclude crossing the obstacle by stepping over it.

(2) Placing low wires 4 inches above ground to prevent personnel from crawling under the obstacle.

g. **Tying procedures**. In tying barbed tape the wrap-around tie (fig. 4-7) should be used, since the sharp bends of other ties weaken the tape. Steel wire rings, crimped on, provide effective ties and may be used where available (fig. 4-8).

h. Splices. Connecting slots at each end of a 50-meter (164 ft.) reel provide a quick method of splicing reels of barbed tape (fig. 4-9). Barbed tape may also be spliced by interlocking the twisted barbs of two separate lengths, then completing the splice by affixing one steel wire ring to each end of the area where spliced (fig. 4-9).

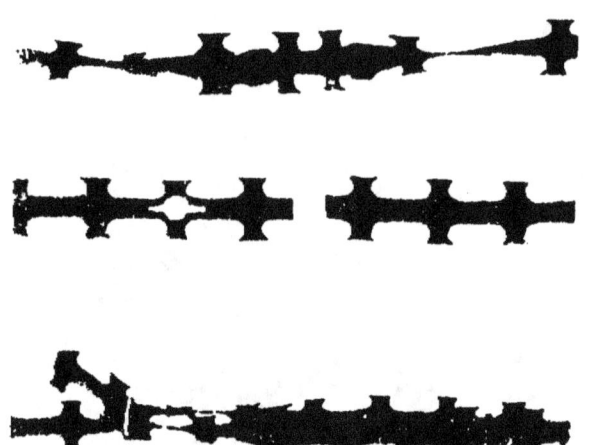

Figure 4-9. Splicing barbed steel tape.

4-4. PICKETS

Wire entanglements are supported on metal or wood pickets.

a. Metal pickets. Metal pickets are issued in two types, screw and U-shaped. The standard lengths are short or anchor, medium, and long (fig. 4-10). The U-shaped picket also comes in an extra long length. Pickets that are serviceable are recovered and used again.

(1) Screw picket. The screw picket is screwed into the ground by turning it in a clockwise direction using a driftpin, stick, or another picket inserted in the bottom eye of the picket for leverage. The bottom eye is used in order to avoid twisting the picket. Screw pickets are installed so that the eye is to the right of the picket, as seen from the friendly side.

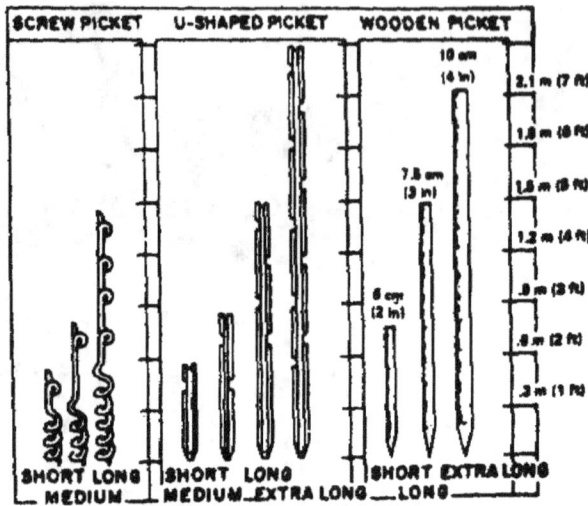

Figure 4-10. Pickets for use with barbed wire.

This allows standard ties to be made easily. Screw pickets tend to be less rigid than other types but are desirable because they can be installed rapidly and silently. When silence is necessary, the driftpin used in installing the pickets should be wrapped with cloth.

(2) U-shaped picket. U-shaped picket is a cold-formed steel picket of U-shaped cross section, pointed at one end for driving. It is notched for wire ties and the pointed end has a punched hole for wires used in bundling the pickets. U-shaped pickets are driven with a sledge hammer. A stake driving cap is used on top of the picket to prevent a sledge from deforming it. Driving the pickets is noisier than installing screw pickets. Noise may be reduced by placing a piece of rubber tire over the driving face of the sledge. The pickets are rigid and sturdy when properly installed and are preferable to screw pickets in situations where noise is not a disadvantage and time is available. The pickets are driven with the hollow surface or concave side facing enemy fire because small arms projectiles ricochet from the convex side. An expedient picket driver which can be locally fabricated is shown in figure 4-11. Constructed as shown it weighs approximately 12 kilograms and is operated by two men. One man holds the picket in a vertical position while the other slides the driver over the picket and starts it into the

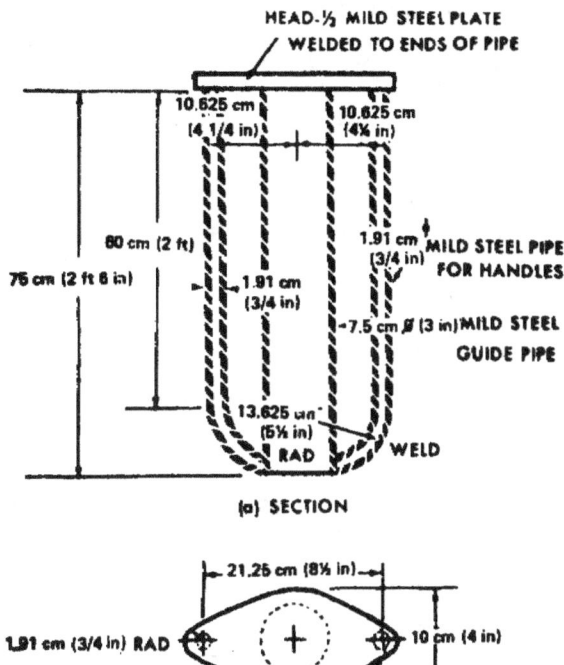

HEAD-½ MILD STEEL PLATE
WELDED TO ENDS OF PIPE

10.625 cm (4 1/4 in)   10.625 cm (4¼ in)

60 cm (2 ft)
75 cm (2 ft 6 in)

1.91 cm (3/4 in) MILD STEEL PIPE FOR HANDLES

1.91 cm (3/4 in)

7.5 cm ∅ (3 in) MILD STEEL GUIDE PIPE

13.625 cm (5¼ in) RAD   WELD

(a) SECTION

21.25 cm (8½ in)

1.91 cm (3/4 in) RAD   10 cm (4 in)

(b) PLAN OF HEAD

Figure 4-11. Expedient picket driver.

ground. Then, both men work the picket driver up and down until the required depth is reached. Short pickets can be driven by turning the picket driver upside down and using the head as a hammer. The bucket of a front loader can be used to push U-shaped pickets into the ground if the tactical situation permits the use of equipment.

(3) Arctic adapter. For erecting barbed wire obstacles with U-shaped drive pickets under conditions where frozen ground prevents driving the pickets, an Arctic adapter is available for anchoring the pickets. The adapter is made of steel and consists of a base plate equipped with an adjustable channel receptacle and two anchor pins. It is anchored by driving the anchor pins through holes in the base place into the ground. One anchor pin drive sleeve with driving pin is provided with each 20 adapters to facilitate anchor pin emplacement. When adapters are not available, a hole can be started with a pick and the picket can be frozen in place by pouring water and snow into the hole.

b. Wooden picket. Expedient wooden pickets of several types may be used.

(1) Round poles 10 cm (4 in.) in diameter are cut to standard picket lengths, sharpened on one end, and driven with a maul. The pickets are used without peeling the bark to prevent the wire from sliding on the picket and to simplify camouflage. Longer pickets are required in loose or sandy soil or when driving through a snow cover. The driving of wooden pickets is not as noisy as the driving of steel pickets, and the noise can be reduced further by fastening a section of tire tread over the face of the hammer or maul. For driving in hard earth, picket tops are wrapped with wire to avoid splitting. Pickets of hardwood, properly installed, are sturdy and rigid.

(2) Dimension lumber ripped to a square cross section may be used instead of round poles. This is equally satisfactory except that is more difficult to camouflage. Such pickets may be camouflaged by painting prior to driving.

(3) Standing trees and stumps may be used as pickets when their location permits.

c. Reference. Table 4-1 lists information pertaining to materials used in the construction of barbed wire entanglements.

4-5. CONCERTINA FENCING

a. Standard barbed wire concertina. The standard barbed wire concertina (fig. 4-12) is a commercially manufactured barbed wire obstacle made of a roll of single-strand, high-strength, spring-steel wire with 4-point barbs attached at 5 cm (2 in.) spacing. Wires forming the coils are clipped together at intervals so the concertina opens to a cylindrical shape 5 to 15 meters (16.4 to 49.2 ft.) long (depending on structure and build of opening) and 90 centimeters (3 ft.) in diameter. The 5-meter (16.4 ft.) length prevents smaller enemy personnel from crawling through the wire as the coils are closer together. Tanglefoot should also be employed in conjunction with the wire to further increase the barrier's effectiveness. The concertina is easily opened and collapsed and can be used repeatedly because the wire returns to its original shape after a crushing force is applied and then removed. The wire

Table 4-1. Wire and Tape Entanglement Materials

Material	Approximate weight		Approximate length		No. carried by one man	Approximate weight of man-load	
	kg	lb	meters	feet		kg	lb
Barbed wire reel................	41.5	91.3	400	1312	½	21	46
Bobbin........................	3.5- 4.0	7.7- 8.8	30	98	4-6	14.5-24.5	32-54
Barbed tape dispenser...........	0.77	1.7	0.45	1.5	20	15.5	34
Barbed tape carrying case.......	14.5	31.9	300	984	1	14.5	32
Standard barbed tape concertina..	14	31.8	15.2	50	1	14	31
Standard barbed wire concertina..	25.4	55.8	15.2	50	1	25	55
Expedient barbed wire concertina.	13.5	29.7	6.1	200	1	13.5	30
Screw pickets:							
Long....................	4	8.8	1.6	6.25	4	16.3	36
Medium..................	2.7	5.9	0.81	2.66	6	16.3	36
Short...................	1.8	3.9	0.53	1.75	8	14.5	32
U-shaped pickets:							
Extra long..............	7.25	16	2.4	7.9	3-4	21.8-29.0	26-64
Long....................	4.5	9.9	1.5	4.9	4	18.1	40
Medium..................	2.7	5.9	0.81	2.66	6	16.3	36
Short...................	1.8	3.9	0.61	2.0	8	14.5	32
Wooden pickets:							
Extra long..............	7.7-10.5	16.9-23.1	2.13	7.0	2	15.4-20.8	34-46
Long....................	5.4- 7.25	11.8-15.9	1.5	4.9	3	16.3-21.7	36-48
Short...................	1.4- 2.7	3- 5.9	0.75	2.5	8	11.0-21.7	24-48

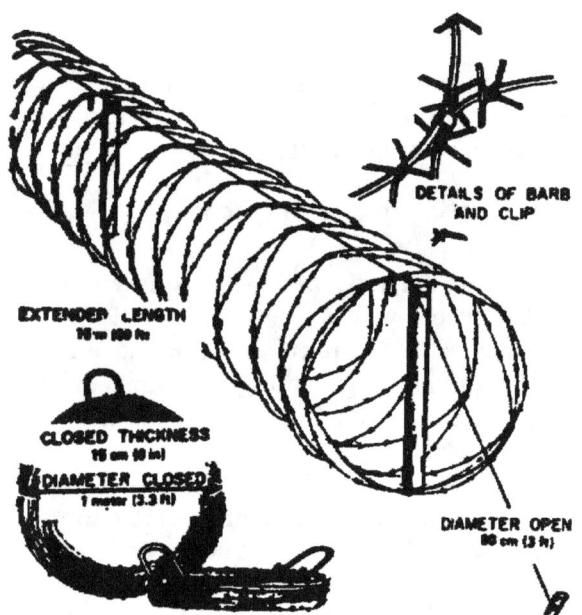

Figure 4-12. Standard barbed wire concertina.

is much harder to cut than standard barbed wire. The concertina weighs 25.4 KG (55.8 lb).

(1) Handling.

(a) To open concertina. The collapsed concertina is tied with plain wire bindings attached to the quarter points of a coil at one end of the concertina. In opening the concertina, these bindings are removed and twisted around the carrying handle for use in tying the concertina when it is again collapsed. Four men open a concertina and extend it to the 5- to 15-meter (16.4 to 49.2 ft.) length, with one man working at each end and others spaced along its length to insure it opens and extends evenly. When necessary, two men can easily open a concertina by bouncing it on the ground to prevent snagging as they open it.

(b) To collapse concertina. Two men can collapse a concertina in the following manner: First all kinks in coils are removed. Loose clips are then tightened or replaced with plain wire. To close the concertina, one man stands at each end of it and places a foot at the bottom of the coil and an arm under the top of the coil. The two men walk toward each other closing the concertina by feeding the wire over their arms and against their feet. When closed, the concertina is laid flat and compressed with the feet. The concertina is tied with plain wire bindings.

(c) To carry concertina. One man easily carries the collapsed concertina by stepping into it and picking it up by the wire

4-10

handles attached to the midpoints of an end coil.

(2) **Staples.** Improvised staples approximately 45 cm (18 in.) long and made of l/2 inch (1.25 cm) driftpins or similar material are used to fasten the bottoms of concertina fences securely to the ground.

b. **Barbed steel tape concertina.** Barbed tape concertina comes in a diameter of 85 cm (33 in.) and an expanded length of 15.2 meters (50 ft.). It is formed of barbed tape wrapped around a high strength, spring steel, core wire. Its configuration, method of handling, and method of employment are similar to standard barbed wire concertina. One roll weighs only 14 kg (31 lbs.).

Section II. Construction Procedures

4-6. ORGANIZATION OF WORK

Table 4-2 gives the materials and manhours required for entanglements of the various types. The normal sizes of work crews are given in the descriptions of the entanglements. For each construction project, the senior noncommissioned officer divides his crew into groups of approximately equal size, based on his knowledge of the skill and speed of each man. He organizes them in such a way that construction proceeds in proper order and at a uniform rate. Each individual must know exactly what his group is to do and his particular job in the group. Each

Table 4-2. Material and Labor Requirements for 300 Meter Sections of Various Wire Entanglements.

Type of entanglement	Lng	Med	Sht	Barbed Wire Reels [1]	No of concertinas	Staples	GPBTO Units [6]	Manhours to erect 300 m of entanglement [3]	Kgs of materials per linear meter of entanglement [2]
Double apron, 4- and 2-pace	100	.....	200	14-15 [19] [4]	.....	.....	.....	59	4.6 [3.5] [5]
Double apron, 6- and 3-pace	66	.....	132	13-15 [18] [4]	.....	.....	.....	49	3.6 [2.6] [5]
High wire (less guy wires)........	198	.....	.....	17-19 [24] [4]	.....	.....	.....	79	5.3 [4.0] [5]
Low wire, 4- and 2-pace	....	100	200	11 [15] [4]	.....	.....	.....	49	3.6 [2.8] [5]
4-strand cattle fence	100	.....	2	5-6 [7] [4]	.....	.....	.....	20	2.2 [1.8] [5]
Triple standard concertina	160	.....	4	3 [4] [4]	59	317	.....	30	8.2 [7.3] [5]
General purpose barbed tape obstacle (GPBTO) .	.....	.....	.....	.....	.....	.....	3	1	2.7

1. Lower number of reels applies when screw pickets are used; higher number when u-shaped pickets are used. Add the difference between the two to the higher number when wood pickets are used.

2. Average weight when any issue metal pickets are used. Estimate truck loads based on vehicle capacity of 2268 Kgs.

3. Manhours are based on the use of screw pickets. Multiply these figures by 0.67 when experienced troops are being used, and by 1.5 for night work. With the exception of triple standard concertina and GPBTO, multiply by 1.2 when using driven pickets.

4. Number of cases of barbed tape required if barbed tape is used in place of barbed wire.

5. Kgs of material required per linear meter of entanglement if barbed tape is used in place of barbed wire and barbed tape concertina is used in place of standard concertina.

6. Based on vehicle emplaced obstacle installed in triple belts.

man should have barbed wire gauntlets. The sequence of operations for each fence is given in the paragraph describing the erection of the fence. The sequence that is outlined should be followed, and as experience is gained, the size and composition of the groups may be varied. For each section of entanglement, all fence-building operations normally proceed from right to left, as one faces the enemy. It may be necessary under some circumstances to work from left to right. If time permits, men should be taught to work in either direction. In case of heavy casualties, the senior officer or NCO will decide what wires, if any, are to be omitted.

a. Construction at night. For night construction the following additional preparations are made:

(1) Tracing tape should be laid from the materials dump to the site of work and then along the line of fence where possible.

(2) Materials should be tied together in man loads, and pickets bundled tightly to prevent rattling.

(3) Wire fastenings of wire coils and pickets should be removed and replaced with string which can be broken easily.

(4) A piece of tape should be tied to the ends of the wire on each reel or bobbin.

b. Supervision. Proper supervision of entanglement construction includes the following:

(1) Proper organization of the work into tasks.

(2) Making sure the tasks are carried out in the proper sequence.

(3) Prevention of bunching and overcrowding of personnel.

(4) Making sure the wires are tightened properly and spaced correctly.

(5) Checking ties to verify that they are being made correctly and at the right points.

c. Construction in combat areas. When working in close proximity to the enemy, the necessary precautions include--

(1) Provision of security around the work party.

(2) Silence.

(3) No working on enemy side of fence unless absolutely necessary.

(4) Use of screw pickets, if available.

(5) Men not working should seek concealment near the work site until they begin work.

(6) Individual weapons must be kept nearby at all times.

d. Wire ties. Wires are tied to pickets by men working from the friendly side of the wire and picket; the wire is stretched with the right hand as the tie is started. The four ties used in erecting wire entanglements are shown in figure 4-13.

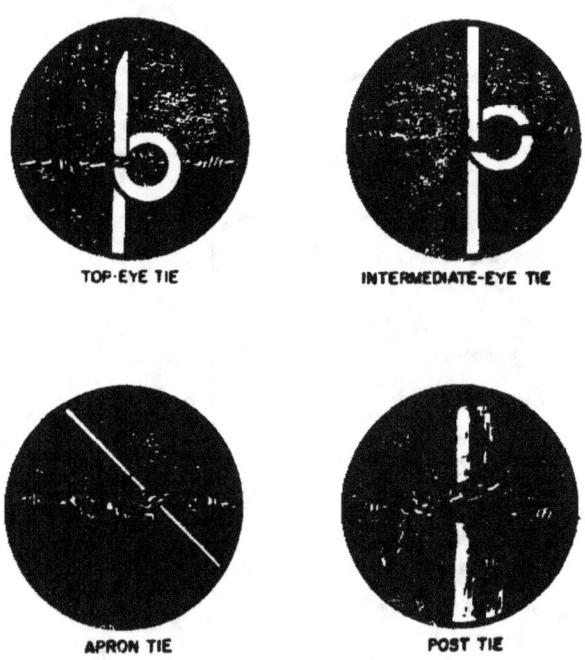

TOP-EYE TIE   INTERMEDIATE-EYE TIE

APRON TIE   POST TIE

Figure 4-13. Ties for erecting entanglements as seen from the friendly side.

(1) **Top-eye tie.** The top eye is used to fasten standard barbed wire to the top eye of screw pickets. It is made in one continuous movement of the left hand (fig 4-14) while the right hand exerts a pull on the fixed end of the wire. This is a secure tie, quickly made, and uses only a short piece of wire.

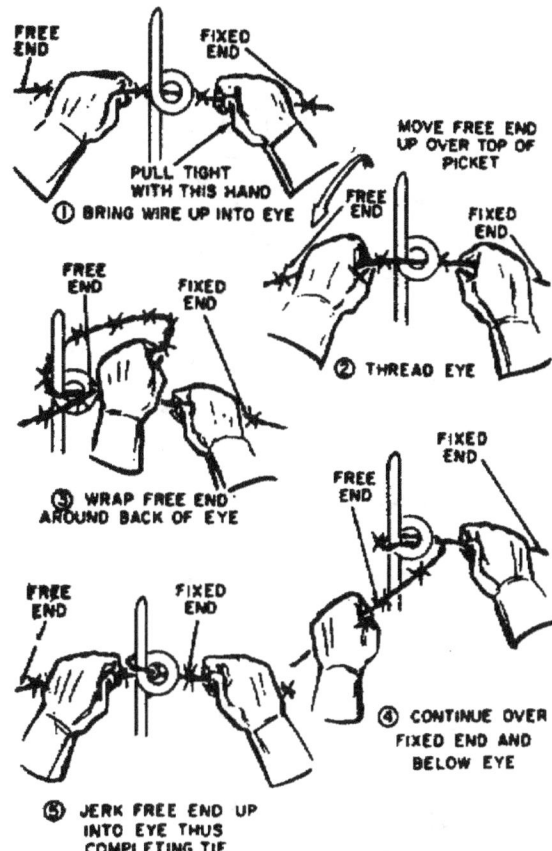

Figure 4-14. Top-eye tie.

(2) Intermediate-eye tie. This tie is used to fasten standard barbed wire to eyes other than the top eye, in screw pickets. It is made as shown in figure 4-15. This tie and the other ties described below require more time to make than the top-eye tie and each uses several centimeters of wire. In making the intermediate-eye shown in figure 4-15, the following points are especially important:

(a) The right hand reaches over the fixed wire and around the picket, with the palm down. The left hand holds the fixed end for tension.

(b) The loops are removed from the free end and wrapped around the picket.

(c) One side of the loop should pass above the eye and the other side below the eye.

(3) Post tie. Standard barbed wire is fastened to wooden pickets or to the steel U-shaped picket with the post tie shown in figure 4-16. The

wire should be wrapped tightly around the post to keep the barbs from sliding down. With the U-shaped picket, the wire wrapping is engaged in a notch in the picket. The method is essentially the same as that of the intermediate-eye tie.

(4) Apron tie. The apron tie is used whenever two wires that cross must be tied together. It is tied in the same manner as the post tie except a wire is substituted for the post (fig. 4-17).

(5) Barbed tape splices. Connecting slots at each end of a 50-meter (164 ft.) reel provide a quick method of splicing reels of barbed tape. Barbed tape may also be spliced by interlocking the twisted barbs of two separate lengths, then completing the splice by twisting a short piece of wire to each end of the area where spliced.

e. Method of installing wires

(1) The end of the wire is attached to the first anchor picket. This is the picket at the right end of a section of entanglement, from the friendly side. Fences are built from right to left as this makes it easier for a right-handed man to make the ties while remaining faced toward the enemy.

(2) A bar is inserted in the reel and the reel is carried for 23 to 27 meters (75 to 88 ft.), allowing the wire to unwind from the bottom of the reel. This is done on the friendly side of the row of pickets to which the wire is to be tied.

(3) Slack is put in the wire by moving back toward the starting point; the ties are then made by two men leapfrogging each other. If available, two men can be assigned to make the ties as the reel is unwound.

f. Tightening wire. After a wire is installed it can be tightened, if necessary, by racking with a driftpin or short stick (fig. 4-18). Wires should not be racked at ties or where they intersect other wires because this makes salvage of the wire very difficult. Fences are similarly racked to tighten them when they sag after having been installed for some time. Wires should be just taut enough to prevent them from being depressed easily

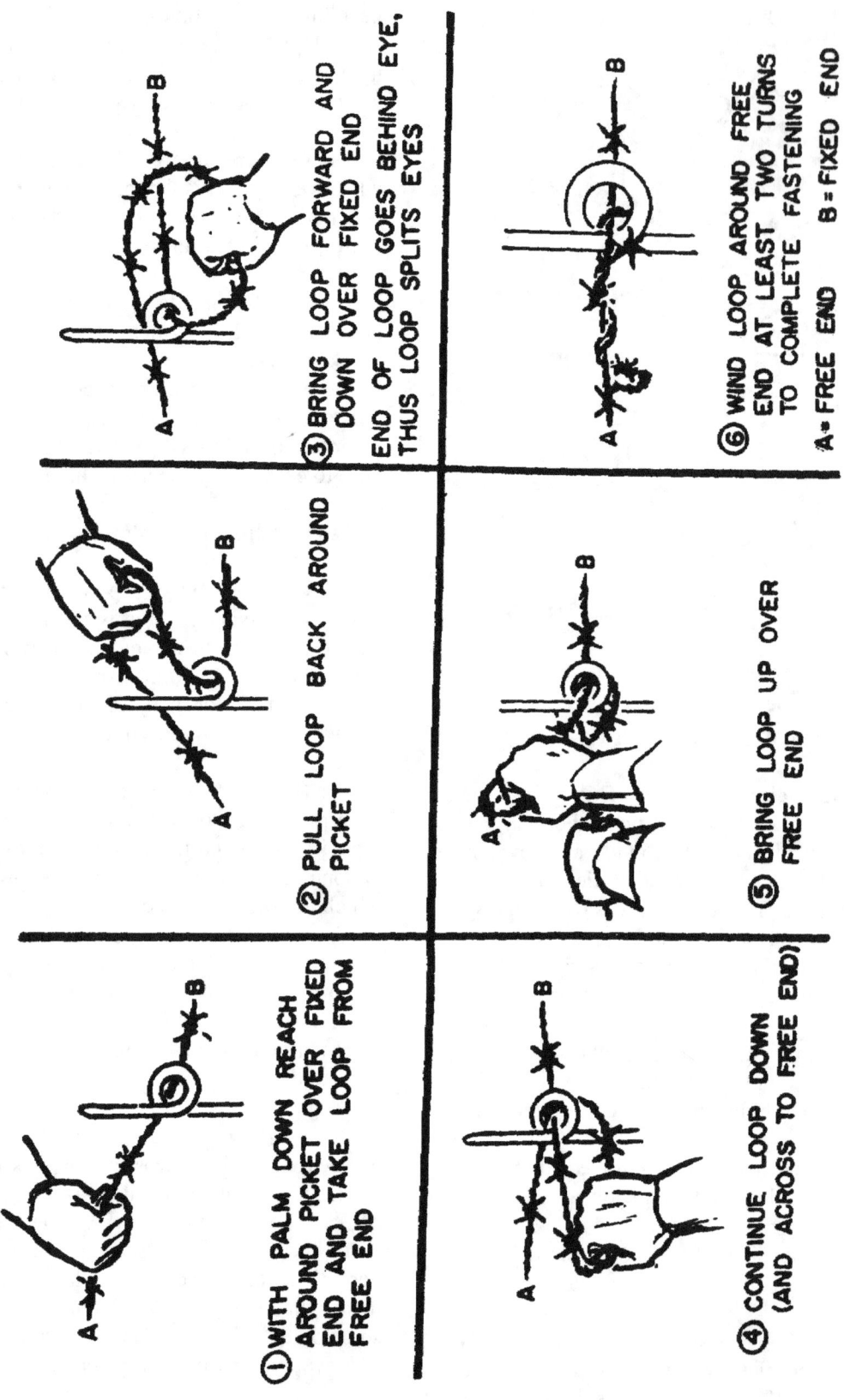

③ BRING LOOP FORWARD AND DOWN OVER FIXED END

END OF LOOP GOES BEHIND EYE, THUS LOOP SPLITS EYES

⑥ WIND LOOP AROUND FREE END AT LEAST TWO TURNS TO COMPLETE FASTENING

A = FREE END   B = FIXED END

② PULL LOOP BACK AROUND PICKET

⑤ BRING LOOP UP OVER FREE END

① WITH PALM DOWN REACH AROUND PICKET OVER FIXED END AND TAKE LOOP FROM FREE END

④ CONTINUE LOOP DOWN (AND ACROSS TO FREE END)

Figure 4-15. Intermediate-eye tie.

by boards, mats, or similar objects thrown across them. If wires are stretched too tightly they are more easily cut by fragments. Barbed steel tape must never be tightened by racking.

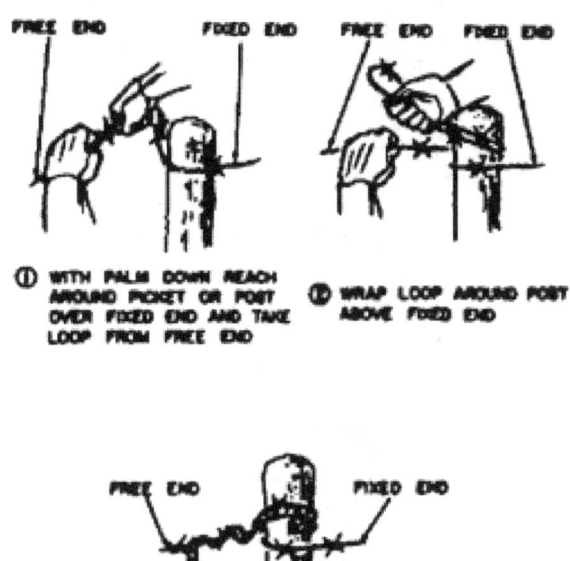

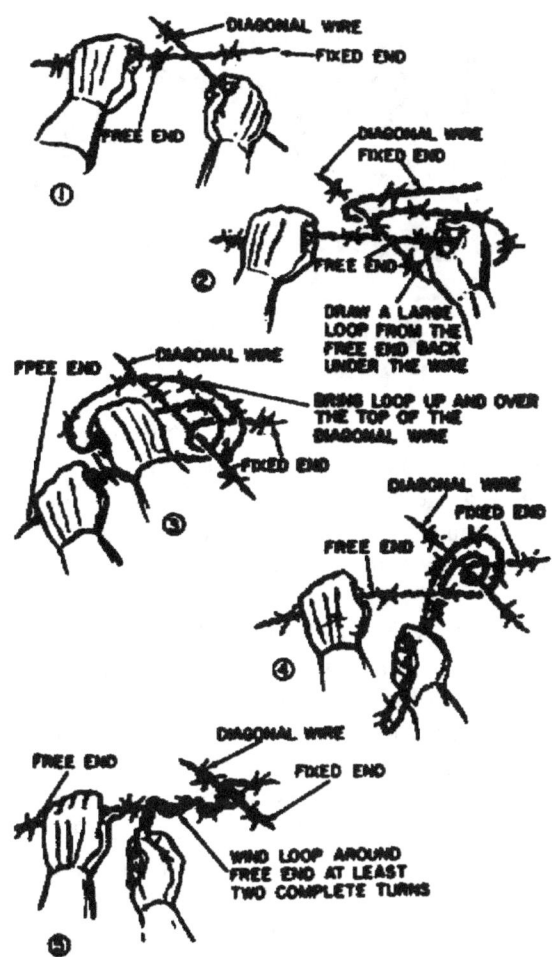

Figure 4-16. Post tie.

4-7.   FOUR-STRAND CATTLE FENCE

a. **Description**. The four-strand center section of a double apron fence can be installed rapidly to obtain obstacle effect, and aprons can be added later to develop it into a double apron fence. In rural areas where wire fences are used by farmers, obstacles in the form of four-strand cattle fences (fig. 4-19) will blend with the landscape. Their design should follow as closely as possible the local custom, usually wooden pickets at about 2- to 4-pace intervals with four horizontal strands of barbed wire fixed to them. They should be sited along footpaths and edges of fields or crops, where they will not look out of place. If conditions permit, this fence may be improved by installing guy wires in the same manner as the diagonal wires of the double apron fence. All longitudinal wires of this fence must start and end at an anchor picket.

b. **Construction**. Eight men may be employed on short sections of this fence up to 16 men on 300-meter (984 ft.) sections. The two operations are laying out and installing pickets, and installing wire.

Figure 4-17. Standard barbed wire apron tie.

Figure 4-18. Tightening wire by racking.

(1) **First operation**. The work party is divided into two groups of approximately equal size. The first group carries

4-15

Figure 4-19. Four-strand cattle fence as viewed from the enemy side.

and lays out long pickets at 3-meter (9.8 ft.) intervals along the centerline of the fence, beginning and ending the section with an anchor picket, and including anchor pickets for guys if needed. The second group installs the pickets.

(2) Second operation. As the first task is completed, men move individually to the head of the fence and are organized into teams of two or four men to install wires. Four four-man teams, two men carry the reel and two men make ties and pull the wire tight. For two-man teams, the wire must first be unrolled for 50 to 100 meters (164 to 328 ft.), then the men come back to the head of the work and make the ties or the wire may first be made up into bobbins to be carried and unwound by one man while the other man makes the ties. The first team installs the bottom fence wire, and draws it tight and close to the ground. Succeeding teams install the next wires in order.

4-8. DOUBLE-APRON FENCE

a. Types. There are two types of double apron fence, the 4- and 2-pace fence and the 6- and 3-pace fence. The 4- and 2-pace fence (fig. 4-20) is the better obstacle of the two and is the type more commonly used. In this fence the center pickets are 4 paces apart and the anchor pickets are 2 paces from the line of the center pickets and opposite the midpoint of the space between center pickets. The 6- and 3-pace fence follows the same pattern with pickets at 6- and 3-pace intervals. For this fence, less material and construction time are required, but the obstacle effect is substantially reduced because with the longer wire spans make it is easier to raise or lower the wires and crawl over or under them.

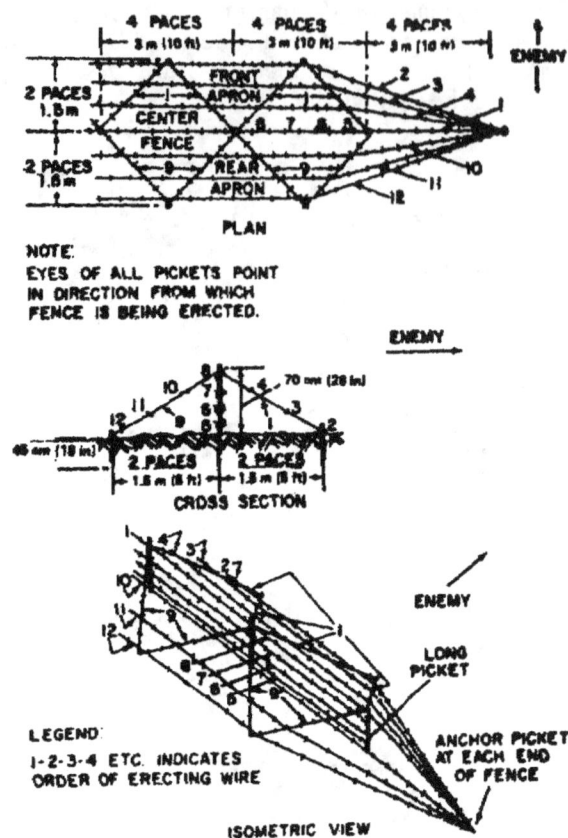

Figure 4-20. Double apron fence.

Except for picket spacing, the 4- and 2-pace and the 6- and 3-pace fences are identical. Only the 4- and 2-pace fence is discussed in detail.

b. Construction. A 300-meter (984 ft.) section of either type of double-apron fence is a platoon task normally requiring 1 1/2 hours, assuming 36 productive men per platoon. There are two operations in building a double apron fence: laying out and installing pickets, and installing wire. The first operation is nearly completed prior to starting the second. The second operation is started as men become available and the first operation has moved far enough ahead to avoid congestion. A platoon is normally assigned to build a 300-meter (984 ft.) section.

(1) First operation. The work party, if not organized in three squads, is divided into three groups of approximately equal size. One squad lays out the long pickets along the centerline of the fence at

4-pace intervals at the spots where they are to be installed and with their points toward the enemy. Another squad lays out the anchor pickets, with points toward the enemy and positioned 2 paces each way from the centerline and midway between the long pickets (fig. 4-21). The spacing is readily checked with a long picket. The third squad installs all the pickets, with the help of the two other squads as the latter finish the work of laying out the pickets. When installed, the lower notch or bottom eye of the long pickets should be approximate 10 cm (4 in.) off the ground to make passage difficult either over or under the bottom wires.

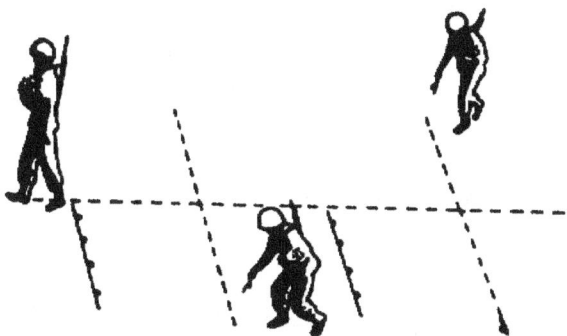

Figure 4-21. Laying out anchor pickets.

(2) **Second operation.** As the groups complete the first operation, they return to the head of the fence and begin installing wire. The order in which the wires are installed is shown in figure 4-20 and is further illustrated in figure 4-22. Care must be taken to avoid having any of the men cut off between the fence and the enemy. The men are divided into two- or four-man groups and proceed to install the wires in numerical order; that is, as soon as the men installing one wire have moved away from the beginning of the fence and are out of the way, the next wire is started. Installation is as follows:

(a) The No. 1 wire is the diagonal wire on the enemy side and is secured with a top-eye tie to all pickets. It is important to keep this wire tight.

(b) The No. 2 wire is the trip wire on the enemy side of the fence and is secured to both diagonals just above the anchor picket with the

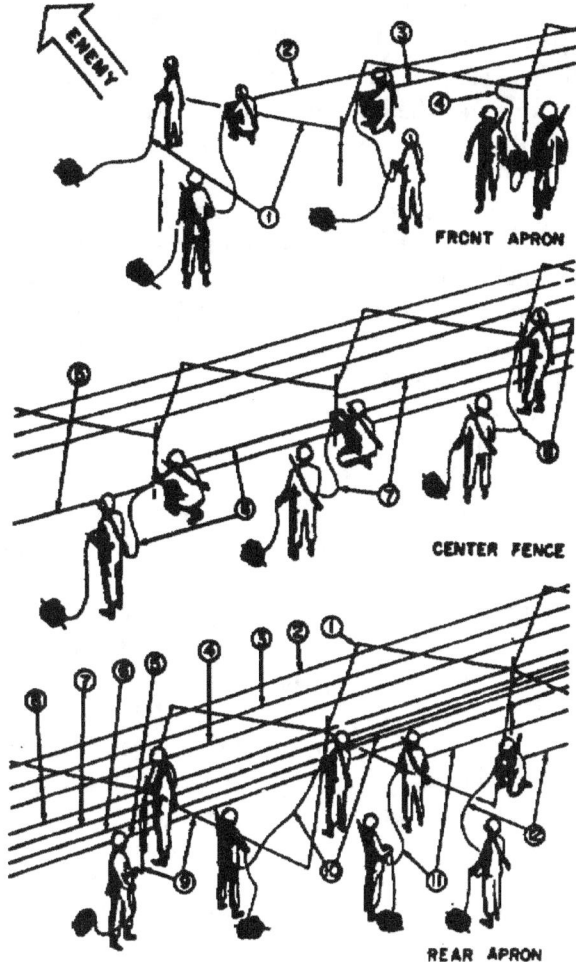

Figure 4-22. Sequence of installing wire in a double apron fence.

apron tie. This wire must be tight enough and close enough to the ground to make passage over or under the wire difficult.

(c) The No. 3 wire is an apron wire on the enemy side of the fence. It is secured to the first diagonal wire, and thereafter to each alternate diagonal, and then to the last diagonal wire. The No. 4 wire is also an apron wire on the enemy side of the fence. It is secured to the first diagonal wire (No. 1), thereafter to the diagonal wires which are not tied to the No. 3 wire, and then to the last diagonal wire. Apron wires Nos. 3 and 4 are equally spaced along the diagonal wire.

(d) The No. 5 wire is the first one

which is not started from the end anchor picket. It is started at the first long picket, and ended at the last long picket. It is secured with the intermediate-eye tie and is stretched tightly to prevent passage over or under it.

(e) Wires No. 6, 7, and 8 complete the center portion of the fence and are secured to the long picket No. 6 and 7 with the intermediate-eye tie. They also start at the first and end at the last long picket. No. 8 is secured with the top-eye ties. These wires (No. 6, 7, and 8) form the backbone of the fence and are drawn up tightly to hold the pickets in position.

(f) No. 9 is the diagonal apron wire on the friendly side of the fence and is secured with the top-eye to all pickets. No. 10 and 11 are apron wires and No. 12 is the tripwire on the friendly side of the fence. Wire No. 12 is installed in the same manner as wire No. 2 (b) above).

(g) If the fence is not satisfactorily tight when installed, wires are tightened by racking as described in paragraph 4-6f.

4-9. STANDARD CONCERTINA FENCES

As an obstacle, in most situations, the triple standard concertina fence is better than the double apron fence. The material for the standard concertina fence weighs about 50 percent more than for a triple standard concertina fence of the same length, but it is erected with about one-half the man-hours. Every concertina fence is secured firmly to the ground by driving staples at intervals not more than 2 meters (6.6 ft.). The staples are used on the single concertina fence and on the front concertina of the double and triple types. The two types of fence are as follows:

a. **Single concertina**. This is one line of concertinas. It is erected quickly and easily but is not an effective obstacle in itself. It is used as emergency entanglement or for the temporary closing of gaps between other obstacles. It is for such purposes that one roll of concertina may be habitually carried on the front of each vehicle in combat units.

b. **Double concertina**. This consists of a

double line of concertinas with no interval between lines. The two lines are installed with staggered joints. As an obstacle, the double concertina is less effective than a well-emplaced, double apron fence. It is used in some situations to supplement other obstacles in a band or zone.

4-10. TRIPLE STANDARD CONCERTINA FENCE

a. **Description**. This consists of two lines of concertinas serving as a base, with a third line resting on top, as shown in figure 4-23. All lines are installed with staggered joints. Each line is completed before the next is started so a partially completed concertina entanglement presents some obstruction. It is erected quickly and is difficult to cross, cut, or crawl through.

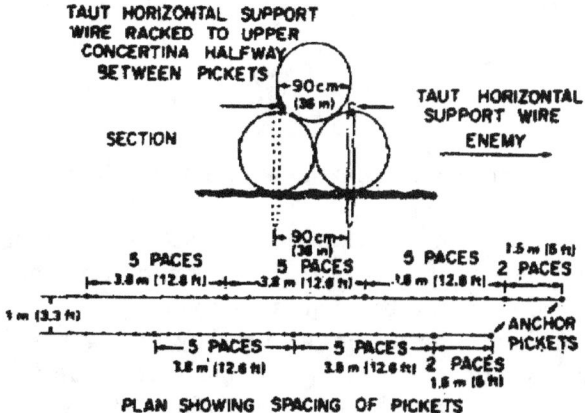

Figure 4-23. Triple standard concertina fence.

b. **Detail**. A 300-meter (984 ft.) section of this fence is a platoon task normally requiring less than 1 hour. There are two operations: carrying and laying out pickets and concertina rolls and installing pickets, and opening and installing concertinas.

c. **First operation**. For the first operation, the work party is divided into three groups of approximately equal size: one to lay out all pickets, one to install all pickets, and one to lay out all concertina rolls.

(1) The first group lays out front row long pickets at 5 pace intervals on the line of fence (fig. 4-24) with points of pickets on line and pointing toward the enemy. The rear row long pickets are laid out on a

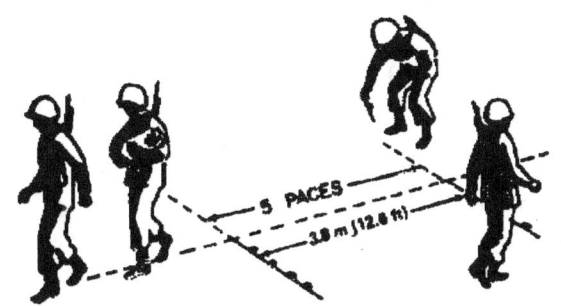

Figure 4-24. Laying out long pickets for triple concertina fence.

line 90 cm (3 ft.) to the rear and opposite the center of interval between the front row long pickets. An anchor picket is laid out at each end of each line, 1.5 meters (5 ft.) from the end long picket.

(2) The second group installs pickets beginning with the front row (fig. 4-25). As in other fences, eyes of screw pickets are to the right. Concave faces of U-shaped pickets are toward the enemy.

Figure 4-25. Installing front row pickets for triple concertina fence.

(3) The third group lays out concertinas along the rows of pickets (fig. 4-26). In the front row, one roll is placed at the third picket and one at every fourth picket thereafter. Sixteen staples accompany each front row concertina. In the second row, two rolls are placed at the third picket and two at every fourth picket thereafter. As each roll is placed in position, its binding wires are unfastened but are left attached to the hoop at one end of the roll.

Figure 4-26. Laying out concertina.

d. Second operation. As they complete the first operation, all men are organized in four-man parties (fig. 4-27) to open and install concertinas, beginning at the head of the fence. The sequence, shown in general in figure 4-27 is as follows:

(1) Open the front row concertinas in front of the double line of pickets and the other two in its rear.

(2) Lift each front row concertina in turn and drop it over the long pickets, then join concertina ends as shown in figure 4-28.

(3) Fasten the bottom of the concertina to the ground by driving a staple over

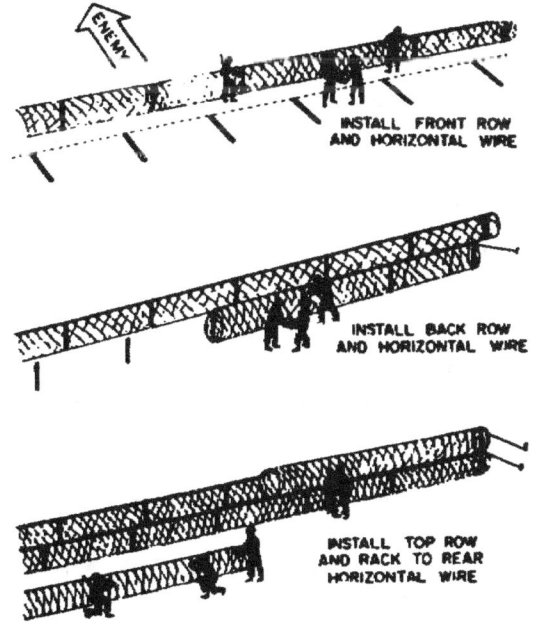

Figure 4-27. Installing concertina.

4-19

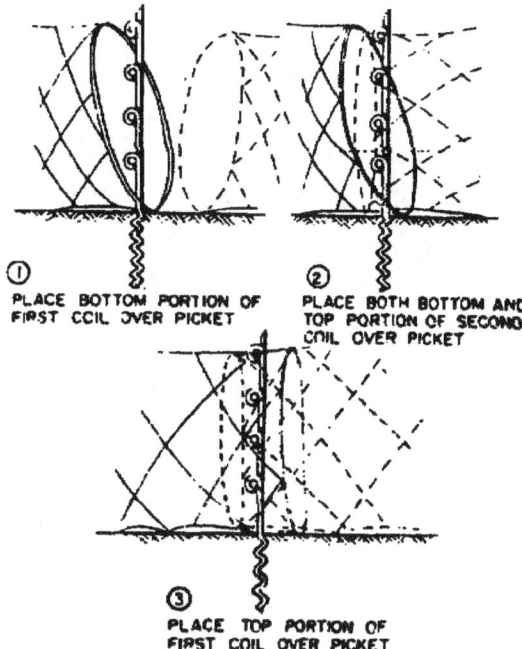

① PLACE BOTTOM PORTION OF FIRST COIL OVER PICKET

② PLACE BOTH BOTTOM AND TOP PORTION OF SECOND COIL OVER PICKET

③ PLACE TOP PORTION OF FIRST COIL OVER PICKET

Figure 4-28. Joining concertina.

each pair of end hoops, one over the bottom of a coil at each long picket, and one at the l/2 and l/4 points of the 3.8-meter (12.5 ft.) picket spacing. Securing the front concertina to the ground is essential and must be done before installing another concertina in its rear unless the enemy side of the entanglement is sure to be accessible later.

(4) Stretch a barbed wire strand along the top of each front row and fasten it to the tops of the long pickets, using the top eye tie for screw pickets. These wires are stretched as tightly as possible to improve the resistance of the fence against crushing.

(5) Install the rear row concertina as described above for the front row concertina.

(6) Install the top row concertina (fig. 4-27), fastening the end hoops of 15-meter (50 ft.) sections with plain steel wire ties. Begin this row at a point between the ends of the front and rear of the lower rows, thus breaking all end joints.

(7) Rack the top concertina to the rear horizontal wire at points halfway between the long pickets. If there is safe access to the enemy side of the fence, similarly rack the top concertina to the forward horizontal wire.

4-11. LOW-WIRE ENTANGLEMENT

a. General. This is a 4- and 2-pace double apron fence in which medium pickets replace long pickets in the fence centerline (fig. 4-29). This results in omission of the Nos. 6, 7, and 8 wires, and in bringing all the apron and diagonal wires much closer to the ground so passage underneath this fence is difficult. This fence may be used advantageously on one or both sides of the double apron fence. The low wire entanglement is used where concealment is essential. In tall grass or shallow water, this entanglement is almost invisible and is particularly effective as a surprise obstacle. However, a man can pick his way through this low wire fence without much difficulty; therefore, for best results it must be employed in depth.

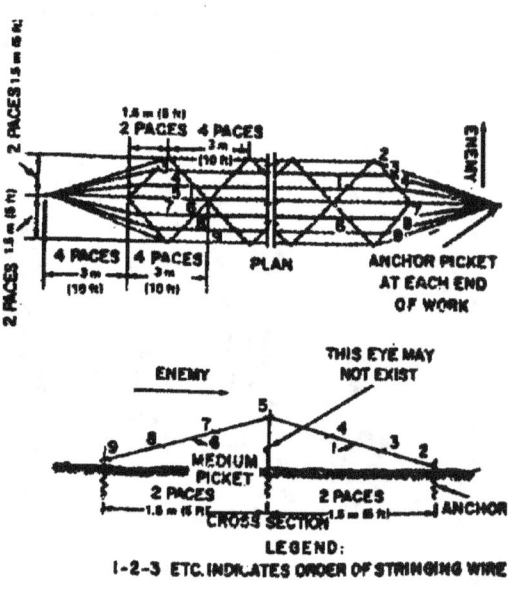

LEGEND:
1-2-3 ETC. INDICATES ORDER OF STRINGING WIRE

NOTE:
EYES POINT IN DIRECTION FROM WHICH FENCE IS BEING ERECTED

Figure 4-29. Low wire fence.

b. Construction. Except for the omission of three wires and the substitution of the medium pickets, this fence is constructed in the same manner as the double apron fence.

4-12. HIGH-WIRE ENTANGLEMENT

a. Description. This obstacle consists of

4-20

two parallel 4-strand fences with a third 4-strand fence zigzagged between them to form triangular cells. With two rows of pickets as shown in figure 4-30, the entanglements is classed as a belt; with one or more additional rows of fences and triangular cells it is a band. To add to the obstacle effect, front and rear aprons may be installed and spirals of loose wire may be placed in the triangular cells.

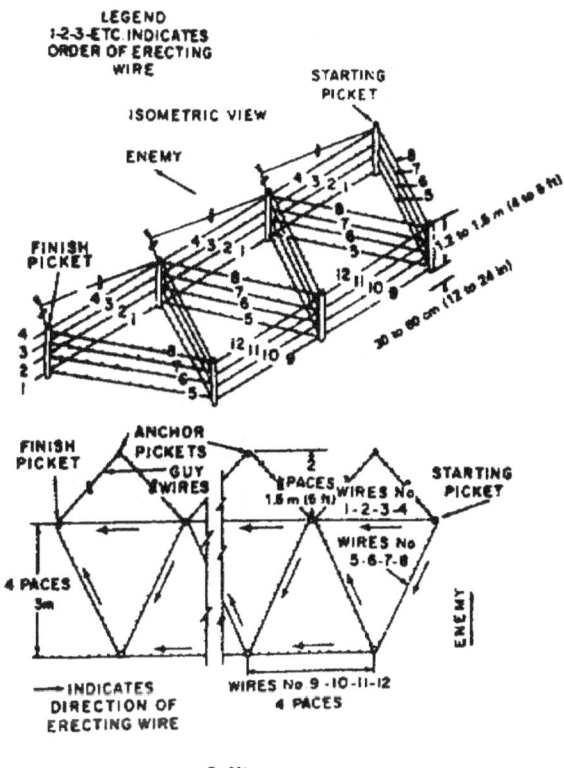

Figure 4-30. High wire entanglement.

b. Construction. A 300-meter (984 ft.) section of high entanglement with two rows of pickets, as shown in figure 4-30, is a platoon task normally requiring about two hours, assuming 38 men per platoon. The two operations are: laying out and installing pickets, and installing wire.

(1) First operation. For this operation the working party is divided into two groups, two-thirds of the men going to the first group and one-third to the second. The first group carries and lays out

pickets, front row first and at 3-meter (10 ft.) intervals. Second row pickets are laid out in a line 3 meters (10 ft.) to the rear of the front row and spaced midway between them. The first group also lays out an anchor picket in line with each end of each 4-strand fence, 3 meters (10 ft.) from the nearest long picket. If guys are needed, anchor pickets are also laid out in lines 2 paces from the lines of the front and rear fences, opposite and midpoint of spaces between the long pickets. The second group installs front row pickets, returns to the head of the fence, installs the rear row, and then installs the anchor pickets. When the first group finishes laying out pickets, they begin installing wire and help finish installing the pickets.

(2) Second operation. As the first task is completed, men move individually to the head of the fence and are organized into teams of two or four men to install wires in the same manner as for the 4-strand fence. The order of installation is as shown in figure 4-30, except if front guys are used they are installed before the No. 1 wire; rear guys after the No. 12 wire. The lengthwise wires of each 4-strand fence begin and end at an anchor picket.

4-13. TRESTLE APRON FENCE

The trestle apron fence (fig. 4-31) has inclined crosspieces spaced at 4.8- to 6-meter (15.7 - 19.7 ft.) intervals to carry longitudinal wires on the enemy side. The rear ends of the crosspieces are carried on triangular timber frames which are kept from spreading by tension wires on the friendly side. The crosspiece may be laid flat on the ground for tying the longitudinal wires in place and then raised into position on the triangular frames. The frames are tied securely in place and

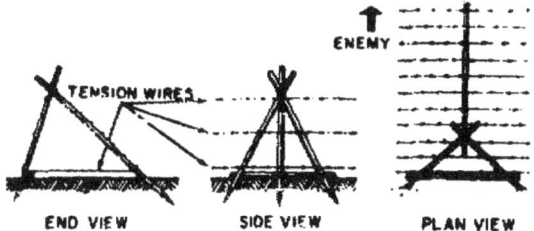

Figure 4-31. Trestle apron fence.

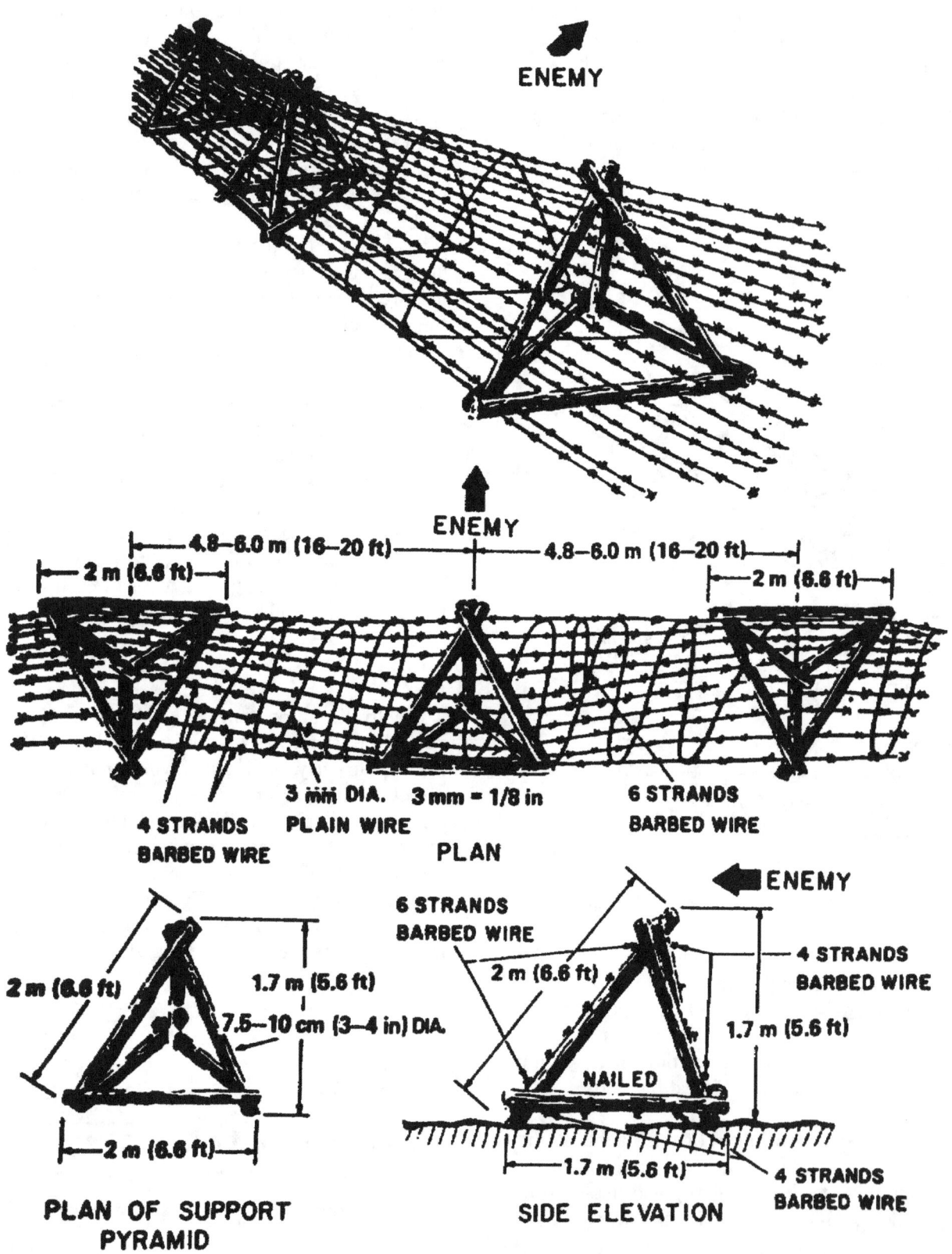

ENEMY

ENEMY

4.8—6.0 m (16—20 ft) 4.8—6.0 m (16—20 ft)

2 m (6.6 ft) 2 m (6.6 ft)

3 mm DIA. 3 mm = 1/8 in 6 STRANDS
PLAIN WIRE BARBED WIRE

4 STRANDS
BARBED WIRE

PLAN

6 STRANDS
BARBED WIRE ENEMY

2 m (6.6 ft) 4 STRANDS
BARBED WIRE

2 m (6.6 ft) 1.7 m (5.6 ft)

7.5—10 cm (3—4 in) DIA. 1.7 m (5.6 ft)

NAILED

2 m (6.6 ft) 1.7 m (5.6 ft) 4 STRANDS
BARBED WIRE

PLAN OF SUPPORT
PYRAMID SIDE ELEVATION

Figure 4-32. Lapland fence.

4-22

held by the tension wires. The fence should be sited in such a way it can be guyed longitudinally to natural anchorages and racked tight.

4-14. LAPLAND FENCE

Figure 4-32 shows the lapland fence which can be used equally well on frozen or rocky ground, and on bogs or marshlands. This fence is wired with six strands of barbed wire on the enemy side, four strands on the friendly side, and four strands on the base. In snow, the tripods can be lifted out of the snow with poles or other means to reset the obstacle on top of newly fallen snow. On soft ground, the base setting of tripods and the base wires give enough bearing surface to prevent the obstacle from sinking.

4-15. PORTABLE BARBED WIRE OBSTACLES

Standard concertinas are readily moved and are well adapted for the temporary closing of gaps or lanes, or for adding rapidly to the obstacle effect of fixed barriers such as the double apron fence. Other portable barbed wire obstacles are described below.

a. Spirals of loose wire. By filling open spaces in and between wire entanglements with spirals of loose wire, the obstacle effect is substantially increased. Spirals for such use are prepared as follows:

(1) Drive four 1-meter (3.3 ft.) posts in the ground to form a diamond 1 by l/2-meter (3.3 by 1.6 ft.).

(2) Wind 75 meters (246 ft.) of barbed wire tightly around the frame. Start winding at bottom and wind helically toward top.

(3) Remove wire from frame and tie at quarter points for carrying or hauling to site where it is to be opened and used. One spiral weighs less than 9.1 kg (20 lbs.) and a man can carry three or more of them by stepping inside the coils and using wire handles of the type furnished with the standard concertina.

(4) If spirals are needed in large quantities,

mount the diamond-shaped frame on the winch of a truck and use the winch to coil the wire.

b. Knife rest. The knife rest (fig. 4-33) is a portable wooden or metal frame strung with barbed wire. It is used wherever a readily removable barrier is needed; for example, at lanes in wire obstacles or at roadblocks. With a metal frame it can be used as an effective underwater obstacle in beach defenses. Knife rests are normally constructed with 3 to 4 meters (9.8 to 16.4 ft.) between cross members. They should be approximately 1 meter (3.3 ft.) high. The cross members must be firmly lashed to the horizontal member with plain wire. When placed in position, knife rests must be securely fixed.

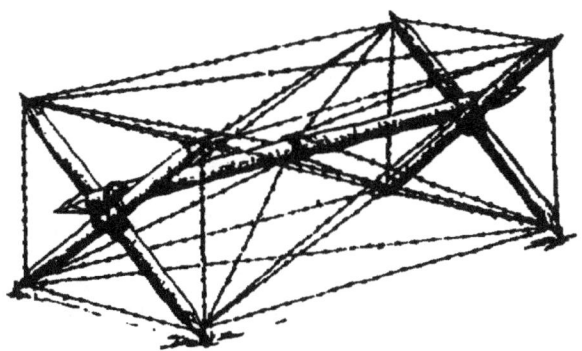

Figure 4-33. Knife rest.

c. Trip wires. Immediately after a defensive position is occupied and before an attempt is made to erect protective wire, trip wires should be placed just outside of grenade range, usually 30 to 40 meters (98 to 131 ft.). These wires should stretch about 23 centimeters (9 in.) above the ground and be fastened to pickets at not more than 5-meter (16.4 ft.) intervals. They should be concealed in long grass or crops on a natural line such as the side of a path or the edge of a field. The Trip wires should be placed in depth in an irregular pattern.

d. Tanglefoot. Tanglefoot (fig. 4-34) is used where concealment is essential and to prevent the enemy from crawling between fences and in front of emplacements. The obstacle should be employed in a minimum depth of 10 meters (32.8 ft.). The pickets should be spaced at irregular intervals of from 75 cm to 3 meters (2.5 to 10 ft.), and the height of the barbed wire should vary

Figure 4-34. Tanglefoot in barrier system.

4-24

between 23 to 75 cm (9 to 30 in.). Tanglefoot should be sited in scrub, if possible, using bushes as supports for part of the wire. In open ground, short pickets should be used. Growth of grass should be controlled to help prevent the enemy from secretly cutting lanes in, or tunneling under, the entanglement.

4-16. COMBINATION BANDS

As noted in paragraph 4-12, the high wire entanglement may be built with additional rows of fences and triangular cells to form bands of any desired depth or may be made more effective by adding front and rear aprons. Other types of fences may be combined in bands to form obstacles which are more difficult to breach than a single belt. Portable barbed wire obstacles may be added as described in paragraph 4-15. The construction of bands of varied types is desirable because this makes it difficult for the enemy to develop standard methods of passage and it permits fitting the obstacles to the situation and to the time and materials available. Six different types of effective combination bands are shown in figure 4-35. Other variations are readily developed.

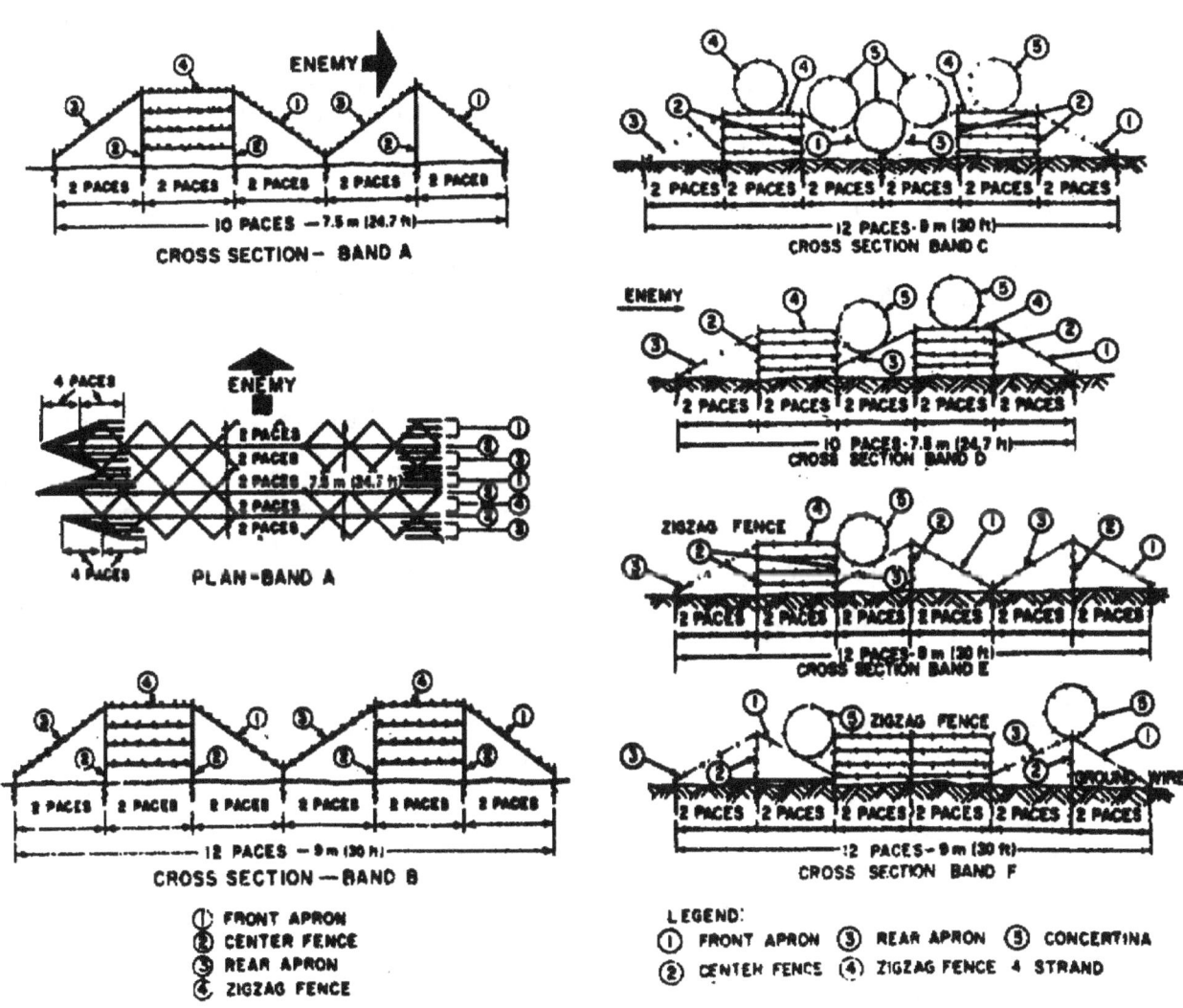

Figure 4-35. Combination bands of wire obstacles.

4-25

Section III. Material and Labor Estimates

4-17. BASIC CONSIDERATIONS

Barbed wire obstacles are constructed primarily from issue materials, thus, both logistical and construction estimates are involved. Table 4-1 gives weights, lengths, and other data required for estimating truck transportation and carrying party requirements. Table 4-2 gives the material and labor requirements for construction of various wire entanglements.

4-18. REQUIREMENTS FOR A DEFENSIVE POSITION

a. When estimating materials and labor requirements for wire entanglements deployed along the FEBA, use the following rules of thumb to determine the effective length of the entanglement:

(1) **Tactical wire:** Front x 1.25 x number of belts.

(2) **Protective wire:** Front x 5 x number of belts.

(3) **Supplementary wire:**

(a) **Forward of FEBA:** Front x 1.25 x number of belts.

(b) **Rear of FEBA:** Unit depth x 2.5 x number of belts.

b. When estimating material and labor requirements for wire entanglements deployed around a perimeter defensive position, use the following rules of thumb to determine the effective length of the entanglements.

(1) **Tactical wire:** Mean perimeter of the wire x 1.25 x number of belts.

(2) **Protective wire:** Mean perimeter of the wire x 1.10 x number of belts.

(3) **Supplementary wire:** Mean perimeter of the wire x 1.25 x number of belts.

c. **Method of estimating.** The following step-by-step procedure is recommended for estimating

material, labor, and transportation requirements for various lengths and types of wire entanglements.

(1) Determine the employment by use, whether Tactical, Protective, or Supplementary wire will be constructed.

(2) Determine the depth of employment by totaling the number of belts of wire.

(3) Determine the effective length of the entanglement by utilizing the appropriate rule of thumb in **a** or **b** above.

(4) In order to utilize table 4-3 to determine the quantities of material and the manhours required for construction, the effective length must be divided by 300. This gives you the number of 300 meter sections you would effectively construct. Carry this number out two decimal places and then round-off to the nearest tenth.

(a) Multiply the number of 300 meter sections times the values in table 4-3 according to the type of wire to be constructed. Pay careful attention to the footnotes for this table. You may have more than one choice of values and various factors may be required to adjust the table values.

(b) The number of 300 meter sections is multiplied by the appropriate value in each column of table 4-2, except for the column entitled **Kilograms of materials per linear meter of entanglement.** The value in this column is the average weight per meter and should be multiplied by the total effective length of the entanglement to determine the total weight of the required materials. Divide the total weight by the vehicle capacity to determine the number of trucks or truckloads required to haul the material. Footnote **b,** to table 4-2 states the vehicle capacity should be 2268 kgs, which equates to 2 1/2 tons. Use of this weight limit will enable you to make an accurate estimate of the number of trucks required, whether 2 1/2 ton cargo or 5 ton dump trucks are used. The 5-ton dump has less than 1/3 the volume capacity of the 2 1/2-ton cargo truck, and the bulk or volume of wire entanglement materials will limit a 5-ton dump truckload to approximately 2 1/2 tons.

SELF TEST

1. In which use of barbed wire is each series of concertinas placed about 10 meters in depth? (Para 4-1f, fig. 4-3)

2. How many more meters of barbed wire are on a full reel than are put on a bobbin? (Para 4-2c and d)

3. What advantage does barbed tape have over standard barbed wire? (Para 4-3e(1))

4. Why are the U-shaped steel pickets used to support wire entanglements emplaced with the hollow surface (concave side) facing enemy fire? (Para 4-4a(2))

5. In which direction should fence-building operations normally proceed? (Para 4-6)

6. How and why are the ends of the wire on bobbins marked? (Para 4-2d(5), 4-6a(4))

7. When a standard barbed wire concertina is being collapsed for transportation or storage, what keeps the bottom of the wire coil from fanning out? (Para 4-5a(1)(b))

8. Which kind of picket is recommended for the construction of wire entanglement in combat areas in close proximity to the enemy? (Para 4-6a(4), fig. 4-10)

9. In the construction of barbed wire entanglements, which tie is used to join two wires that cross? (Para 4-6d (4), fig. 4-13, 4-17)

10. In the construction of a four-strand cattle fence, which fence construction team installs the third strand from the top? (Para 4-7b(2))

11. What size unit is normally assigned the task of constructing a 300-meter section of double-apron fence? (Para 4-8b)

12. Which wires (numbered in sequence of installation) form the backbone of a double-apron fence? (Para 4-8b(2)(e), figs. 4-20, 4-22)

13. What does wire No. 12 of a double-apron fence have in common with wire No. 2? (Para 4-8b(2)(b) and (f))

14. After the pickets for a triple concertina fence have been installed, where is the first roll of concertina placed by the personnel that lay out the wire? (Para 4-10c(2), fig. 4-26)

15. Why is a strand of barbed wire stretched tightly along the top of front row concertina sections in the construction of a triple standard concertina fence? (Para 4-10d(3))

16. What barbed wire obstacle is used equally well in snow, rocky ground, or marshland? (Para 4-14)

17. Which barbed wire obstacle is constructed about 23 centimeters above the ground? (Para 4-15c)

    Situation: Given perimeter defense:

                 Tactical wire mean perimeter = 800 meters

                 Protective wire mean perimeter = 600 meters

                 Supplementary wire mean perimeter = 1000 meters
                      (See figure 4-36)

18. Estimate the amount of material, the truckloads, and the manhours required to construct one band (three belts in depth) of tactical wire using 4 and 2 pace double apron design. The fence will be constructed during daylight hours by inexperienced troops using U-shaped pickets and barbed tape. (Para 4-17 and 4-18)

19. Estimate the amount of material, the truckloads, and the manhours required to construct one belt of triple standard concertina for protective wire. The fence will be constructed during the daylight hours by experienced troops using U-shaped pickets and barbed wire. (Para 4-17 and 4-18)

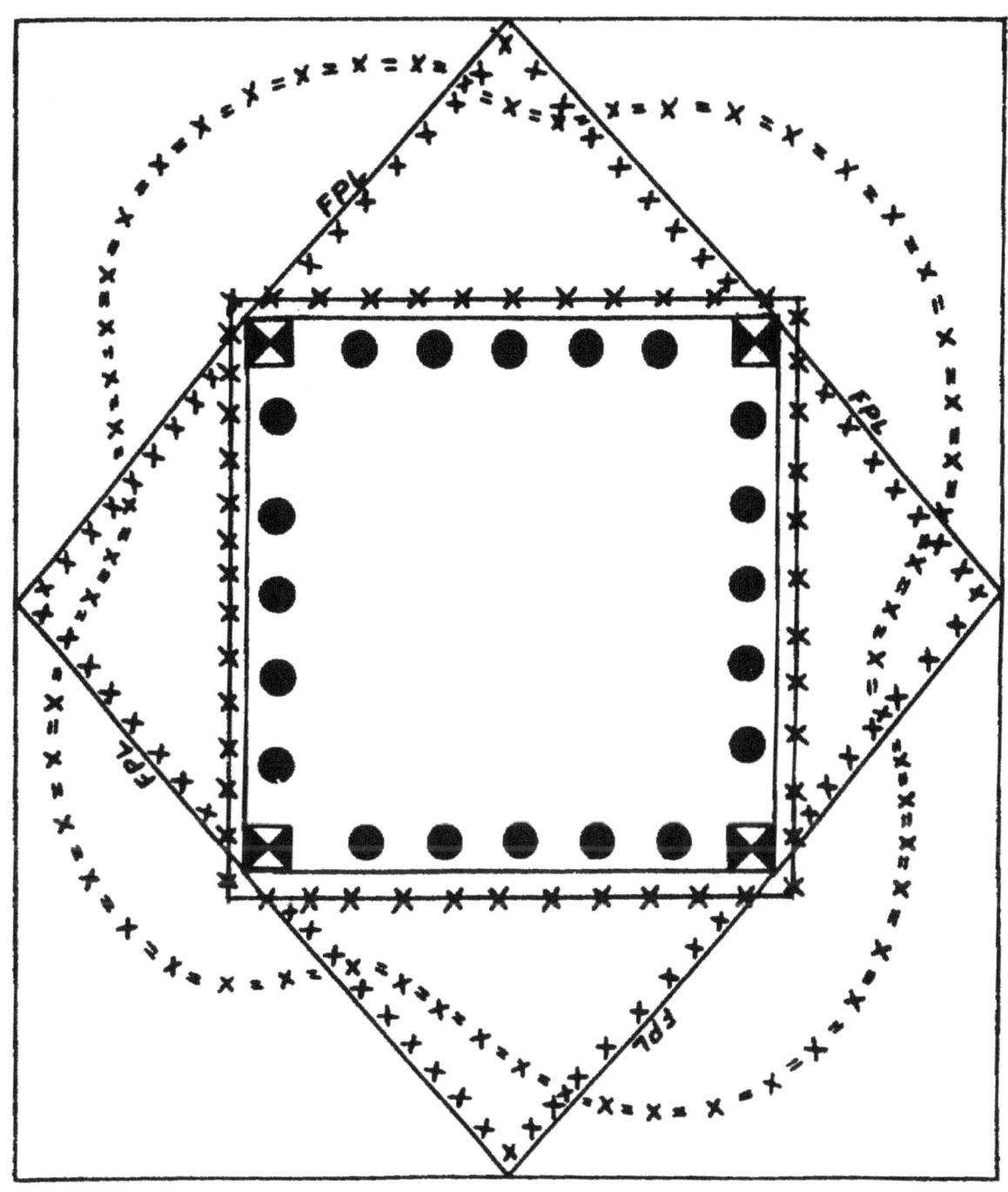

x x x Tactical wire   (800 meter mean perimeter)

x=x=x Supplementary wire   (1,000 meter mean perimeter)

x—x—x Protective wire   (600 meter mean perimeter)

Figure 4-36. Base camp (perimeter) defense.

4-29

LESSON 5

CAMOUFLAGE
(Protection Against Enemy Surveillance)

CREDIT HOURS.. 2

TEXT ASSIGNMENT.. Attached memorandum.

LESSON OBJECTIVES

Upon completion of this lesson on protection against enemy surveillance you should be able to accomplish the following in the indicated topic areas:

1. **Direct Surveillance.** Discuss the advantages and disadvantages of direct methods of surveillance.

2. **Indirect Surveillance.** Discuss the advantages and disadvantages of indirect methods of surveillance.

3. **Aerial Photography.** Discuss the advantages of oblique aerial photography as a method of indirect surveillance.

4. **Radar.** Describe how the ultra high frequency radio signals of radar are used to detect objects and installations.

5. **Doppler and SLAR Radar.** Discuss the advantages and disadvantages of doppler and SLAR radar in surveillance of military objectives and activities.

6. **Infrared.** Describe the two types of infrared detectors (active and passive) and protective measures required by units or activities.

7. **Factors of Recognition.** Discuss the factors of recognition -- shape or pattern, color or tone, texture, shadow, position, size, movement, sound, and smell -- and counter measures for protection.

8. **Siting.** Discuss terrain patterns and protective measures used to take advantage of pattern characteristics.

9. **Discipline.** Discuss night discipline and sound discipline and the control of tracks shine, and debris as elements in effective countersurveillance.

10. **Concealment Principles.** Discuss the three fundamental ways of concealing installation and activities -- hiding, blending, and disguising.

11. **Concealment of Field Fortifications.** Discuss the concealment consideration in the siting of field fortifications.

12. **Concealment of Artillery.** Discuss factors which lead to detection and prevention measures required.

13. **Concealment of Bivouacs.** Describe the sequence of countersurveillance measures structured in four stages -- planning, occupation, maintenance, and evacuation.

ATTACHED MEMORANDUM

Section I. Introduction

5-1. IMPORTANCE OF COUNTERSURVEILLANCE

a. Throughout history soldiers have employed techniques of camouflage to conceal themselves or their intentions from the enemy. Successful concealment adds the value of surprise in attack and provides security in defense. Although modern warfare employs increasingly complex and deadly weapon systems and highly sophisticated electronic surveillance devices, the necessity and importance of deceiving the enemy remains.

b. The essential part of any military deception is proper application of countersurveillance techniques and principles. Correctly used, countersurveillance can spell the difference between victory and defeat; to an individual, it can mean the difference between life and death. Small semi-independent units must furnish their own security, reconnaissance, surveillance, and countersurveillance. They must be able to exist for long periods of time with a minimum of control and support from higher headquarters. As a result, their success depends to a large extent upon their ability to remain undetected by the enemy.

5-2. DIRECT AND INDIRECT METHODS OF SURVEILLANCE AVAILABLE TO THE ENEMY

To be effective, camouflage measures must counter the detection methods available to the enemy. It is, therefore, necessary to understand surveillance methods: how each type of surveillance is employed, its advantages, its disadvantages, and how to achieve concealment from those detection methods the enemy is most likely to use. There are two broad categories of surveillance, direct and indirect.

a. Direct. When methods of detection are direct, the observer uses his senses, principally sight, hearing, and smell, to gather information about the existence, identification, or scope of enemy activity. Of these, by far the most important is sight. The human eye has a remarkable range sensitivity -- a

candle flame had been seen from a distance of 30 miles on a clear dark night. The ears are also sensitive -- tests indicate a ticking watch can be heard 20 feet away. Even though concealment from visual observation is complete, the sounds of voices, footfalls, or running engines easily give away a position. The sense of smell is often overlooked. The ability to detect and identify characteristic odors can lead to detection of the enemy. Under ideal conditions, cigarette smoke can be identified from a distance of a quarter of a mile; exhaust fumes and cooking odors carry even farther.

(1) Advantages of direct methods of surveillance. Direct methods of surveillance have many advantages:

(a) They provide immediate information on which action may be based.

(b) The information obtained is easily evaluated because it is natural and familiar.

(c) The human eye, ear, and nose are normally sensitive and accurate receivers.

(d) Movement is usually detected by direct observation.

(2) Disadvantages. There are four major disadvantages to direct methods of surveillance.

(a) There is no permanent record of the information obtained.

(b) Atmospheric conditions and time of day may hamper observation.

(c) The observer's experience and mission may limit the information obtained.

(d) Human error may cause incomplete or incorrect information.

b. Indirect. Indirect methods of surveillance include all of the mechanical, electrical, and chemical devices which extend the range of the human senses. Many of these devices record the detected image on film or tape. They include both ground and aerial cameras, infrared devices, chemical (olfactory) sensors, ground-to-ground and air-to-ground radar, and starlight scopes. All such devices have the effect of reducing or eliminating the protection once afforded by distance or darkness. To be effective, camouflage efforts must be designed to defeat these devices (table 5-1) as well as direct methods of surveillance.

(1) Advantages of indirect methods of surveillance. Among the advantages of indirect methods of surveillance are the following:

(a) Observations may be conducted from points out of range of enemy fire.

(b) Areas inaccessible to ground observers may be monitored by indirect methods.

(c) Certain spectrums, such as near and far infrared, which are invisible to the unaided eye, may be detected and recorded with special sensors or film.

(d) Most indirect detection devices provide a permanent record on film or tape. These recorded images, such as aerial photography and side-looking airborne radar as remote sensor imagery. All such imagery can be enlarged for more detailed study of suspect areas, can be thoroughly examined at leisure, and may be duplicated and distributed to other echelons for simultaneous use. Imagery of the same area repeated over a period of time can reveal tell-tale changes in the appearance of the terrain that would otherwise go unnoticed.

(2) **Disadvantages.** There are several disadvantages in the use of indirect methods of surveillance. Among these are the following:

Table 5-1. Surveillance Devices and Countersurveillance Means

Surveillance Device	Detection Capability	Countersurveillance Protective Means
1. Aerial Photo		
(a) Infrared film	reflects — differences between fresh and dried out vegetation	paints, fresh vegetation
(b) C D Film	high reflectant; reflects differences	paints, fresh vegetation; nets
(c) Color film	true color; reveals non-matching colors	improve camouflage
2. Radar		
(a) ground to ground (doppler)	detects movement; line of sight	slow, controlled movement; defilade; radar scattering materials; nets
(b) Air to ground (SLAR)	similar to aerial photo; but also can penetrate fog, haze	radar scattering materials; nets; dig in.
3. Infrared		
(a) Active	line of sight; reflectant-artificial vs. natural material differences revealed	defilade, eliminate contrasts of tone and color
(b) Passive	sensitive to heat rays (nets not effective against this)	reduce heat pick up by attenuating heat radiation; use of defilade and brush
4. Starlight scope	greatly amplifies reduced light to permit visual perception under night conditions	same measure as against visual detection in daylight
5. Olfactory sensors	detect chemical compounds	avoid unnecessary use of fuel burning engines, exhaust control; use of converters

(a) Time is needed to process and distribute the imagery.

(b) Bad weather may ground aircraft, obscure subjects, or interfere with electronics reception, especially doppler radar, and passive infrared devices.

(c) Skilled and trained personnel are needed both to operate complex electronic equipment and to interpret the imagery obtained.

(d) Special stereo-photography and stereoscopic viewing equipment is necessary to obtain a three-dimensional view with aerial photographs.

Section II. Indirect Surveillance Devices

5-3. AERIAL PHOTOGRAPHY

a. Detection capability. By far, the most commonly used surveillance method is photography, both ground and aerial. Aerial photography is indispensable in camouflage inspection and detection, revealing and recording data often unnoticed by the unaided eye. Film sensitivity has kept pace with the development of high resolution lens systems, making modern aerial cameras capable of recording minute detail from very high altitudes. Camouflage measures that are aimed only at ground observers will fail if the enemy has any aerial surveillance capability. Good camouflage must be three-dimensional to counter aerial surveillance.

b. Types of aerial photography. There are two major types of aerial photography in common use for surveillance purposes, **vertical** and **oblique**. Photography from multiple camera installations combining the two types, and from scanning-type (panoramic) cameras is also used. Most vertical photography is planned and flown for map-making purposes. Aerial photography for mapping purposes must meet very exacting requirements and must be flown under carefully controlled conditions. When available, such photography is invaluable to surveillance personnel. It is seldom obtainable, however, under combat conditions. Reconnaissance and surveillance needs are more often met by various kinds of oblique photography (fig 5-1), which cover a greater area with fewer flights. Many of the factors which provide the controlled geometry of mapping photography are disregarded in reconnaissance flights. When necessary, even pictures taken with hand-held cameras from helicopters or other small aircraft can provide valuable information. For purposes of camouflage

detection, it should be remembered in areas of moderate to rugged relief, defilade may limit the information recorded on low altitude oblique photography.

5-4. RADAR

Radar detecting devices emit radio signals, usually in the form of pulses of an ultrahigh frequency, which are reflected from the object being viewed and received back at the point of transmission. By analyzing these minute reflected signals, the characteristics of the object under observation may be determined. Two types of radar equipment are commonly used for surveillance purposes: ground-to-ground (doppler) radar, and air-to-ground radar, which includes side-looking airborne radar (SLAR).

a. Doppler radar is a line-of-sight device used primarily to detect movement. Because it is line-of-sight, maximum use of defilade is the best means of avoiding detection by doppler radar. Very slow, controlled movement is effective against certain types of these devices. Doppler radar is less effective when it is raining because of the resulting clutter in the reception of pulses.

b. Air-to-ground radar is generally used with film or tape to record the reflected pulses. The resulting imagery is similar in appearance to aerial photography and has been extensively used for mapping purposes in areas of heavy cloud cover, where light sensitive film cannot be used. The radar waves penetrate fog, haze, or smoke and return an accurate indication of the shape of the terrain. This penetrating quality of air-to-ground radar waves is invaluable in

Low Oblique

Figure 5-1. Low oblique photograph.

detecting hidden radar-reflectant equipment. It is important to remember foliage cover alone cannot be relied upon completely to defeat detection by air-to-ground radar. Concealment from this form of radar depends upon reduction or scattering of the reflected pulses, achieved by digging in, defilade, or the use of special radar-scattering screening materials.

5-5. INFRARED

a. There are two types of infrared detectors: active (near) emits electromagnetic energy not visible to the human eyes; passive (far) is sensitive to the longest, or thermal wavelengths of the spectrum, and detects, rather than emits energy.

b. Active infrared, like doppler radar, emits line-of-sight waves. It also detects the different reflectant qualities of natural and artificial materials. Any of the measures which reduce or eliminate the contrast between objects and their natural backgrounds are effective countermeasures against this type of surveillance. These include tree canopy, cut green vegetation, net screening systems, and all camouflage paints used for pattern painting.

c. Concealment from passive infrared depends upon reducing heat emission of subjects which are hotter than their surroundings. Therefore, some insulation or shield must be used. Defilade, heavy brush, or even tree cover will at least attenuate the heat radiation; to what extent depends upon the density or thickness of the cover. It should also be noted screening nets, although they reflect active infrared waves, do not shield a hidden object which emits heat from detection by passive infrared devices. These devices are affected by rain, however, which can cause sufficient clutter in the receiver to render them ineffective.

5-6. OTHER TYPES OF SENSORS

a. **Starlight scopes** are special optical devices which greatly amplify reduced light to permit visual perception under night conditions.

Countermeasures include all of the means of concealment from visual detection in daylight.

b. **Olfactory (chemical sensors).** Various kinds of sensors can detect and identify certain chemical compounds associated with military activities or equipment. In general, the effectiveness of such devices can be reduced by avoiding unnecessary operation of any fuel-burning engine, and by keeping all engines in efficient operating condition to cut down on the discharge of exhaust fumes. Another measure is the installation of converters which break down detectable chemical compounds into components which do not affect the sensors.

Section III. Factors of Recognition

5-7. GENERAL

All objects, especially those of military significance, have certain characteristics that help to determine their identities. These characteristics, called **factors of recognition**, must be hidden or disguised to prevent detection by any form of enemy surveillance. Ground observers rely on six such factors of recognition related to appearance: shape, color, texture, shadow, position, and movement. In addition, sounds and smells provide identifying clues. These factors, with the exception of movement, sound, and smell, are also important to the aerial observer and photo interpreter, although his viewpoint differs somewhat. When studying black and white photography, including infrared, he considers tonal values instead of color. Pattern as well as shape is another factor in photo interpretation. The arrangement of certain objects may be apparent to the aerial observer and reveal items hidden to the ground observer. Finally, the relative size of objects, especially buildings, provides still another clue. The perceptive observer or interpreter relies on deductive reasoning, based on one, several, or all of these factors to detect and identify anything of military significance. Therefore, camouflage measures must be designed to eliminate everyone of these tell-tale factors, and to conceal from airborne as well as ground-based

surveillance. One factor overlooked may not conclusively identify an object, but it will invite closer inspection, which often spells detection.

5-8. FACTORS

a. **Shape or pattern.** Shape is probably the most important single factor in recognizing the objects around us. It is also of great importance in recognizing objects from their photographic images. Items of military equipment, such as trucks, tanks, and guns, have distinctive outlines, making them easy to identify, on the ground or on photographs. Thus, it is very important to avoid any position which creates a silhouette against the sky or a contrasting background. The characteristic shape of an object can be hidden or altered by the use of screening nets, branches of foliage, tree canopy, or digging in. One of the objectives of pattern painting is to alter the apparent shape of objects. Seen from the air, man-made features usually are regular in form, or have straight or smoothly-curved lines. Examples of these are buildings, highways, and railroads. Natural features, such as streams, shorelines, or wooded areas, are generally irregular in shape. In addition, the way objects are arranged on the ground sometimes creates distinctive patterns which are easy to identify by aerial observers. Examples of such patterns are military posts, ammunition dumps, and housing developments. The orderly rows of trees in an orchard, seen from the air, contrasts sharply with the random growth of natural vegetation. To avoid detection, avoid creating a characteristic pattern that reveals a military activity (fig 5-2)

b. Color or tone. Strong, bright, sharply-contrasting colors are quickly noticed, and can even be seen through screening nets. Color is also an important factor when color or camouflage detection (CD) aerial film is used for surveillance. Colors which do not blend properly into the surrounding terrain are immediately apparent on color photographs. The red-blue/green color contrast on CD film reveals poor camouflage as well as objects that are not camouflaged at all. On black-and-white and infrared photos, tones of gray indicate differences in color, textures, or infrared reflectance. To counter the revealing factor of color or tonal differences, all military equipment and clothing should blend as much as possible with the surrounding terrain, and should be infrared reflectant. Darker shades are usually less noticeable than lighter shades of the same color. Camouflage materials such as paints, nets, and clothing are available in different seasonal and climate color blends to match as

Figure 5-2. Trees bordering air strips cut in irregular patterns rather than in straight lines, to avoid creating a tell-tale pattern.

closely as possible the surrounding terrain. If cut foliage is used, it must be kept fresh and replaced when necessary to retain its infrared-reflectant qualities.

c. **Texture.** Closely related to tone, texture refers to the ability of an object to reflect, absorb, or diffuse light. It may be defined as the relative smoothness or roughness of the surface. A rough surface, such as a field of grass, reflects little light and casts many shadows on itself. Consequently, it appears very dark to the eye or on a photograph. A smooth surface, such as an airstrip, even though it might be painted the same color as the surrounding terrain would show up as a lighter tone on a photograph. Very smooth, almost textureless surfaces reflect both natural and artificial light. This is known as shine, one of the most revealing breaches of camouflage discipline. Every effort must be made to eliminate the shine from smooth surfaces, including windshields, headlights, lenses of glasses, boots, even skin. Covering these surfaces with rough-textured materials or mud will reduce or eliminate the reflection of light. Texturing materials can be applied to smooth paved surfaces to help them blend with the surrounding ground and reduce tonal contrasts.

d. **Shadow.** The shadow of an object often provides the only clue in determining its identity. Viewed from directly above, water towers, smoke stacks, power line towers, and similar tall structures appear as circles or dots. Their shadows, however, reveal their characteristic outlines, as though viewed from the side, and help to establish their identities. Sometimes it may be more important to disrupt the shadow of an object than it is to conceal the object itself.

e. **Position or site.** The locations of certain objects with relation to other features can identify many photo images not easily recognized by themselves. Factories or warehouses are usually beside a railroad or railroad siding. Schools may be identified by their adjacent athletic fields. A water tower next to a railroad station and a silo next to a barn would be difficult to distinguish from each other were it not for the nearby railroad tracks or cultivated fields. In creating simulations of disguising military items, it is important to retain a logical relation to other nearby features, in a plausible and convincing site.

f. **Size.** The size of unknown objects on a photograph as determined from the scale of the photography or a comparison with known objects of known size aids in their identification. Both the relative and the absolute sizes are important. For example, in a built-up area, the smaller buildings are usually dwellings and the larger buildings, commercial or community buildings. Large important structures can be easily identified by their size. The roof of such a structure can be painted, walkways added, and foliage carefully placed to create the illusion of several small insignificant buildings.

g. **Movement.** Although the factor of movement seldom reveals the identity of an object by itself, it is the most important one for revealing existence. Even though the other factors of recognition have been completely eliminated, an enemy observer will be attracted to the area if movement is not controlled. He may even be concentrating his attention elsewhere but he will not fail to detect movement in another area through his peripheral vision. It should also be remembered movement can be detected by ground-to-ground radar. To reduce the chances of detection, quick or unnecessary movement should be avoided. Move slowly and carefully, following the natural lines of the terrain as much as possible.

h. **Sound.** Sound has pitch, loudness, and tone, which can be used to identify its nature and origin, and to pinpoint its exact location. Carelessness with regard to sound discipline can reveal the kind and quantity of equipment and even the size of a unit. All tell-tale sounds, even whispering, should be kept to a minimum, especially at night. When sound cannot be avoided, its identity can sometimes be masked by so-called "sound screens", which are stronger sounds created by the firing of machine guns or artillery pieces; the running of tanks, prime movers and tractor engines along a broad front; or by the operation of sound projection stations which imitate various battle sounds.

i. Smell. The factor of smell was relatively ignored for a long time as a means of detection except by close ground observers. Yet the characteristics exhaust from fuel-burning engines, cooking odors, and campfire and tobacco smoke as clues which can linger long enough to lead the enemy directly to your position. The development of chemical and olfactory sensors make is possible to detect traces of such odors no longer discernible by the human nose. The best defense against this factor of recognition is to avoid creating tell-tale odors if possible. Good maintenance of fuel-burning engines, and strict discipline while in bivouac are measures that will reduce the creation of traceable odors.

Section IV. Methods of Countering Factors of Recognition

5-9. THREE PRINCIPLES

In the previous paragraphs you learned about the various methods of direct and indirect surveillance, and how the factors of recognition are used to detect and identify military personnel, equipment, or activity. To counter these factors, the principles of camouflage have been developed, and despite the sophistication of modern techniques, are essentially the same today as they were in ancient times. Good camouflage now, as then, is based on three principles: siting, discipline, and construction.

5-10. SITING

Siting for camouflage is choosing the most advantageous position in which to hide personnel, equipment, or activity. Every type of terrain has some characteristic which may be used to aid concealment (fig. 5-3). Proper siting, taking maximum advantage of these characteristics, can reduce and sometimes eliminate the need for artificial camouflage. The factors which govern site selection are as follows:

a. Mission. The most important consideration in the selection of a site for any military use is the mission of the unit. However excellent a site may be from the concealment standpoint, if it in any way inhibits the accomplishment of the mission, it is useless.

b. Size. The site must be of sufficient size to permit proper dispersal for effective operation. Such dispersal is necessary not only for concealment, but also to reduce losses from enemy fire.

c. Terrain patterns. Terrain can be divided into four general types, each of which has a distinctive and characteristic appearance from the air. The site chosen must provide concealment without disturbing or altering the characteristic pattern of the terrain. The four terrain types are: agricultural, urban, wooded, and barren.

(1) Agricultural. The controlled lines created by cultivation, such as fence lines, hedgerows and furrows, are the most prominent characteristic of agricultural terrain. In flat areas, this may appear as a checkerboard pattern resulting from different types of crops. In more rolling country, the curved parallel lines of contour plowing or terracing are typical. In any case, siting in such rural areas must conform with the existing pattern, leaving it unaltered in appearance.

(2) Urban. Cities, towns, and villages also have controlled lines, in these cases created by the regular pattern of streets, bordered on each side by buildings and carefully spaced trees. Most urban areas provide abundant concealment with numerous shadowed areas and large warehouses, factories, or garages.

(3) Wooded. Wooden terrain is characterized by irregular forest outlines, streams, and relief features. In densely

WRONG

RIGHT

Figure 5-3. Example of proper siting and dispersal of tents in sparsely vegetated terrain (barren).

wooded areas, the tree canopy provides excellent concealment from most visual or camera surveillance. Even sparsely wooded areas afford some protection if proper dispersal is practiced.

(4) Barren. Irregular terrain features, without the controlled man-made lines of agricultural or urban areas are also typical of barren terrain. These features consist of washes, drifts, and other irregular folds, scattered rock accumulations, and scrub growth. The best siting measures for such areas are to make maximum use of the shadowed parts of the terrain, and of defilade.

5-11. DISCIPLINE

The second basic condition for the achievement of success in any camouflage effort is the strict maintenance of camouflage discipline, by both the unit as a whole and the individual soldier. This means avoidance of any activity that changes the appearance of an area or reveals the presence of military equipment (table 5-2). Camouflage discipline is a continuous, around-the-clock necessity and applies to every individual. If the rigid routine of such discipline, both visual and audio, is not followed by one man, the entire camouflage effort will fail. Carelessness and laxness will undoubtedly reveal the position to the enemy. Tracks, spoil, and debris are the most common signs of concealed military activity or objects.

a. Tracks. Tracks are especially revealing to the aerial observer. They indicate type, location, strength, and even intentions of a unit. Often a single track across an area of low vegetation is clearly visible. This is especially true in the early morning hours when there is a heavy dew. The gradual turns of wheeled vehicles are distinguishable from the skidding turns of a track laying vehicle. Tracks should follow closely and be parallel to hedges, fences, cultivated fields, and other natural terrain lines in order to remain inconspicuous from the air (fig. 5-4). Tracks should always continue past the position to a logical termination. On short stretches, exposed tracks may be erased by brushing out, or by covering with leaves and debris.

b. Tracks in snowy areas. In snow covered terrain, concealment of tracks is a major problem. Even in light snow, tracks make strong shadow lines visible from great distances. Sharp turns should be avoided because the resulting snow ridges cast even heavier shadows. The same principles stressed throughout this discussion apply to snow covered terrain, with a bit more emphasis on following natural shadow-casting terrain lines. It is also important all vehicles keep to the same tracks. Vehicles leaving the tracks or road may achieve short periods of track concealment by driving directly into or away from the sun, as

Table 5-2. Camouflage Disciplinary Measures

Revealing Element	Disciplinary Measures*
Siting Deficiencies	Have vehicle movement and emplacement conform to terrain patterns. Strictly follow unit SOP in planning, occupation, maintenance, and evacuation of an area.
Tracks	Strict conformity with track plan by member of unit. Stay on existing routes if possible. Have tracks continue past location to logical destination. Locate tracks close to and parallel to hedges, fences, and cultivated fields. Follow terrain lines.
Shine	Cover with nonreflecting material such as burlap, brush, mud, etc. Conceal mess kits, watch crystals, etc.
Sound	Minimize sound of engine exhausts, troop activity, etc. Use of sound screens.
Spoil and Debris	Cover or place to blend with surroundings.
Smell	Avoid creating tell-tale odors if possible.
Shadows	Locate vehicle within larger shadow (such as cast by a building). Locate vehicle so that its shadow is cast on an irregular object such as roadside trees and brush, rocky hillside, etc.
Snow Covered Terrain	Take advantage of dark features of the landscape (woods, etc). Use drags to smooth out tracks in snow.

*These measures should be included in a detailed unit SOP.

shadows cast by these tracks will not be apparent until the sun strikes them from an angle. Short lengths of tracks may be obliterated if they are not too deep, by trampling them with snowshoes.

c. Shine. Siting and track discipline do much to conceal a vehicle, but shine can nullify the best site and finest track discipline. Shine is always present when there is light in the sky, sunlight, moonlight, or the light of flares. It is caused by the reflection of light from windshields, windows, mess kits, watch crystals, and other such smooth almost textureless surfaces. Even the lenses of field glasses, when used in direct sunlight, can reflect a bright shine similar to that of a mirror. These danger spots must be concealed by any means. The betraying nature of shine should never be underestimated. Even under heavy overhead cover, shiny objects may be revealed through the smallest of gaps. They should be covered with nonreflecting material such as blankets, tarpaulins, burlap, or even mud.

d. Night discipline. No less important is strict observance of blackout rules. At night, windows, hatches, entrances, and other openings through which light can shine must be covered with shutters, screens, curtains, and other special opaque materials to prevent enemy ground and air observers from noticing the interior illumination. Fires can be lighted only in specially designated and equipped areas. Smoking is forbidden near the enemy, as is the display of lights of any type. Combat and transport vehicles can be allowed to travel only with their lights turned off or obscured. Aerial photographs taken at night by the light of flares or by the use of image intensification equipment can pick up breaches in camouflage discipline, which are more likely to occur at night than in the daylight hours. Consequently the same standard of camouflage discipline must be adhered to by night as by day.

e. Sound discipline. Troops must pay special attention to sound camouflage during night movement and apply all principles of scouting and patrolling. During nighttime river crossings, the noise from the paddles should be muffled. Revealing sounds from tank and truck movement or from engineering work can be muffled by sound screens.

f. Spoil and debris. Spoil and debris must be covered, or placed to blend with the

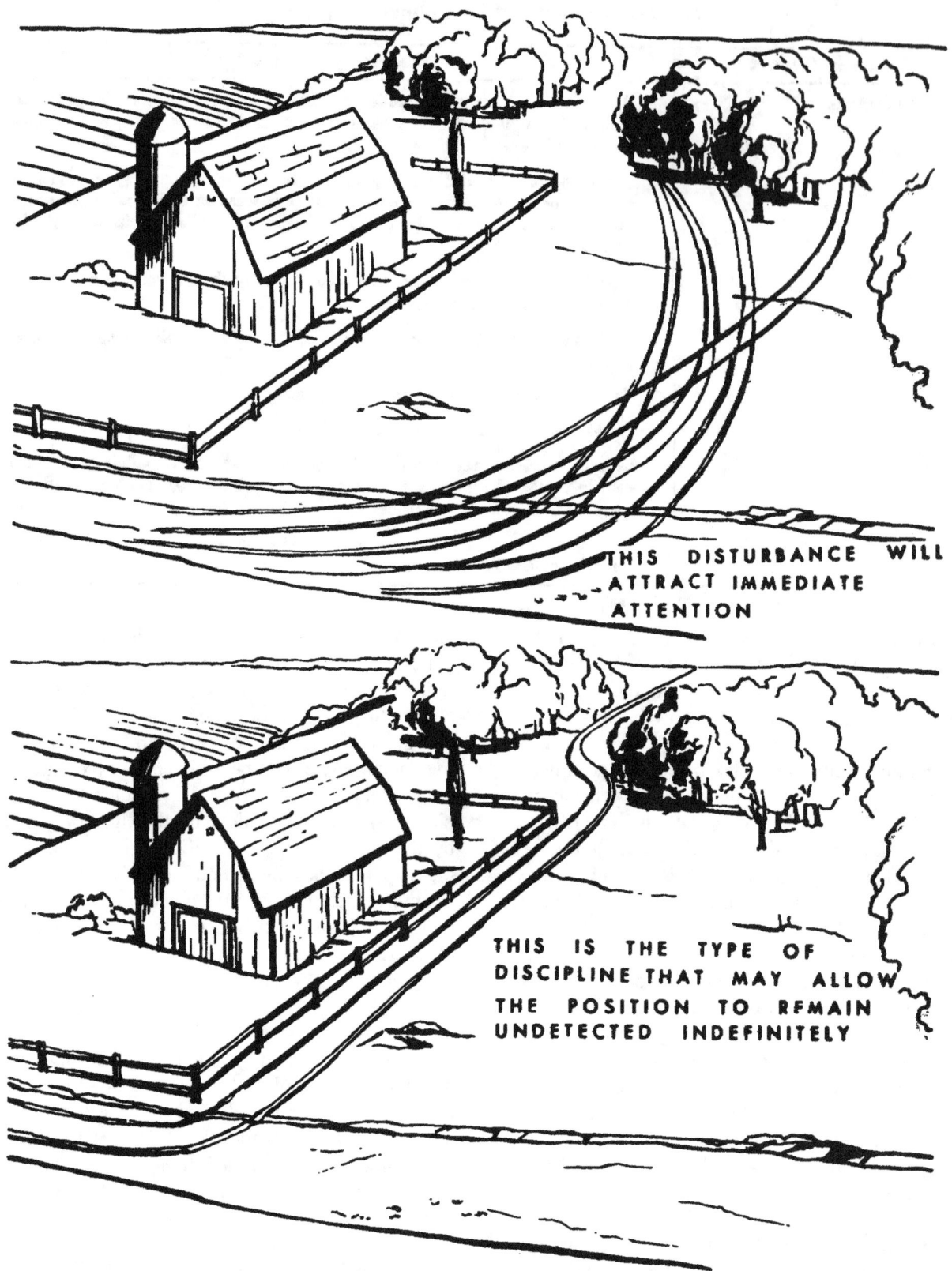

Figure 5-4. Track discipline.

surrounding. Excess dirt from digging fortifications can be dumped in streams or spread inconspicuously along roads. Under no circumstances should any trash or litter be left where it can be seen, even after a unit has vacated an area.

5-12. CAMOUFLAGE CONSTRUCTION.

The third and final principle on which good camouflage is based is camouflage construction. When the terrain and natural vegetation are such that natural concealment is not possible, artificial camouflage is added. Artificial or natural materials are used to help blend the object or individual with the surrounding terrain. Camouflage construction should be resorted to only when siting and discipline cannot produce the desired concealment. Natural materials are preferred over artificial materials, since the former resembles the surrounding vegetation of terrain. If artificial materials are used, they must be arranged to blend with the surroundings to the greatest possible degree. They must be of sturdy construction to withstand varying weather conditions, and must be constantly checked and maintained. The construction work must be hidden, with the work parties observing the strictest discipline. If possible, all engineering work should be carried out at night, with all traces of the night's activities camouflaged before morning. There should be no disruption of the terrain pattern; no destruction of plants or trampled grasses; nor should there be any new roads or open ditches visible. This is difficult to do, but unless discipline is maintained during such construction, there is little point to the camouflage effort.

5-13. BASIC CONCEALMENT METHODS IN COUNTERSURVEILLANCE

After the unit or an activity has been sited, there are three fundamental ways of concealing installations and activities: hiding, blending, and disguising.

a. Hiding. Hiding is the complete concealment of an object from any form of enemy observation by some type of physical screen. Sod over the mines in a minefield hides the mines; the overhead canopy of trees hides the objects beneath it from aerial observation; a defilade hides objects from ground observation; a net hides objects beneath it; a road screen hides the obstacle behind it. In some cases, the screen itself may be invisible to the enemy. In other instances, while visible to the enemy, a screen conceals the amount and type of activity behind it. Problems of concealment have been made more difficult by the development of electronic surveillance devices. Concealment from visual observations is no longer enough. The detection capability of the enemy must be determined; if it includes remote sensory equipment such as near or far infrared devices or radar devices, appropriate counter measures must be employed.

b. Blending. Blending is the use of natural or artificial materials to reduce or eliminate contrast and make individuals or equipment appear to be part of the background or surrounding terrain. For example, the individual can apply stick face paint to the exposed areas of the skin, can add burlap and foliage to his helmet, and can stain or paint his clothing in a mottled pattern so he will blend into the background. Vehicles and other equipment are pattern painted to alter the identifying angles of their shapes and make them less conspicuous.

c. Disguising. Disguising is the third method of camouflage. It consists of changing the appearance of troops, material, equipment, or installations in order to mislead the enemy as to their true identity. For example, supplies or ammunition can be stacked and covered with hay to resemble the haystacks of the region. The roof and surroundings of a large military building can be altered to create the impression of several small unimportant structures.

d. Simulations. A simulation, sometimes called a "dummy" or "decoy", is a false representation of actual personnel, equipment, or material employed to give the appearance of the real item. Although strictly speaking, simulations are not camouflage measures, they are often associated with camouflage techniques in large-scale deceptive operations. Simulations are openly displayed to draw enemy attention away from the true military targets, which have been concealed by one or more of the camouflage techniques discussed above.

Section V. Countersurveillance Methods for Field Fortifications and Artillery

5-14. FIELD FORTIFICATIONS

a. Siting. After the demands of the military situation and the mission have been met, siting with proper background is the first consideration given to the concealment of a fortification. From the standpoint of ground observation, the emplacement should be sited to avoid creating a silhouette against the sky or against a background of contrasting color. To avoid air observation, the emplacement should be located under trees, bushes, or in dark areas of the terrain.

(1) It is equally important that the concealing cover chosen is not isolated, since a lone clump of vegetation or solitary structure is a conspicuous hiding place and will draw enemy fire whether the enemy sees anything or not.

(2) The natural look of the terrain should not be disturbed. This is the best accomplished by removing or camouflaging the spoil.

(3) Natural terrain lines, such as edges of fields, fences, hedge-rows, and rural cultivation patterns are excellent sites for emplacements to reduce the possibility of aerial observation (fig. 5-5). Regular geometric layouts are to be avoided.

b. Construction. Before any excavation is started, all natural materials, such as turf, leaves, forest humus, or snow are removed and placed inside to be used later for restoring the natural appearance of the terrain. Concealment while constructing an elaborate fortification is vital.

c. Covers. When a position cannot be sited under natural cover, camouflaged covers are valuable aids in preventing detection. Materials native to the area are preferred, but when using materials (fig. 5-6) over an emplacement they must be replaced before they wilt and change color, leading to detection. Artificial materials may be used effectively, such as those made to simulate tall grass, bushes, stumps, and rocks, whichever the terrain calls for. They are valuable principally against aerial observation. They are light in weight and may be easily pushed out of the way.

d. Machine gun positions. The machinegun receives the close attention of enemy troops and its concealment must be as perfect as possible. Usually, machinegun emplacements are hasty, in which case camouflage means siting to best advantage and then using any materials at hand.

e. Mortars. Mortars should always be sited in defilade. Since a mortar covering a designated target area has a wider choice of position than the other smaller weapons, such defilade can almost always be found and concealment from direct ground observation is fairly easy. Proper siting in shadow and broken ground pattern, making certain there is the necessary overhead clearance for firing, together with intelligent use of natural and artificial materials offer the required mortar concealment from the air.

5-15. VEHICLES

a. Revealing factors. A badly concealed vehicle can lead to much more than just a lost vehicle; it may mean discovery of a unit, disclosure of an important tactical plan, or complete destruction of an installation. Camouflage of vehicles depends not only on concealing the vehicles themselves, their shine, shadow, and shape, but equally on preventing and concealing their all-revealing tracks. (It must be remembered that enemy ground and aerial observation is drawn

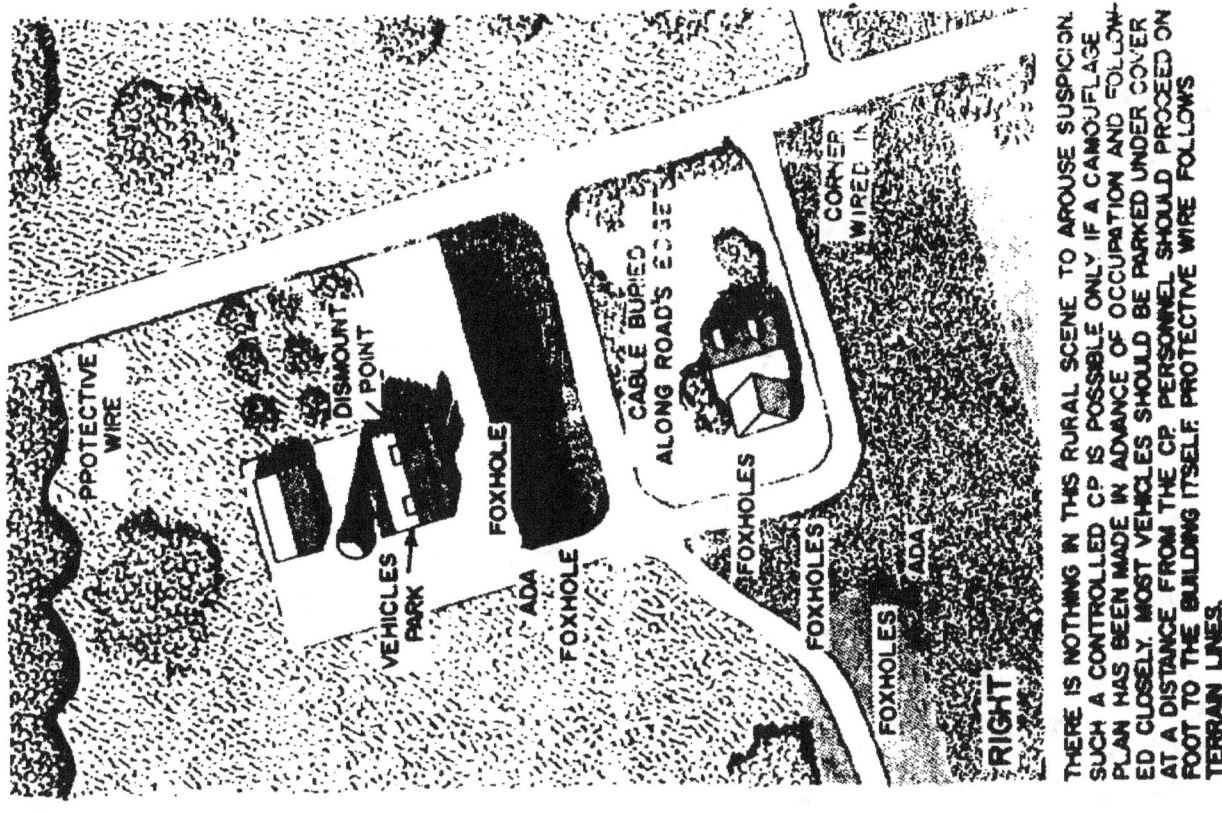

THERE IS NOTHING IN THIS RURAL SCENE TO AROUSE SUSPICION. SUCH A CONTROLLED CP IS POSSIBLE ONLY IF A CAMOUFLAGE PLAN HAS BEEN MADE IN ADVANCE OF OCCUPATION AND FOLLOW-ED CLOSELY. MOST VEHICLES SHOULD BE PARKED UNDER COVER AT A DISTANCE FROM THE CP. PERSONNEL SHOULD PROCEED ON FOOT TO THE BUILDING ITSELF. PROTECTIVE WIRE FOLLOWS TERRAIN LINES.

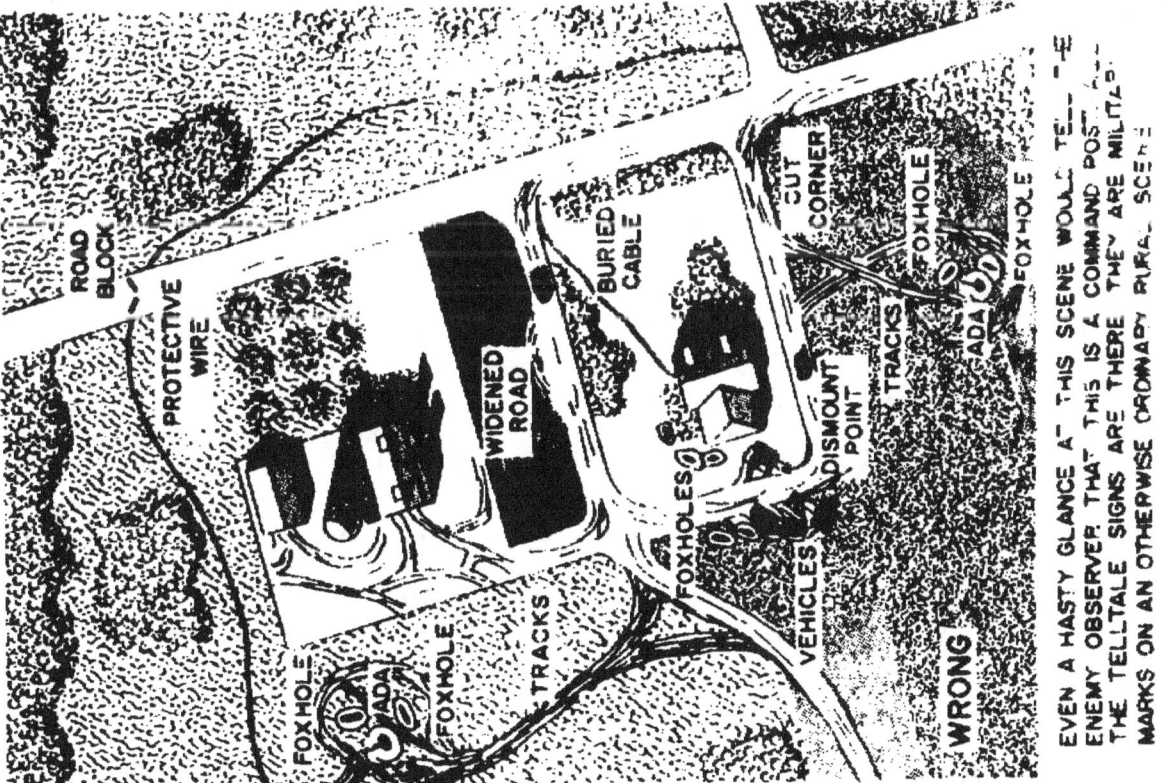

EVEN A HASTY GLANCE AT THIS SCENE WOULD TELL THE ENEMY OBSERVER THAT THIS IS A COMMAND POST. THE TELLTALE SIGNS ARE THERE THEY ARE MILITARY MARKS ON AN OTHERWISE ORDINARY RURAL SCENE.

Figure 5-5. Layout of a command post.

Figure 5-6. Camouflage using natural materials.

quickest by anything that moves, and that nothing can be done to conceal vehicles moving through undergrowth or along exposed routes.)

(1) Tracks. Control of the tracks made by vehicles of all types is one of the more critical aspects of camouflage discipline. Poorly concealed tracks can reveal not only position, but the types and numbers of the vehicles that left them. Tracks are sometimes more visible from the air than from the ground.

(2) Shine. Shine is a revealing factor which applies especially to vehicles. The many smooth surfaces on vehicles reflect even low intensity light. Windshields, headlights, metal housings, and similar reflecting surfaces must be covered.

(3) Shadow. The shadow cast by a vehicle is a revealing factor which must be concealed as

part of any vehicle camouflage measures. Also important are the smaller shadow areas contained within the vehicle itself, such as the shadow line of a truck body in and around the cab, beneath the fenders, within the wheels, and in the open back of the cargo space.

b. Camouflage measures.

(1) Siting and dispersion. As is always the case in camouflage, the goal of good vehicle siting is to occupy the terrain without altering its appearance. To accomplish this, vehicles should be parked under natural cover whenever available. When cover is inadequate, they should be parked so the shape of the vehicle will disappear into the surroundings. Before a driver can site his vehicle to take advantage of the concealment possibilities of his surroundings, he must know how the different terrains look from the air. In combat zones this knowledge is as important as knowing how to drive the vehicles.

(2) Track discipline. The most reliable way to eliminate tracks as a factor revealing details about vehicles is to continually practice the principles of track discipline. Vehicles should follow and parallel existing terrain lines, such as hedges, fences, and field line. Tracks should always continue past their destination to a logical termination. Whenever possible, using existing roads whenever possible prevents the creation of new, easily-spotted tracks across fields or open country. Even the comparatively small amount of timber which must be cut down to clear a roadway through a wooded area leaves gaps in the overhead cover that are clearly seen from the air. Partially concealed roads do exist, however, and they are better than exposed ones. Reconnaissance parties should locate them. Any gaps in overhead cover on such a road can be concealed by erecting overhead screens of either artificial or natural materials. On short stretches, exposed tracks may be erased by brushing leaves and debris over them. All concealed routes should be marked in advance of use and guards should be posted to insure minimum disturbance in the area.

(3) Track plan. If possible, before a unit occupies a position, a quartering party should first make a reconnaissance and layout a concealed on-way track plan. No vehicle should enter the new area until then. This plan should be laid out to fit into the terrain pattern as inconspicuously as possible by taking advantage of existing roads, overhead cover, and shadow casting lines. Many factors must be considered in such a plan: duration of occupation; time allowed for entering and leaving; size, character, and mission of occupying unit; distance from the enemy; and weather effect on visibility. A standard track plan is impossible - an individual solution is required for each position. In addition to laying out a plan on the ground itself, a plan should be sketched on either a map overlay or a sketch of the area. Parking areas should be indicated as well as those portions of routes to be patrolled by traffic guides.

(4) Training. Since a unit may have to occupy a position without prior reconnaissance, unit camouflage training must insure all personnel are trained to follow terrain patterns and utilize all overhead cover, when possible. Particular attention must be directed to training of vehicle drivers, so they will follow these rules automatically, even in the absence of NCO's and officers. The officers and NCO's must instruct all personnel that when the first

vehicle enters an area, guards must be stationed at critical points to direct traffic. This prevents unnecessary vehicle slowdown, stopping, or jamming on a roadway.

(5) Using shadows. In addition to the shadow cast by the vehicle itself, which must be disrupted as much as possible (fig. 5-7), there are shadows cast by larger objects which, under certain circumstances, can provide concealment for limited periods. Whether or not a shadow cast by a large object is reliable enough to conceal a parked vehicle depends upon the geographical latitude, the time of year, and the time of day. For example, in the northern hemisphere in winter, when the sun remains fairly low in the sky, there is usually sufficient shadow on the north side of a building or other large object to safely conceal a parked vehicle. In the summer, when the sun is high overhead, there is little or no shadow on the north side. Similarly, shadows on either the east or west side are available for half a day only. When these variables are completely understood, parking in a shadowed area can provide good short-term concealment. In certain instances, parking on the sunny side and close to a larger object throws the vehicular shadow on the object, concealing or disrupting it enough to

Figure 5-7. Throw the shadow onto something irregular.

prevent detection, against for short periods only.

(6) **Use of natural materials.** While good siting and dispersion are essential, sometimes they are not enough. Greater concealment can be achieved by supplementing these measures with natural materials to break up the shape and shadows of the vehicles. Materials are almost always available near a parking site and can be erected and removed quickly. When cut foliage is used, it should be replaced as soon as it starts to wither. Altering the color of vehicles or adding texture to them are other ways to supplement siting and dispersion. Color may be changed by applying mud to the body and tarpaulin. Texture may be added all over or in pattern shapes by attaching leaves, heavy grass, or coarse sand to the surface with an adhesive.

(7) **Pattern painting.** Pattern painting of a vehicle is not a cure-all. It is, however, a valuable supplement to other camouflage measures. Added to good siting, dispersion, discipline, and the use of nets, it increases the benefits derived from such measures. Vehicle patterns are designed to disrupt the cube shape of vehicles from all angles of view, to disrupt shadows, and to tie in with the shadow at the rear of a vehicle when it is faced into the sun, as well as the large dark shadow areas of windows, mudguards, wheels, and undercarriage. The standard patterns and colors described in TC 5-200 have been specifically designed both for effective concealment and ease of accomplishment.

(8) **Nets.** When natural materials are insufficient or unavailable, camouflage nets are used to conceal vehicles. The lightweight plastic modular screening nets are easy to use, quickly erected, and quickly removed. They provide some protection against air-to-ground radar, as well as infrared devices. Even if the nets themselves are detected, they still conceal the identity of the vehicle.

(9) **Digging in.** In a desert, or any open barren terrain, the lower an object is to the ground, the smaller is its shadow and the easier it is to conceal from aerial observation. When the situation permits, every effort must be made to dig in important vehicles. Not only are they more easily

concealed but they are also protected from fragments. An excavation is made, with a slanting approach and the vehicle is parked in the pit. Sandbags are used to form a revetment for protection and the whole thing is covered with a net. The net is sloped gently out to the sides and staked down. Finally, the vehicle tracks to the position are brushed out or covered.

5-16. ARTILLERY

a. Revealing factors. As is the case with all other impedimenta of warfare, skillful concealment of artillery weapons can add immeasurably to the element of surprise and thence to the defeat of the enemy. Enemy observers are trained to search for certain definite signs which indicate the presence of artillery - imperfectly camouflaged weapon positions, blast areas, litter, paths or wheel tracks, and in the case of a missile site, the excessive earthworking scars in the terrain pattern necessitated by a level firing pad and fueling entrances and exits, and other necessary activities. Even though the weapons themselves are hidden, such signs are dead giveaways of the presence of artillery. These signs may not of themselves indicate the exact nature of the position, but they do attract enemy attention and invite more careful observation.

b. Camouflage measures.

(1) **Governing factors.** Camouflage measures vary with the situation and are affected by the following:

(a) There will be little opportunity to camouflage positions extensively when their occupancy will be of short duration. If it should develop that the weapons must remain longer, their locations can then be improved by better siting and hiding.

(b) When the batteries are deployed for a coordinated attack, the location of each battery and of each piece should be carefully selected.

(c) In a defensive action, extensive camouflage is developed. Utmost precaution must be taken to deceive the enemy as to the location of the installation.

(2) Siting. The exact position for the elements of a battery, within the assigned area, must possess several qualifications:

(a) The required field of fire.

(b) Room for dispersion of weapons, vehicles, and other equipment organic to the battery.

(c) Opportunity to establish communications without creating attention getting ground scars and paths.

(d) Opportunity for access and supply routes. It is desirable to have routes available to the front, flanks, and rear. This is important in situations where it may be necessary to make sudden changes in position. When personnel, ammunition, equipment, and other supplies are moved into position, they must follow a prepared traffic plan.

(3) Pattern painting. Pattern painting of artillery pieces can be an effective aid to concealment and is designed for use in varying terrains (TC 5-200). Standard patterns are available for some types of artillery, and are being developed for the others.

(4) Screening systems. Whenever natural concealment is impossible or difficult, the lightweight plastic screening system provides a quick and effective means of concealment. The lanyards used to fasten the modules together, if more than one are needed, are designed for quick release when the weapons must be raised and fired. Wire netting, suitably garnished with dyed burlap strips or other material, is heavier and bulkier, but holds its form, is durable, and is invaluable for positions of a relatively permanent nature.

Section VI. Countersurveillance Measures for Bivouacs

5-17. INTRODUCTION

The problems of concealment of bivouacs, command posts, and field service installations are similar within the various geographic terrain areas. Each is an activity in which personnel and equipment are closely grouped in a particular area for more than a few hours. Elements of the unit are concentrated in a smaller area than usual and, except for security elements, the men are less alert than when engaged in combat. The breaches in camouflage discipline which can occur when a unit has occupied an area over a period of time must be avoided. A thorough reconnaissance of the terrain to be occupied should be accomplished prior to occupation, taking into consideration the tactical situation and camouflage. This eliminates confusion when moving into the area, prevents unnecessary camouflage construction, and insures an orderly occupation of the area.

5-18. METHODS AND PROCEDURES

a. Siting. Proper siting can contribute significantly to solving the problem of concealment.

An ideal bivouac area, for example, is a large wooded area containing many existing routes of approach. Such an ideal place is seldom found. Military units should be sited, when possible, to take advantage of terrain features such as shadow, terrain lines, rocky areas, villages, farms and defilades. The individual must be ready to fit himself and his equipment inconspicuously into any type of terrain.

b. Camouflage discipline SOP. Next to siting, the standing operating procedure (SOP) of camouflage is the most important element of the camouflage of bivouacs. The SOP is based on the principle that everyone in the unit understands camouflage discipline. This SOP provides for the following measures:

(1) Covered areas for drying laundry at specified times.

(2) Measures for disposal of empty cans and other bright articles that shine.

(3) Striking of shelter tents during the day except under heavy cover or in rain or fog.

(4) Siting of latrines under cover with paths well marked and concealed.

(5) Elimination of latrine screens except when specifically ordered.

(6) Concealment of spoil from kitchen, refuse pits, latrines, and foxholes.

(7) Withholding fire at enemy planes as appropriate.

(8) Maintaining strict camouflage discipline during the night as well as during the day.

c. Development of bivouac. There are four critical stages in the development of a bivouac. In the order in which they occur, they are: planning, occupation, maintenance, and evacuation.

d. Planning stage. Frequent bivouacs are characteristic of mobile warfare. In such warfare, there is seldom time or facilities to erect elaborate constructions for concealment. Bivouacs are usually hastily occupied and quickly evacuated. Camouflage measures are hasty in nature, and dependent upon local natural materials. The most important elements in the planning stage of a bivouac are performed by the advance and quartering parties.

(1) Advance party. The advance party should consist of a representative from the headquarters that ordered the move, a representative from each subordinate unit and, if possible, someone particularly knowledgeable in camouflage techniques. This party should make a thorough reconnaissance of the area proposed and then divide the area into subordinate unit areas. The quartering party from each subordinate unit then makes its reconnaissance of the assigned area, taking into consideration both the tactical and camouflage capability.

(2) Quartering party. Before going into the area the quartering party should be as familiar as possible with the terrain and the ground pattern through a careful study of available maps and aerial photographs. They must be fully acquainted with both the tactical plan and the camouflage requirements. The quartering party should designate dispersal points and concealment areas for the subordinate units, select cutting areas for natural materials, tape motor park and roadways, and post traffic signs and guides. Critical elements which the quartering party must keep in mind are:

(a) Mission of the unit. The tactical plan and its demands, which normally include the concealment of the bivouac, must be satisfied as completely as possible.

(b) Access routes. Effectiveness of concealment depends greatly on a well-prepared and well-maintained track plan. Roads within bivouac areas are normally planned with only one entrance and one exit, and for one-way traffic through the area. A simple loop or a loop with a bypass is preferable to a complex road net.

(c) Existing concealment qualities of the area.

(d) Area in relation to the size of the unit. The area should be large enough to afford natural concealment through dispersion, taking advantage of terrain features and natural materials.

(e) Concealment of the perimeter defense element of the position. Even though other elements of a bivouac are well concealed, a conspicuous perimeter defense may betray the position.

e. Occupation stage. The occupation stage is limited to the period during which the unit is moving into the bivouac area. A carefully controlled traffic plan is mandatory during this stage. Guides posted at route junctions should be fully informed of the camouflage plan. One of their duties is to enforce camouflage discipline. Vehicle turn-ins must be taped or wired to prevent widening of corners. Foot troops should follow selected and marked paths through the area.

(1) Dispersion. Dispersion should be automatic and should provide for a minimum of 50 square meters per man and no less than 20 meters between tents. Vehicles will seldom be less than 50 meters apart in ordinary terrain or less than 100 meters in desert areas. The kitchen area should be carefully selected to provide for the various parts of the kitchen. The three main congested areas that must be dispersed are the food dispensing area, mess kit washing area, and eating area.

(2) **Immediate camouflage measures.** Camouflage is not something applied as an afterthought to other activities. Camouflage measures must be immediate and continuous. Vehicles and equipment should be concealed as soon as they are properly sited. Immediate steps should be taken to obliterate vehicle and equipment tracks. This may be accomplished by using leaves, brush, or other natural materials to cover up tracks. In sandy areas a drag or rake can be used to eliminate tracks.

(3) **Tracks.** When it is impossible to stay on existing routes and paths, three courses are open to the unit.

(a) Make new paths and tracks along existing terrain lines. New tracks adjacent to and paralleling such lines are far less conspicuous than fresh tracks breaking a "clean" area.

(b) If a new path in an open area must be made, extend it beyond its destination to a natural termination, such as a junction with a road. This false section must appear as well traveled as the true section. A new route must enter the concealed area some distance from its destination. Turnarounds are to be avoided. A traffic-control plan which includes a one-way system of travel must be strictly enforced.

(c) In some cases, tree tops can be pulled and wired together to cover exposed areas. A more elaborate and difficult procedure (possible only in somewhat prolonged bivouacs) is the construction of overhead screens to conceal small sections of newly created paths and roads. This is a time consuming operation and should be considered only as a last resort in such temporary operations as bivouacs.

f. **Maintenance stage.** The maintenance stage of a bivouac commences when the unit has arrived in the area and terminates when the last element departs. If the occupation stage has been successful from a camouflage standpoint, the maintenance stage is relatively easy. Successful maintenance involves frequent ground inspection of the bivouac area, active patrol measures for camouflage discipline, and, if possible, aerial observation and photography and the correction of defects.

(1) **Kitchen areas.** Critical activities of a unit in bivouac are those which call for the congregation of troops: water facilities, and messing. Mess facilities must be centrally located in a well-concealed area. The track plan must be rigidly enforced. Mess areas should provide ample space for mess lines, wash lines, and eating. Artificial overhead cover may be necessary to conceal mess areas. Garbage disposal pits should be accessible, but not too close to the mess area. The spoil from the pits must be carefully concealed. In the kitchen, if cooking stoves other than issue gasoline burners are used, the problem of smoke should be met by constructing a baffle above the stove so the smoke is well dispersed. The baffle itself should be camouflaged and concealed from aerial view.

(2) **Night discipline.** Camouflage discipline at night is just as important as daylight camouflage discipline. The same rigid rules as for daylight must be observed because the enemy can use infrared surveillance equipment and aerial photography to detect any breach of night camouflage discipline. Night photographs are surprisingly revealing. Taped paths must be followed and blackout control must be enforced. No lights or fires are to be permitted except under adequate concealment such as inside lightproof tents, dugouts, and caves. Equipment and articles of clothing are concealed at night to prevent reflection or shine from the light of aircraft photoflares.

g. **Evacuation stage.** The camouflage of a bivouac is not terminated when the unit moves out. An evacuated area can be left in such a state of disorder that aerial photographs taken by the enemy will reveal the strength of the unit which occupied it, the kind of equipment carried, and the direction in which it went. It is part of camouflage discipline to leave the area looking undisturbed because friendly advancing troops may want to use the same area. Decoy bivouacs may sometimes be used as part of the tactical plan, during occupation or after departure.

h. Geographic areas

(1) **Open terrain.** Concealment in terrain which lacks natural overhead cover, such as open fields or the outskirts of villages, depends mainly on careful siting, dispersion and effective camouflage discipline. Shelter tents should be pitched along lines which are normal in the terrain pattern, such as fence and hedge lines, or beside folds in the ground or other shadow-casting irregularities in the ground surface. Disruptive patterns made with charcoal, paint, mud, or plant stain may be applied to tents to help blend them with their environment. During the daytime, tents should be struck and concealed with natural materials. If time permits, equipment should be at least partially dug in and spoil placed around it to minimize the shadows. Spoil lightens in color as it dries out and must be toned down with other natural materials.

(2) **Snow-covered terrain.** Although camouflage in snow-covered terrain follows exactly the same principles as other camouflage, it presents several special problems. A blanket of snow often eliminates much of the ground pattern, making blending difficult. Differences in texture and color disappear or become less marked. However, snow-covered terrain is rarely completely white, and by taking advantage of dark features in the landscape, a unit on the move or in bivouac may often blend itself successfully into the terrain.

(a) Good route selection in snow-covered terrain is usually more important than any other camouflage measures because exposed tracks are difficult to conceal. If, in selecting a route, advantage is taken of the dark features of the landscape, tracks will blend in very well. However, this does not mean exposed tracks in open terrain of this nature cannot be concealed or toned down.

Tracks may be concealed by using a drag to smooth out the snow or to slope the tracks obliquely at the sides in order to minimize their shadows. When moving into a bivouac area, extreme care must be exercised to avoid leaving exposed tracks pointing toward the site to be occupied. One method of eliminating this is to continue tracks past the entrance to the bivouac area to a predetermined destination. Skis and snowshoes should not be used near the bivouac since their marks (tracks) are more sharply defined and more easily seen than foot tracks. To help avoid detection, personnel, vehicles, and materials should be restricted from open areas.

(b) Vehicles may be pattern painted or painted a solid white, depending on the terrain. This applies to tentage and other facilities as well as vehicles. Bivouacs which have been well concealed in snow for some length of time can be identified easily when the snow melts, unless precautions are taken. This is because the compacted snow on much-used paths melts more slowly than virgin snow and leaves clearly visible white lines on a dark background. When this occurs, the compacted snow must be broken up and spread out to speed up melting.

(c) Tents should be dug into the snow, close to bushy trees whenever possible. The outline of the tent is broken by placing white camouflage parkas on the tent or by pattern painting. In forest areas, a bough platform supported by the nearest trees can be built above the tent. This diverts the smoke coming from the stove pipe. Otherwise the smoke can be easily seen from long distances, especially on extremely cold mornings. Snow shoe and ski racks should be located under bushy trees.

(3) **Desert or barren areas.** Experience in the desert has taught much about concealment in areas that do not have large trees. Areas comparable to the desert as far as camouflage is concerned, are unplowed fields, rocky areas, grasslands, and other sparsely cultivated areas. Certain kinds of predominately flat terrain have shadows which are made by folds in the

ground and which are deep enough to allow some concealment by siting. Proper use of nets will accomplish much in rendering objects inconspicuous in areas where very little or no natural materials are available. This type of terrain offers few advantages for successful siting. In desert terrain, the identity of objects is hidden by keeping each installation as low to the ground as possible, by using nets to break up characteristic form, and by creating gently sloping outlines. Even in essentially barren terrain, excellent concealment is possible when the configuration of the ground is irregular enough to produce a strong shadow pattern. Bivouacs should be dispersed in the shadows of underbrush and among natural terrain features such as gullies and rocks. Tents are to be painted with canvas preservative to match the terrain color.

SELF TEST

1. There are two broad categories of surveillance -- direct and indirect. Define these two methods. (Para 5-2a and b)

2. Give two advantages of direct surveillance. (Para 5-2a(1))

3. Give two advantages of indirect surveillance methods. (Para 5-2b(1))

4. There are two major types of aerial photography in common use for surveillance purposes -- vertical and oblique. Which type is most commonly used and why is this so? (Para 5-3b)

5. What expedient can be used to obtain oblique photography from helicopters or other small aircraft? (Para 5-3b)

6. Low altitude oblique aerial photography provides valuable information on ground activities. What terrain features may limit its effectiveness? (Para 5-3b)

7. There are several devices for indirect surveillance. Which type of device uses radio signals or ultrahigh frequency to transmit reflected signals from which characteristics of the object under observation may be determined? (Para 5-4)

8. What means besides foliage cover should be used to prevent detection by air to ground radar? (Para 5-4b)

9. Infrared devices are also used in surveillance. Which type of infrared device detects and is sensitive to the aerial wavelengths (heat emission)? (Para 5-5a, c)

10. What measure of insulation can be used to attenuate the heat radiation of an object and thereby help prevent detection by passive (far) infrared detectors? (Para 5-5c)

11. Against which type of infrared device are screening nets effective? (Para 5-5c)

12. Starlight scopes are special devices which greatly amplify reduced light to permit visual detection under night conditions. What countermeasures can be used against detection by those devices? (Para 5-6a)

13. Effective countersurveillance depends upon three principles or concepts which govern all implementary plans and activities? What are those principles? (Para 5-9)

14. Concealment of activities and objects is an objective of the countersurveillance plans of a unit. What are the three techniques used in concealment of objects or activities? (Para 5-13)

15. The site chosen must provide concealment without disturbing or altering the characteristic pattern of the terrain. What are the four types of terrain? (Para 5-10c)

16. In choosing a site for an activity or unit, there is one requirement (other than size and meeting mission requirements) that all locations must have. What is this requirement? (Para 5-10c)

17. Tracks of vehicles are usually easily detected. How is their destination obscured? (Para 5-15b(2)

18. A one-way track plan of the site should be laid out. How is this done? (Para 5-18d(2)(b))

19. In a desert, or any open barren terrain, the lower an object is to the ground, the smaller is its shadow and the easier it is to conceal from aerial observation. Knowing this, what would be your first step in concealing a vehicle under these conditions? (Para 5-15b(9))

20. The maintenance of camouflage while a unit is in position is vital to its security. What actions can be taken periodically to determine if the camouflage is continuing to be effective? (Para 5-18f)

ANSWERS TO SELF TESTS

LESSON 1...**Purpose and Requirements of Field Fortifications**

1. Fortification plans should provide the desired degree of protection, and make provisions to bring the maximum volume of effective fire on the enemy as soon as possible.

2. Hasty shelters and emplacements are normally constructed by the combat units occupying the position.

3. Development of fortifications can be accomplished in 3 steps:

   (1) Digging in quickly
   (2) Improving with available materials.
   (3) Refining, using stock materials.

4. Protection against conventional weapons is best provided by constructing a thickness of earth and other materials. This is done by digging into the ground so personnel and equipment offer the smallest target possible to the line of sight of the weapon.

5. Craters, even if developed, are susceptible to being overrun by tracked vehicles.

6. The skirmisher's trench is used when immediate shelter from heavy enemy fire is required and existing defiladed firing positions are not available.

7. A minimum thickness of 30cm (12 in.) of icecrete will resist penatration of small arms fire.

8. Craters, skirmisher's trenches, and prone emplacements can be developed into foxholes.

9. The separation of units and individuals; dispersion is the primary means of increasing protection against nuclear weapons.

10. The firing apertures are cut at 45° to the direction of the enemy.

11. The overhead cover for foxholes (fabric) will support 45cm (18 in.) of soil over any emplacement.

12. The purposes of the cushion layer and burster layers of the heavy overhead cover are –

    Cushion layer – absorb the shock of detonation or penetration.

    Burster layer – cause detonation of the projective before it can penetrate into the lower protective layers. (Para 1-42a(2)(4))

13. A 45cm (18 in.) earth cover is effective against fragmentation (shrapnel) effects of mortars, artillery, and rockets. (Para 1-37e)

14. The purpose of a standoff in front of a protective structure is to detonate shells and thereby reduce their subsequent penetrating effect. (Para 1-39)

15. The airmobile division engineer battalion is equipped to construct artillery firebases in areas where ground transport is prohibitive. (Para 1-23)

16. The major tasks in Phases I, II, and III of firebase construction are --

Phase I Secure site and clear area for helicopters.

Phase II Construct howitzer positions, bunkers, expand perimeter, fields of fire, etc. (Tactical construction)

Phase III Construct final defensive structures, infantry TOC, artillery FDC, etc.

17. Increase in moisture decreases the resistance of soil to the penetration of rounds. (Note 2, Table 1-6)

18. In wooded areas, it is necessary to provide light overhead cover to protect personnel from the shrapnel of tree bursts. (Para 1-44)

19. The walls of the air transportable underground assault bunker are sloping making it easier to extract the bunker from the ground. (Para 1-45a)

20. The plywood perimeter bunker has plywood revetment (soilbin) walls approximately 0.6 meters (2 ft.) thick and capped to prevent moisture from seeping into the soil fill. (Para 1-46)

1. Trenches are excavated as fighting positions and to connect individual foxholes, weapons emplacements, and shelters in the progressive development of a defensive area.

2. Trenches are difficult to camouflage and are easily detected, especially from the air.

3. The crawl trench is used to conceal movement into or within a position and to provide a minimum of protection.

4. Crawl trenches should be 24 to 30 inches in depth and about 24 inches wide.

5. The berm line is located about 18 inches from the front edge of the trench.

6. The trench is dug to a depth of 3 feet below ground level. At this point, a man can fire in a kneeling or crouching position.

7. The crest of the parapet should be irregular to aid concealment.

8. If spoil is available, the rear parapet should be higher than the front parapet to prevent silhouetting of soldier's heads when firing.

9. Parapets can be omitted to aid concealment or when ground provides background and protection to firer's rear.

10. A sump is dug at the lowest point to prevent the floor of the trench from becoming wet and muddy.

11. The necessity of revetment of walls may sometimes be postponed or avoided by sloping the walls of the excavation.

12. In most soils a slope of 1:3 or 1:4 is sufficient.

13. Wall sloping can seriously reduce the protection provided due to the increased width of the trench at ground level.

14. Facing type revetment serves mainly to protect revetted surfaces from the effects of weather and damage caused by occupation.

15. Facing type revetment can be used when soils are stable enough to sustain their own weight.

16. Methods of supporting the facing revetment are timber frames and pickets.

17. Sandbags are uniformly filled about 3/4 full.

18. Sandbags are placed so side seams on stretchers and choked ends on headers are turned toward the revetted face.

19. Two pieces of equipment that can expedite the filling of sandbags are the intrenching machine and the funnel.

20. Dummy trenches should be dug 18 inches deep with brushwood laid in the bottom.

1. An obstacle is employed to stop, or divert enemy movement by means other than firepower.

2. An obstacle used to protect an installation against infiltration or sabotage is classified as a nontactical obstacle.

3. An escarpment 1.5 meters high is an effective obstacle for both vehicles and personnel. Slopes must be approximately a 60 percent incline to stop the movement of tanks unless trees, rocks, or unfavorable soil is on the slope. Rivers must be over 150 meters wide and over 1.5 meters deep and swamps 1 meter deep before they become a major obstacle.

4. Punjis are an antipersonnel obstacle and are effective in jungles where the movement of troops is limited to marching.

5. Wherever it is feasible to have an obstacle under direct observation, trip flares may be used as a warning device to indicate that the enemy has encountered the obstacle. This will alert the unit prepared to supply the firepower.

6. Caltrops are used with barbed wire to make a more effective antipersonnel obstacle. Caltrops are designed to cause injury by penetrating the footwear.

7. A trapezoidal ditch may be camouflaged with snow to make it resemble a standard trench (fig 3-6). The enemy vehicles that are able to cross a standard trench will fall through the camouflaged portion of the excavation and be entrapped.

8. Demolition placed in a culvert under the road is the most satisfactory method for cratering roads. If a culvert is not available, a hole may be dug into the road and a charge placed at the bottom of it. Placing a charge on the road is unsatisfactory because it can be seen. A charge placed in vegetation will ordinarily be alongside the road, which is ineffectual unless the charge is extremely large or of an atomic demolition munitions (ADM) type.

9. The earth used to fill crib obstacles should preferably be obtained by digging a shallow ditch in front of the obstacle.

10. Posts used as an antivehicular obstacle are buried 1.5 meters in the ground either at a slight angle toward the enemy or vertically, projecting between 75 and 120 cm above ground level.

11. Bush-type trees with heavy branches and thick foliage should be use for abatis wherever possible because the branches reduce the momentum of the vehicle. The trees should be at least 6 meters high and 60 cm or more in diameter.

12. Steel hedgehogs can easily be moved by the enemy; therefore, these obstacles must be kept under observation and covered by fire.

13. Concrete cube obstacles are usually cast in place because of the weight involved and the simplicity of making the forms in which they are made.

14. A truck used as a roadblock should be emplaced and have the wheels damaged or removed to prevent it from being pulled out easily.

15. Antitank and antipersonnel mines should be placed between dummy road obstacles.

16. Beyond the depth of 3 fathoms (5.54 meters), the Navy minesweepers are responsible for clearing boat and shipping lanes.

17. Beach obstacles should force the enemy landing craft to unload at low tide several hundred meters seaward of the high water mark. This makes the enemy cross a wide expanse of obstacle-studded beach and be vulnerable to fire.

18. Antiboat obstacles are emplaced from wading depth at low tide to wading at high tide.

19. Timber tetrahedron's are pinned and wired to a triangular frame which is weighted in place with rocks. The anchorage may be improved by driving a post through the obstacle and into the ground.

20. The rock wall is an expedient type of underwater obstacle made of rock found in the area. The rock pillar and the log ramp require wood and other material to construct and secure which takes them out of the expedient category. The hedgehog is a prefabricated obstacle.

LESSON 4...**Barbed Wire Entanglements**

1. A series of barbed wire concertinas should be placed about 10 meters in depth to construct a roadblock to stop wheeled vehicles.

2. Barbed wire is issued in reels of 400 meters of wire. It is taken off the reels and put on bobbins with 30 meters of wire on each when used to repair entanglements or build short lengths of fence. Thus, 400 meters of wire on a reel and 30 meters on a bobbin is a difference of 370 meters (more barbed wire on a full reel than on a bobbin).

3. Barbed tape weighs one-third as much as equal lengths of standard barbed wire.

4. U-shaped steel pickets are driven with the hollow surface (concave side) facing enemy fire because enemy small arms projectiles ricochet from convex sides and may cause casualties.

5. All fence-building operations normally proceed from right to left, as one faces the enemy.

6. A piece of white tracing tape should be tied to the end of the wire on each bobbin or reel to facilitate finding it.

7. To close a concertina, one man at each end places a foot at the bottom of the coil to keep it from fanning out while they walk toward each other to compress the concertina.

8. Screw pickets should be used when constructing wire entanglements in proximity to the enemy. These pickets can be installed with less noise.

9. The apron tie is used to tie together two wires that cross. It is tied in the same way as the post tie, except that the apron tie is a wire-to-wire tie and the post tie is a wire-to-post tie.

10. Barbed wires of a four-strand cattle fence are installed from the bottom up. The first team which has been organized for this work puts on the bottom wire and team 2 installs the second wire from the bottom (third wire from the top).

11. The construction of a 300-meter section of either a 4- and 2-pace or a 6- and 3-pace double-apron is normally assigned to a platoon.

12. Wires numbers 6, 7, and 8 (rear apron) form the backbone of a double-apron fence. They hold the pickets in position.

13. Both wire No. 2 and wire No. 12 are trip wires. Wire No. 2 is installed on the enemy side and wire No. 12 on the friendly side of a double-apron fence.

14. The personnel that lay out the concertinas drop the first roll at the third picket in the front row. The other rolls are placed at every fourth picket from where the first roll was dropped.

15. A strand of barbed wire is stretched tightly along the top of front row concertina sections in the construction of a triple standard concertina fence to increase the resistance of the fence against crushing.

16. The Lapland fence can be used equally as well on frozen or rocky ground and in snow, bogs, or marshlands. The wire is attached to tripods (fig 6-32) instead of pickets.

17. Trip wires are stretched about 23 centimeters above the ground. The tanglefoot is constructed at heights varying from 23 to 75 centimeters. Spirals of loose wire are wound around a form of 1-meter posts on which the wire is extended from the bottom of the posts (above ground) to the top. A knife rest is approximately 1 meter high.

18. Tactical Wire:

800 m mean perimeter x 1.25 3 belts = 3000 m effective length

$$\frac{3000}{300} = 10.00 \text{ sections}$$

$$10.0 \times 100 = 1000 \text{ long pickets}$$
$$10.0 \times 200 = 2000 \text{ short pickets}$$
$$10.0 \times 19 = 190 \text{ cases barbed tape}$$
$$\frac{3000 \times 3.5}{2268} = 4.6 \text{ or } 5 \text{ truckloads}$$

$$10.0 \times 59 \times 1.2 = 708 \text{ manhours}$$

19. Protective Wire:

600 m mean perimeter x 1.10 x 1 belt = 660 m effective length

$$\frac{660}{300} = 2.20 \text{ sections}$$

$$2.2 \times 160 = 352 \text{ long pickets}$$
$$2.2 \times 4 = 8.8 \text{ or } 9 \text{ short pickets}$$
$$2.2 \times 3 = 6.6 \text{ or } 7 \text{ reels barbed wire}$$
$$2.2 \times 59 = 129.8 \text{ or } 130 \text{ concertinas}$$
$$2.2 \times 317 = 697.4 \text{ or } 698 \text{ staples}$$
$$\frac{660 \times 7.9}{2268} = 2.2 \text{ or } 3 \text{ truckloads}$$

$$2.2 \times 30 \times \tfrac{2}{3} = 44 \text{ manhours}$$

1. Direct surveillance requires the observer to use his senses of sight, hearing, and smells to gather infractions about the existence, identification, or scopes of energy activity. Indirect surveillance methods include all of the mechanical, electrical, and chemical devices which extend the range of the human senses.

2. Two advantages of direct surveillance methods are:

    a. Immediate information is provided.

    b. The information is easily evaluated because it is natural and familiar.

3. Two advantages of indirect methods of surveillance are:

    a. Observation may be conducted from points out of range of enemy fire.

    b. Most indirect detection devices provide a permanent record on film or tape. Such images can be enlarged and imagery of the same area can be repeated over a period of time to reveal tell-tale changes in the appearance of the terrain that would otherwise go unnoticed.

4. Reconnaissance and surveillance needs are more often met by various kinds of oblique photography, which also cover a greater area with fewer flights than does vertical photography.

5. Hand held cameras can be used in helicopter and small aircraft to get valuable information on the terrain and activities below.

6. In areas of moderate to rugged relief, defilade may limit information recorded on low altitude oblique photography.

7. Radar detection devices emitting radio signals, usually in the form of pulses of an ultrahigh frequency, produce minute reflected signals from which the characteristic of the object under observation may be determined.

8. As foliage alone cannot be relied upon completely to detect air-to-ground radar, digging in, defilade, or special radar-scattering screening materials should also be used for concealment.

9. Passive (far) infrared detectors are sensitive to thermal wavelengths and concealment depends on reducing the heat emission of objects which are hotter than their surroundings.

10. Defilade, heavy brush, and tree cover will attenuate heat radiation and thus help protect from passive (far) infrared detectors.

11. Screening nets reflect active infrared waves but do not shield a hidden object which emits heat from detection by passive infrared devices.

12. Countermeasures against starlight scopes include all means of concealment from visual detection in daylight.

13. All camouflage or countersurveillance plans and activities are effectuated through siting, discipline, and construction.

14. Concealment of an object or activity can be achieved through the technique of hiding, blending, and disguising.

15. The four types of terrain are agricultural, urban, wooded, and barren.

16. The site chosen must provide concealment without disturbing or altering the characteristic pattern of the terrain.

17. Tracks should always continue past their destination to a logical termination.

18. In addition to laying out a plan on the ground itself, a plan should be sketched on either a map overlay or a sketch of the area.

19. When the situation permits, every effort must be made to dig in important vehicles.

20. Successful maintenance involves frequent ground inspection, active patrol measures for camouflage discipline, and, if possible, aerial observation and photography and the correction of defects.

Table 1-1. Characteristics of Personnel and Individual Weapons Emplacements

| Type of emplacement or shelter | Protection afforded [1] | | | |
| | Nuclear weapons effects | | Conventional weapons | |
	Fortification protection factor [2]	Thermal effects	Tracked vehicles	Artillery fragments
Improved crater	90	Fair	Virtually none	Better than in open.
Skirmishers trench	95	Fair	Virtually none	Better than in open.
Prone emplacement	85	Good	Virtually none	Fair
Open one man foxhole	65	Very good	Good	Good
Open one man foxhole with offset	20	Excellent	Very good	Excellent
One man foxhole with half cover	55	Very good	Fair (−)	Very good
One man foxhole with half cover and offset	20	Excellent	Very good	Excellent
Open two man foxhole	65	Good	Good	Good
Deepened two man foxhole	55	Very good	Good	Very good
Two man foxhole with half cover	60	Very good	Fair to good	Very good
Two man foxhole with offset	15	Excellent	Very good	Excellent
Two man foxhole with half cover and adjoining shelter	30	Excellent	Good	Excellent
Open fighting trench (25' length) [4] 7.5m	85	Good	Fair	Fair
Fighting trench with full cover (25' length) 7.5m	70	Excellent	Fair	Very good

[1] Protection afforded assumes the occupants of fortifications are in the most protected position of their fortifications. For most
[2] See app C.
[3] Assumes normal digging capability in daylight with trained troops.
[4] May include wooden framing and braces.
[5] See metric conversion table, app B.

Table 1-1. Characteristics of Personnel and Individual Weapons Emplacements (Continued)

Total construction time in man-hours for construction with D-handle shovels and ordinary carpentry tools [1]					Weight and vol...			
Revetment materials for cover support only		Complete revetment		No revetment materials used	Revetment materials for cover support only			
					Corrugated metal construction		Sized lumber construction	
Corru-gated metal constr.	Sized lumber constr.	Corru-gated metal constr.	Sized lumber constr.		Weight (lb.)	Volume (cu. ft.)	Weight (lb.)	Volume (cu. ft.)
N/A	N/A	N/A	N/A	0.5	N/A	N/A	N/A	N/A
N/A	N/A	N/A	N/A	0.5	N/A	N/A	N/A	N/A
N/A	N/A	N/A	N/A	1.5	N/A	N/A	N/A	N/A
N/A	N/A	3.5	4.5	2.0	N/A	N/A	N/A	N/A
9.0	14.0	10.0	16.0	N/A	50 (22 kg)	0.6 (.17 cu m)	180 (8 kg)	5.5 (1.6 cu m)
2.5	3.0	4.5	5.5	N/A	10 (4.5 kg)	0.1 (.03 cu m)	20 (9 kg)	0.6 (.17 cu m)
10.0	14.0	12.0	18.0	N/A	60 (27 kg)	0.7 (.2 cu m)	200 (90kg)	6.0 (1.7 cu m)
N/A	N/A	6.0	8.0	3.0	N/A	N/A	N/A	N/A
N/A	N/A	8.0	10.0	5.0	N/A	N/A	N/A	N/A
4.0	4.0	8.0	10.0	N/A	15 (6.7 kg)	0.2 (.06 cu m)	32 (14.4 kg)	1.0 (.3 cu m)
20.0	30.0	22.0	35.0	N/A	120 (54kg)	1.5 (.42 cu m)	400 (180 kg)	12.0 (3.4 cu m)
11.0	17.0	13.0	22.0	N/A	100 (45 kg)	1.2 (.34 cu m)	560 (252 kg)	18.0 (5.1 cu m)
N/A	N/A	28.0	32.0	21.0	N/A	N/A	N/A	N/A
27.0	29.0	35.0	40.0	N/A	240 (108 kg)	4.0 (1.1 cu m)	360 (162 kg)	11.0 (3.1 cu m)

...rtifications protection decreases as the angle of sight from the position to the center of the weapon burst increases.

ne of materials

Complete revetment			
Corrugated metal construction		Sized lumber construction	
Weight (lb.)	Volume (cu. ft.)	Weight (lb.)	Volume (cu. ft.)
N/A	N/A	N/A	N/A
N/A	N/A	N/A	N/A
N/A	N/A	N/A	N/A
190 (85 kg)	3.5 (1.0 cu m)	240 (108 kg)	8 (2.4 cu m)
240 (108 kg)	4.0 (1.2 cu m)	420 (108 kg)	13.0 (3.8 cu m)
200 (90 kg)	3.5 (1.0 cu m)	200 (90 kg)	8.0 (2.4 cu m)
250·(112 kg)	4.0 (1.2 cu m)	440 (198 kg)	14.0 (4.0 cu m)
280 (126 kg)	5.0 (1.4 cu m)	320 (144 kg)	10.0 (2.8 cu m)
300 (135 kg)	5.5 (1.6 cu m)	375 (168 kg)	12.0 (2.4 cu m)
280 (126 kg)	5.0 (1.4 cu m)	350 (159 kg)	11.0 (3.1 cu m)
380 (171 kg)	6.0 (1.7 cu m)	700 (315.kg)	22.0 (6.2 cu m)
460 (207 kg)	7.0 (2.0 cu m)	880 (396 kg)	28.0 (7.9 cu m)
490 (220 kg)	8.0 (2.4 cu m)	710 (319 kg)	22.0 (6.2 cu m)
730 (328 kg)	12.0 (3.6 cu m)	1060 (477 kg)	33.0 (9.3 cu m)

Table 1-2. Characteristics of Crew Served Infantry Weapons Emplacements

| Type of emplacement or shelter | Protection afforded [1] | | |
| | Nuclear weapons effects | | Conve... |
	Fortification protection factor [2]	Thermal effects	Tracked vehic...
Open horseshoe type M60 machinegun emplacement	70	Good	Fair
Open 2 one-man foxhole type light machinegun emplacement	65	Very good	Good
Horseshoe type machinegun emplacement with full cover	55	Very good	Fair
2 one-man foxhole type machinegun emplacement with ½ cover and adjoining shelter	30	Excellent	Good
Pit type emplacement for 3.5 inch rocket launcher	80	Fair	Fair
81-mm mortar emplacement	80	Fair	Virtually none
4.2-inch mortar emplacement	85	Good	Virtually none
Recoilless rifle position (mounted)	80	Fair	Virtually none

[1] Protection afforded assumes the occupants of fortifications are in the most-protected position of their fortif...
[2] See app C.
[3] Assumes normal digging capbility in daylight with trained troops.
[4] May include wooden framing and braces.
[5] See metric conversion table, app. B.

Table 1-2. Characteristics of Crew Served Infantry Weapons Emplacements (Continued)

weapons	Total construction time in man-hours for construction with D-handle shovels and ordinary carpentry tools [footnote]					Revetment materials for cover sup[...]		
	Revetment materials for cover support only		Complete revetment		No revetment materials used	Corrugated metal construction		Si[...] co[...]
Artillery fragments	Corru-gated metal constr.	Sized lumber constr.	Corru-gated metal constr.	Sized lumber constr.		Weight (lb.)	Volume (cu. ft.) m³	Weight (lb.)
Fair to good	N/A	N/A	5.0	7.0	2.0	N/A	N/A	N/A
Good	N/A	N/A	6.0	7.0	4.0	N/A	N/A	N/A
Very good	9.0	11.0	11.0	14.0	N/A	190 (85.5kg)	4.0 (1.1 cu m)	250 (112.5kg)
Excellent	15.0	22.0	19.0	28.0	N/A	250 (112.5kg)	2.5 (.7 cu m)	630 (283.5kg)
Fair	N/A	N/A	5.0	6.0	3.0	N/A	N/A	N/A
Fair	N/A	N/A	12.0	N/A	N/A	N/A	N/A	N/A
Fair	N/A	N/A	29.0	N/A	N/A	N/A	N/A	N/A
Fair	N/A	N/A	N/A	N/A	30.0	N/A	N/A	N/A

:ions. For most fortification protection decreases as the angle of sight from the position to the center of the weapon burst incre[...]

Table 1-2. Characteristics of Crew Served Infantry Weapons Emplacements (Continued)

Weight and volume of materials [1]				
t only	Complete revetment			
lumber truction	Corrugated metal construction [4]		Sized lumber construction	
Volume (cu. ft.) m³	Weight (lb.)	Volume (cu. ft.) m³	Weight (lb.)	Volume (cu. ft.) m³
N/A	280 (126kg)	5.0 (1.4cu m)	450 (212kg)	14.0 (4.0 cu m)
N/A	530 (238kg)	10.0 (2.8 cu m)	640 (288kg)	20.0 (5.7 cu m)
7.0 (2.0 cu m)	720 (324kg)	13.0 (3.7 cu m)	890 (400kg)	27.0 (7.6 cu m)
20.0 5.7 cu m)	520 (234kg)	7.5 (2.1 cu m)	850 (382kg)	30.0 (8.5 cu m)
N/A	110 (49kg)	1.0 (.3 cu m)	160	5.0 (1.4 cu m)
N/A	210 (94kg)	3.0 (.9 cu m)	N/A N/A	N/A N/A
N/A	370 (166kg)	6.0 (1.8 cu m)	N/A N/A	N/A N/A
N/A	N/A	N/A	N/A	N/A

www.ingramcontent.com/pod-product-compliance
Lightning Source LLC
Chambersburg PA
CBHW082132290526
45794CB00008B/3011